DIARY OF A SEA CAPTAIN'S WIFE

DIARY OF A
SEA CAPTAIN'S WIFE
Tales of Santa Cruz Island

by

MARGARET HOLDEN EATON

1876–1947

Edited by

JANICE TIMBROOK

McNally & Loftin, Publishers
Santa Barbara

McNally & Loftin, Publishers
P.O. Box 1316
Santa Barbara, CA 93101

Composition & Printing by Kimberly Press, Inc.
Goleta, California

Library of Congress Catalog Card Number 80-81722

ISBN: 0-87461-033-8 — Soft Cover

TABLE OF CONTENTS

PREFACE

Margaret Eaton and her husband Ira were well known to Santa Barbarans in the early part of this century as operators of the Pelican Bay Camp on Santa Cruz Island. Beginning humbly with small-scale commercial fishing, seal hunting, and passenger charters, the Eatons gradually developed a unique resort that came to be popular among writers, film companies, and people from all over the country.

Working from her diary and her memories, Mrs. Eaton wrote this extraordinary story of her life over a period of many years, until her death in 1947. She is remembered by her daughter, Vera Eaton Amey, as a fearless and compassionate woman. Mrs. Amey has done admirably well in sorting through mountains of pages, letters, clippings and photographs to organize her mother's manuscript. She has also painstakingly consulted other sources to confirm, as much as possible, the accuracy of these recollections.

With the passage of time—half a century and more—corroboration becomes increasingly difficult, and inconsistencies have inevitably crept in. The reader who would use *Diary of a Sea Captain's Wife* as a historical reference is asked to bear this in mind. The true significance of Margaret Eaton's story lies in its appeal as the personal account of a woman living in a man's world, in a time and place remote from today's urban society.

> Janice Timbrook
> Associate Curator,
> Santa Barbara Museum of Natural History

ACKNOWLEDGEMENTS

I would like to thank the following friends for the help they have given me: Mrs. Richard Cagnacci of Santa Barbara for developing a very fitting title for my mother's story; Mr. I. A. Bonilla for his help in editing; and Mrs. Joy Bonilla for her encouragement in my efforts to get the material assembled.

Vera Eaton Amey

Childhood and Leaving Home

I WAS BORN in Quebec, Canada, on February 22, 1876, the second youngest of eight children. The St. Lawrence River flowed behind our house, and at high tide the water came right up to the kitchen door. My father, Patrick Holden, was captain of his own tugboat, and from the back steps I would watch his boat working on the river, towing large sailing ships carrying freight or passengers to the wharf. In the wintertime the river was frozen, and Father would be away working logging camps in Savannah or New Orleans.

Since my father was away so much, I was understandably closer to my mother, around whom my life revolved. Eliza Holden, like most mothers in those days, was always busy with the many tasks involved in caring for her large family—washing, mending, and cooking. Delicious aromas would emanate from her kitchen—pots of stew and soup on the wood stove, and cookies, cakes and pies in the oven. Going about her work, she would always sing beautiful hymns; both our parents were Roman Catholics. All us children were raised in that faith and taught to be proud of it and of our wonderful family. My younger brother Michael and I spent many happy hours at home with our mother while the older children were in school.

This peaceful and contented life was shattered when our mother suddenly died. I was only five years old at the time and my baby brother three, both too young to understand what had happened. The family was broken up; the older children went to live with relatives, but Michael and I were sent to a Catholic convent, really an orphanage. Wrenched away from my mother, father, brothers and sisters, and from my home

1

and all familiar surroundings, I felt immense despair, confusion and loneliness.

After six years in the convent, we were allowed to see our
family occasionally—one day every three months. One time I
spent the whole day just watching the river and the boats. I
told my brother and niece that someday I would have a boat of
my own to ride around in all day. They laughed and said,
"Girls don't have boats—only men do." But I knew I would
have a boat. These visits only made me more dissatisfied and
unhappy with life in the convent. When Michael was old
enough to help on the tugboat, Father took him out of the convent; I was left there, even though I was two years older. Re-
belling against this unfairness, I ran away to my aunt's house
and refused to go back to the convent. She sent me to a private
school for the rest of the term, and the next fall I was enrolled
in an academy for young ladies in St. Paul, Minnesota.

During my second year at the academy, I was called back
home to Quebec when my father became seriously ill. I had
always thought of him as an invincible man of the outdoors,
and his death came as a terrible shock to me. At seventeen I
was a full orphan, and overcome with bitterness at having
both my parents taken from me. My faith in God's wisdom
began to waver.

After Father's death, the family scattered and I went to live
with some cousins. Finally I came to accept the fact that I must
earn my own living. I accepted a position as a lady's maid with
an elderly, semi-invalid woman and after six months moved to
Toronto with her. A year later the lady died, and once again
I had lost someone who had become very dear to me.

Shortly after this, while sitting on a park bench in Toronto
and wondering what I ought to do next, I happened to meet
two young ladies I had known in the convent years before.
They were working as waitresses in a Toronto hotel, but were
about to leave for California to work at the Coronado Hotel in
San Diego. They said there were great opportunities to make
money out there. The pay was twenty dollars a month, plus
room and board and plenty of "side money." California seemed

like the other side of the world to me, and I was reluctant to leave my home for an unfamiliar place and a job at which I had no experience. But two weeks later the girls wrote from San Diego that they had secured a job for me as a waitress at the Coronado, and all arrangements were to be made for my transportation by the hotel's head office.

And so I decided to leave my homeland for an unknown future in California. I never returned to Canada, and (except for my younger brother Michael, who visited twenty-five years later) never saw my brothers or sisters again.

After a three-day train trip, I arrived in southern California and was amazed to see live palm trees and groves of orange and lemon trees. When the train stopped in San Bernardino, I had to get out, run down the street, and throw my arms around the first palm tree I came to, to be sure it was real. Everything was so different from Canada! I was very glad to see my two friends who met me at the station in San Diego.

The Coronado was a first-class hotel catering to wealthy people. A hundred and fifty waitresses were employed there. We all lived in a dormitory and were required to wear uniforms—black shoes and stockings, black dress with starched white collar and cuffs at breakfast, and white dress, collar and cuffs at dinner. I started work that first evening terrified I would make awful mistakes, as I was completely inexperienced. However, the people were very understanding, and soon I learned to take the orders and serve them well. Between breakfast and dinner the girls had time to themselves, which was usually spent on the beach enjoying the sun and the sound of the waves washing on the sandy shore. With such warm temperatures and constant sunshine, this certainly did not seem like winter; in Quebec everyone would be bundled in furs this time of year.

I continued working at the Coronado through the winter season. Then I was sent with six other girls to Albuquerque, New Mexico, to open a new hotel, the Alvarado. I stayed there that summer and fall. It was so hot, and I longed for the beautiful ocean and sea breeze of San Diego. Then word came that

a man named Potter was opening a new hotel in Santa Barbara, a prospect which caused great excitement among the
waitresses. Everyone wanted to go to Santa Barbara. I was
delighted when I got the news that I had been hired. Once
again I was on my way to a new home and new adventures.

CHAPTER I

Santa Barbara Beginnings
1902–1905

The Potter Hotel — A Beautiful Town — I Meet Ira Eaton —
Our Wedding — The House on Victoria Street — Learning to
Cook — Ira Builds a Boat — Our First Child

THE POTTER was an immense hotel near the beach in Santa
Barbara. I walked there from the depot and was shown to my
room in one wing of the hotel, where all the staff lived. Like
the Coronado, the rule here was that we could do as we wished
after working hours, but we had to be in before ten o'clock at
night when the gates were locked. As I started to work that
evening I remembered my first uncertain night waiting table
a year ago; but now I was an experienced waitress and proud
of my work.

The girls said Mrs. Potter was "breaking into society," and
nearly all the elite of Los Angeles were at the hotel—Ned
Greenway, the Crockers and the Tobins, all good for five dollars a day side money. There were also prominent people from
the east, including both John D. Rockefellers, Senior and Junior, and their wives. Old John Senior thought he was very
generous when he handed me fifty cents.

The food the hotel gave the staff was mostly stale leftovers
from the day before, and it was generally not worth eating. By
ten in the morning we were nearly starved, so we learned to
smuggle fresh food back to our rooms by wrapping it in napkins and shoving it down our stockings. Then we would gather
to feast on steaks, chops, bacon, rolls, popovers, eggs—the
hotel provided the guests with the best of everything—while
the girls told of the good times they had the night before.

5

Being new in town, I stayed very close to the hotel at night
for the first week or two and did not go out with the girls. But
after working hours during the day, my roommate Hilda and
I would stroll along the main street of the town, which I found
to be very quaint and interesting. Horses, hitched to carriages
and driven by coachmen, pranced up and down the street; the
livery stables did a thriving business. There were rambling
adobe houses and frame store buildings, and in many places
there were wooden sidewalks. The post office was a very dirty
building; the men spat and threw their match stubs on the
floor, and the room was always full of smoke. At the upper end
of State Street was the old Arlington Hotel, famous among
waitresses all over the world. Because of the elderly women it
catered to, we called it "The Old Ladies' Home." Sometimes
we walked on to the Old Mission where we were received by
a priest who showed us through the building, and we would
climb the stairs to get a better view of the town.

Arlington Heights—later called the Riviera—was having a
boom, with lots selling for two and three hundred dollars
apiece. But I thought, who wants to pay two hundred dollars
for a pile of rocks up on a hill? Oak Park was just starting to
boom, too. Hope Ranch was a beautiful drive. There were no
houses, but a watchman would open the iron gates, collect the
toll, and let you drive through, telling you not to race your
horses but to drive carefully.

Sometimes we would walk on the beach or sit on a bench
watching the surf pound on the shore. I would think about how
I loved this beautiful Santa Barbara with the ocean at the
front door and the mountains standing guard at the back, and
I decided I would like to make this my home.

One night at dinner Hilda asked me to a party with twenty
couples, as they were short one girl. At first I hesitated, but
she told me that I must start to go out sometime. It was to be a
hayride out to Old Town in Montecito where they would have
an old-time dance. So I agreed to go. After work the wagon
was waiting, and Hilda introduced me to my partner, whose
steady girl could not come that evening. He was a slim young

man about five feet nine inches tall, clean-shaven, with dark hair, light blue eyes, and a decidedly winsome smile. He helped me into the wagon and sat down beside me. His name was Ira Eaton.

On the hayride all the boys and girls were in such good spirits, throwing rice over everybody. My partner tried to keep me brushed off, as I did not join in the pranks; I was the new girl and very shy. We arrived at the hall in Old Town, and then the dancing began to the music of an old-time Spanish orchestra. Between dances my partner told me Margaret was a pretty name, and he would like to call me that instead of "Miss Holden." He said that although people generally called him "Ike," he wanted me to call him "Ira."

After the dance we all piled into the hay wagon and started home. On the way, my escort asked to meet me the following evening and we could go for a walk. I told him no, that he already had a girl, but he said she was not really his steady girl and anyway he liked me better. So I agreed to go, but only if four of us went together, not just the two of us. Back in town, we drove up State Street in the hay wagon, all of us singing. We stopped at a restaurant as most of the crowd were hungry. We kept the help on the run, but everyone was good-natured. Most of the boys, including Ira, had beer. I asked for tea, and the crowd gave me a teasing about that.

After a couple of hours of fun, we went home to the Potter Hotel, but there was no way to get in as everything had been locked up. We would be caught if we went in through the main entrance. Ira finally climbed the fence and opened the side gate for us. It was four o'clock in the morning when we went to our rooms for a few hours' sleep.

The next evening I worked late, and every little while Hilda came in to tell me my boyfriend was waiting outside. Finally work was over and I went out. Ira was sitting on the fence that enclosed the hotel, where all the boys waited to meet their girlfriends. Hilda, her friend, Ira and I went to the Olympic, the same restaurant where we had been the night before. It was owned by a pleasant, good-looking Italian man named Miratti.

We had a good steak, and that night I drank a glass of beer.

All the boys in town, even those who lived in the upper part of town, ditched their girls to pay court to the Potter Hotel waitresses. Dances were held for us at the old armory. After a while Milo Potter decided to arrange dances for his help at the hotel, in the big dining room. The Potter Hotel orchestra played, and the best refreshments the hotel could afford were served.

I began to keep company steadily with Ira. In the evenings I could not get through my work fast enough. I felt so let down until I was sitting beside Ira on the fence. Soon I had gotten over my shyness, and every evening on meeting and parting we kissed. Some nights we would go to the Last Chance Saloon at the corner of State Street and Cabrillo Boulevard. It was a ramshackle old building, and as you walked across the floor you expected to fall through any minute. We would have beer and sandwiches and talk for hours. I usually got home in the small hours, and Ira would boost me over the eight-foot gate. I often ripped my pants in the effort to get over that gate, but Ira never knew it. Eventually we started going to the main entrance, where Ira would give a tip to the old grey-haired watchman to let me in.

After I had known Ira about six weeks, we were sitting on a bench one night watching the moon reflected on the water, the waves breaking on the shore, and the heavens crowded with stars. Ira had one arm around me, his other hand holding both of mine. He told me how much he loved me, and asked me to marry him. He knew he was asking a great deal of me to give up my job, as I was making more per day than he was, but we could start out together on his salary of twenty-one dollars a week at the Union Mill and Lumber Company. I said I loved him very much but hated to give up my job; I could still work after we were married as so many of the girls did. Ira said his wife was not going to work, but keep house for him. He would do everything he could to make me happy. Of course, I finally said I would marry him and give up my job. I had loved him from the very first night I had met him on the hayride.

Our wedding day was September 2, 1903. The ceremony was held at Ira's sister's house at 1223 Garden Street, and all neighbors provided flowers for the occasion. When we had finished all the decorating I was very tired and had a slight headache. Ira suggested I have a drink of whiskey to settle my nerves, but being very opposed to liquor I took a cup of strong black tea instead, and felt much better.

My wedding dress was white organdy and lace. My hair had been washed and waved, tied on top with a large white ribbon, and my two wide red braids hung down below my waist. Ira's sister Lillian was the bridesmaid, his cousin Roscoe Seeley the best man, and his four-year-old niece Juanita Eaton the ring-bearer. As Ira put the ring on my finger he gave my hand a gentle squeeze, and I thought how wonderful he was. I made up my mind I would always try to do the best I could to make him happy. As everyone was congratulating us and wishing us all sorts of happiness, the best man quietly drew Ira aside and reminded him about the wedding fee of five dollars. In all the confusion of getting married, Ira had not thought of that part of the ceremony, so he turned to me and asked if he could borrow the money as he was short. I knew he had paid the last of his week's wages for his suit, so I hunted for my pocket-book and gave him the five dollars. I actually paid for my own marriage.

Then we all piled into the dining room and had a huge feast of everything you could mention, including baked chicken and roast turkey. The wedding cake was a work of art, more than five feet around and in three layers decorated with pink and white hearts and candy roses. We were given some beautiful presents, silverware and serving pieces. Father Eaton called Ira and me from the table and in front of the whole company had us stand one on each side of the parlor door. He had bored a hole over the door and inserted a piece of cotton rope; he handed me one end of the rope and Ira the other. Then he told us to pull as hard as we could to see who was stronger. Of course Ira pulled the rope from me. Father Eaton said that signified we would always pull together, and that the man should always lead and the woman follow. This was a very old-fashioned custom of the early days.

When the feast was over and the guests were getting ready to leave, a cab and two horses came to the front gate, and my new husband took me for a ride all around the town. I felt very proud. Then we went to the Eatons' home at 322 East Victoria Street, where a room was ready for us.

The next day we arranged to board with Ira's sister Lillian until we could save enough money to start housekeeping. Also, I did not know how to cook and Ira hoped his mother and sister, both excellent cooks, could teach me.

We had been married about three weeks, when one Saturday night Ira wanted to go downtown alone to visit with the boys. I said very well, I would stay home and mend his socks. He promised to be home about nine o'clock. I did my mending and fell asleep; I woke up about eleven and Ira had not come home yet. I lay there and waited uneasily for an hour, then went to Lillian's room and asked her if anything could have happened to him. She told me not to worry, he would be home in a little while. I could not sleep, and finally about two o'clock got Ira's cousin Roscoe to go downtown and try to find him. Soon they came back together, and Ira explained to me later that he had been in a poker game trying to win thirty-five dollars to pay for his new bicycle.

That was the first time I regretted having left my job as a waitress at the Potter Hotel to get married. If I had not been so much in love with my husband, I believe I would have gone back to the hotel the very next morning and asked to be taken on again. Later I found out that Ira tended to keep very late hours when he was out in the evenings.

After awhile I decided it was time we started up housekeeping, so when Ira was through work at the mill we would roam around looking for houses to rent. On Victoria Street we discovered a little house with a red rosebush climbing all over the front, and in back a tall shrub covered with white, bell-shaped flowers. I thought, if I have flowers on the outside, I can arrange the inside. The house had a peaked roof and a sliding front door; it may at one time have been a barn. Inside were four square rooms of equal size. We decided to rent the house for four dollars a month, and after work each day Ira could build closets and otherwise fix it up.

With new wallpaper, second-hand furniture, wood stove and tin bathtub, and things given to us by Ira's parents, our new home was soon ready. We moved in on a Saturday, had a cold supper, and went out to buy groceries for our meals on Sunday. A large steak costing seventy-five cents made quite a hole in the week's paycheck, but we wanted to celebrate. Early the next morning Ira started a fire in the wood stove and said, "Margaret, let's go outside and watch the smoke curl up out of the chimney."

"But Ira, my hair is not braided yet." I was just combing it, and it reached down below my waist.

"Never mind," he said. "You look just beautiful with your golden hair hanging down." My hair was really quite red. I slipped on a bungalow apron and went outside with him. He put his arms around my neck and hugged me tightly, telling me how beautiful I was. As we stood there watching the smoke curling out of the chimney, such a homey feeling came over me. For our first breakfast we had bacon and eggs, coffee for Ira and tea for me. I washed the dishes in the dishpan set on the kitchen table (padded with the *Morning Press*) and then threw the dishwater down the privy. With all the wood ashes from the stove thrown in too, the privy would always be in sanitary condition.

Ira was busy cleaning up the yard, so I suggested that I would fix the dinner. He said that would be fine if I thought I could handle it, but to be sure to call him if I needed help. I cooked our beautiful juicy steak in a frying pan on the wood stove, and everything was going well until the time came for me to season the meat after turning it. I forgot I had taken the top off the pepper box to fill the shaker for the table, and the entire contents of the box poured out onto my expensive steak. I was sure it was ruined, but Ira just told me to wash it off under the faucet, which I did. He finished cooking the steak and made some very good gravy too. I felt terrible, for I had planned to make my first dinner turn out perfectly. But Ira was very nice about it and said the meal was a great success anyway. After dinner I borrowed some cookbooks from Ira's mother.

The next morning as Ira was leaving for work I asked him what he would like for his lunch, and he suggested beef stew. So I ordered the meat and opened the cookbook for instructions. The Potter Hotel often served creamed meats on toast, so I thought instead of thickening the stew I would pour it over toast in a tureen and keep it warm on the stove until Ira came home for lunch. When he arrived his dinner was waiting for him, and it smelled so good. But when he took the cover off the tureen, he got a funny look on his face. All you could see was toast and more toast! It had soaked up every drop of gravy. The potatoes were cooked to mush. I didn't even show him my rock-hard biscuits, which I had made with baking soda since I had no baking powder. Another failure; my eyes filled with tears. But once again Ira was so nice; though he didn't touch the toast he ate the meat and vegetables. He comforted me and said I would do better next time, then kissed me and left for work again.

I felt so bad about that spoiled dinner that I stayed home and cried all afternoon. I thought how much I would like to go back to my job at the Potter Hotel where there was no cooking to worry about. I discovered that I could cry better than I could cook. But we loved each other, so I must try to make the best of things.

We lived very economically and I began to figure that we could put away part of Ira's salary for savings. It cost us only about thirty dollars a month to live. We spent about five dollars a week for groceries; rent was four dollars a month and water one dollar. We used coal oil for light, so there were no gas and electricity bills to pay. Wood did not cost us anything, as the mill gave free wood to those who worked there. I did all our washing. Ira allowed himself a dollar a week for tobacco, and we permitted ourselves the luxury of going downtown to see moving pictures on Saturday nights. They were shown on a canvas screen in a large tent on lower State Street; the seats were camp chairs and there was sawdust on the floor. So our expenses were not many. I had three hundred dollars in the bank from my job, and if we could save some of Ira's pay as well we would have quite a nest egg.

Then about six months after we were married Ira said he would like to build a boat to run around the Santa Barbara harbor. He knew I had been born on the waterfront in Quebec, and we had talked a great deal about the ships on the St. Lawrence River. But I was against the idea as I was expecting a baby and knew we would need all the money we could save for that event. Ira said he would have a partner to share expenses and would buy the lumber at the mill and do the work himself. Still I objected, but it was obvious that Ira had his heart set on a boat and nothing I could say would change his mind.

So Ira started building his boat in Father Eaton's back yard next door. He would get up every morning at six and go over to inspect the work done the night before until I called him to breakfast at seven. At noon when he came home for lunch he would go over and look at the boat again. When he came home from work at five o'clock, he would ask me to call him when supper was ready and work on the boat until six. After supper he went right back and worked on the boat until nine or ten at night, and sometimes as late as midnight. All this time, our conversation at home (what little time he was home) was about boats and the money to be made in fishing, sealing, or abalone-picking. I could not understand why he would want to leave his job at the mill which paid regularly every Saturday; this boating business seemed too uncertain.

Soon the partner wanted out of the boat project, as his wife, also expecting a baby, was giving him a lot of trouble. So Ira bought his share; I gave him the money I had been trying to hold in the bank to pay for the arrival of our baby. The next Saturday night I opened Ira's pay envelope to give him his fifty cents for tobacco (he had cut himself down from a dollar) and got a weak feeling in the pit of my stomach. There was only ten dollars in the envelope—the rest had gone to pay for lumber for the boat. I managed to look up at him and smile. I would show him I could be just as game as he was.

It was not easy to eat, pay bills and build a boat on twenty-one dollars a week. Somtimes Ira would have to stop buying lumber when the bills got too large. But marine catalogs started coming to the house, and Ira began to talk of an engine for the boat. Originally it was to have been just a little sailboat, but Ira said the engine was important because if he was caught out in the channel with a load of fish and no wind, he would lose his catch. It was useless for me to argue with him; he always had a line of talk I couldn't overcome.

All Ira's friends who were interested in boats came over every night to check on the progress and tell stories. Ira would bring them into the house, spread out the boat plans, and they would stay and talk until midnight. Though this parade of people and the hammering next door bothered me quite a bit, I tried to stay out of the way and pay no attention. I had other things to worry about. My baby was expected to arrive soon and I began making the layette, though I couldn't afford much; all our money was going for the boat.

In December, 1904, my first baby was born—a beautiful six-pound, auburn-haired girl. We named her Corinne Irene, and called her Irene. Six days after she was born there was a heavy rainstorm; somehow I caught cold and became very sick. Mother Eaton moved me into her house so I could be more comfortable, but she also took sick and a nurse was hired to take care of me, thus adding more to the large bills we already had. I stayed in bed for over four weeks, and all through this siege of sickness Ira never mentioned the boat or worked on it. After I began to feel better, I moved back into our little house. Ira had things all cleaned up and helped me around the house until I was really strong again. Then he went back to working on the boat.

One of the men who came over regularly to look at the boat was a Captain Colis Vasquez, who had a forty-foot, two-

masted schooner called the *Peerless*. He used her to haul crawfish to town from the different fishing camps on the islands,
and to catch seals which were then sold to zoos and circuses.
On one trip from the islands he brought us four big crawfish.
By this time my cooking had improved, but I had never cooked
or eaten crawfish. Captain Vasquez showed me how to boil
them; they squirmed when they hit the water, which I didn't
like, but when they were done I had to admit they tasted
delicious.

When Captain Vasquez came to visit, he and Ira would stay
up late talking about who else was building boats and all the
competition there was on the waterfront. He promised to teach
Ira all he could, as he knew the boating business from A to Z.
He also said that whenever he had engine trouble, Ira could
fill the seal orders for him. As the boat progressed, Ira became more and more enthusiastic about all the money he would
be making with it. Also, he would be able to bring home plenty
of fish, which he was fond of eating, and that would save on
the grocery bill. I figured that would be something anyway.

Early in March there were terrible southeast storms. The
wind howled and the rain poured. All the small skiffs and punts
were washed ashore on East Beach, and many larger boats
sank at their moorings or were battered against Stearns
Wharf. Our friend Captain Vasquez took the *Peerless* to the
islands to ride out the storm, and when he came back he said
it was the worst he had ever experienced. The ocean had
washed high up on the shore at Santa Cruz Island, tearing out
trees and boulders, and the heavy rains had destroyed roads
inland on the island. Every canyon was a running river of
mud, and the ocean for half a mile out was the color of mud.
Naturally I had visions of what would have happened to our
boat if it had been in the water—it would have gone ashore
just like all the other boats, and all the money that we had
spent on it would have been lost. But nothing could daunt Ira;
he said that if the men had put their boats out to the winter
anchorage, they would not have lost them. That settled the
boat question for some time.

Ira worked harder than ever to get his boat finished and in the water, for since so many had been lost there would be more call for boats. The engine had arrived from the east, been paid for and stored in the warehouse on the wharf. Almost every evening Ira would tell me who all had been to help him: the Bates boys, the Bagley boys, Don Leach, Wes Thompson, Owen O'Neill and others. He planned to repay them all by giving them trips back and forth to the islands when the boat was done. With all these friends helping him, Ira's boat was soon ready to launch.

CHAPTER II

The *Irene*

1905–1908

Our Boat is Launched — Ira's First Charter — Sealing and
Fishing — San Nicolas Island — Crawfish Season — Wreck of
the *Colman* — The Painted Cave — Sir Reggie — Our Baby
Dies — Santa Rosa and Santa Barbara Islands — Vera is Born
— Joaquin Miller — Christmas at the Fish Camp — The *Irene*
is Lost — The New Boat

AFTER THE STORMS came a week of beautiful weather, and it
was decided that our boat would be launched on the high tide
Sunday morning, March 16, 1905. Saturday night Ira was
busy loading the boat onto a lumber wagon he had borrowed
from the Santa Barbara Lumber Company at the foot of State
Street. The team of horses was fed and bedded in Father
Eaton's barn so things would go smoothly in the morning.

On Sunday Ira and I were out of bed at five, for this was
our day of days, the culmination of so much hard work. Father
Eaton and Wes Thompson, the driver of the team, came over
for breakfast, then went out with Ira to put the finishing
touches on the boat. When all was in readiness and the team
hitched up to the wagon, Wes guided the horses slowly out of
the back yard and into the alley. Turning south onto Garden
Street, we formed quite a parade—Father Eaton driving his
horse and buggy on the left side of the boat, Ira walking on
the right, and I abreast of them on the sidewalk wheeling the
baby in her buggy. Along the route were all our friends and
neighbors, waving and shouting encouragement. They had all
been so kind and never said a word about all the hammering
that had gone on so long. We reached the foot of the street

17

and turned west onto the Boulevard. A large crowd of men was waiting at the Last Chance Saloon, glasses of beer in hand. As the boat passed by they all good-naturedly threw their beer at the hull. It seemed as if everyone in Santa Barbara was gathered along the beach and wharf to see the launching.

Just before the boat was pulled into the water, she was officially christened. One of Ira's best friends, Don Leach, broke a bottle of soda pop over her and named her the *Irene,* after our baby. The horses pulled the wagon as far out into the water as they could walk, and when the team was unhitched, Ira and several of his friends hopped aboard. Captain Vasquez was standing by in the *Peerless,* caught the tow line thrown to him and, amid much shouting and waving of hats and handkerchiefs, pulled the *Irene* into the water. As I stood there watching, I cried with joy and thanked God for all the favors he had shown my husband so far.

When the anchor was thrown out and the *Irene* was at her mooring, I headed home to fix supper for all the boys. I was so happy, I decided I must do my part to help things go right in this boating business. The crowd ate plenty of fish chowder, cake and coffee that night, and decided to make the first trip in the *Irene* the following Saturday across the channel to the islands.

The next weekend the boys left early on the *Irene*'s trial voyage. Returning that evening from the islands, they all came up to the house for supper again, bringing with them a mess of fish they had caught. They had a wonderful trip, stopping at Valdez Harbor where they cooked breakfast over a bonfire on the beach, and then cruising down the coast to Pelican Bay. After dinner on the beach at Little Pelican they had a short siesta, then sailed home without having to start the engine.

The following week, Ira bought lumber to install seats on the *Irene*. Being new, she looked good to the public, and there would be some demand for her to carry passengers. Ira still spent every spare moment on the boat while working eight hours a day at the mill.

One day Ira said he would take the baby and me for a picnic. He borrowed his father's horse and buggy, I put up a lunch, and we drove out to the Rutherford ranch in Goleta. After I had spread our lunch on the grass, Ira said he thought he would like to leave the mill and run his boat himself; if you allowed someone else to run your business, they did not give it the interest they should. He also knew he was inhaling fine ground glass from his mill work, and thought that was why he had stomach trouble. I told him to do what he thought best, and that Saturday he notified his boss that he would not report for work after the first of May.

When the first of May came, Ira invited a group of school-teachers out for a moonlight ride up the coast and back. When he got home late that night he told me the same group had chartered the boat for a trip to the islands in two weeks. I asked if there were any young, good-looking girls in the party, and he said there were quite a few; in fact, the girl who had chartered the boat was very good-looking. She had about the best figure he had ever seen. Well, I thought, I had a very good figure myself until the baby came.

On Sunday, May 14, the party of schoolteachers went to the islands. It was ten o'clock when Ira got home, tired but happy. They stopped at Valdez Harbor for breakfast, then visited Forney's Cove at the west end of the island, went down to Gull Rock and around the south side. They landed at Smugglers' Cove for a lunch of fruit salad, sandwiches and hot coffee, then boarded the boat again and started around the east end of the island for home, making about an eighty-five mile trip for the day. As Ira was eating supper I asked him about that good-looking girl.

"Well," he said, "when we rounded San Pedro Point there was a heavy northwest wind blowing. That girl was sitting close to her boyfriend and I was at the wheel. I noticed she was very quiet, though she had been the life of the party all day.

Pretty soon she was feeding the fish over the side of the boat. She turned pale, then yellow, and then she fainted. I called for water and threw some on her face, but she did not revive. We stretched her out on the deck of the boat and one of the girls opened her shirt-waist to remove her corset, as they thought it might be pressing on her heart. And lo and behold, that girl had padded busts!"

I pointed out that she did have a very good figure but it was borrowed. Ira conceded that mine, after all, was natural, and I thanked him for the compliment.

On May 29 the *Irene* had her first work from another boat. Captain Vasquez and the *Peerless* had an order for seals, and also an agreement to bring back some Chinese fishermen from the island. He turned the party of Chinese over to Ira, and when Ira brought them back they gave him half a sack of abalones, shelled, pounded and ready to eat. Did we have a feast! When cooked, these abalones tasted something like oysters. What we could not eat Ira passed around to his friends.

The *Irene* was becoming very popular. In rapid succession she was chartered for fishing trips up the coast and to the islands by Henly Booth (the city attorney), C. P. Austin, Ed Stevens and a party of his friends, and Mr. J. C. Reynolds. I did not have to put up lunches for Ira and his helper, Danny Pico, very often; the parties usually invited the men to eat with them. Ira and Danny would gather driftwood and start a fire for each group, which was appreciated.

One day Ira came home all excited—he was to make his first trip to San Miguel Island. Mr. Reynolds, Mr. Basil Faulding, and Mr. Breasely were going over, taking Captain Short along as pilot; Ira was to drop them off and call for them in about ten days. As soon as he returned the *Irene* was chartered by another party, Mr. Huron Rock, Mr. Cameron Rogers, and Mr. Frank Knoll. They went to Fry's Harbor and caught quite a mess of fish on the way over, which Ira cooked for their lunch. The roast chicken and sandwich lunch they had brought along went begging, and Ira brought it home to me. On the way home they sighted a large whale and a swordfish, but as they had already spent so much time they didn't stop to look. Then Mr. C. C. Felton and a party of New Yorkers had a very successful fishing trip. They caught the largest albacore landed for some time in Santa Barbara—it weighed eighty-seven pounds. In those days large fish were caught more for sport than for food, being thought too coarse to eat; so Mr. Felton gave the fish to Ira, who sold it in Chinatown for three cents a pound. That money went to help buy Ira a white cap and white duck trousers to wear on the boat.

Then it was time for Ira to go over to San Miguel to bring back the party of young men he had left off at the wharf at Cuyler Harbor ten days before. The party brought back plenty of Indian relics such as skulls and arrows, and several interesting shells they had picked up on the beach at low tide. Ira said San Miguel looked very desolate from the boat, and in the harbor there was a huge rock just covered with thousands of seagulls. He wanted to take a week to explore the area sometime, as it seemed to be such an unusual place.

All this news was very interesting to me. I was beginning to think that perhaps I should not have been so worried about the boating business after all.

Next Ira made arrangements to take two of the oldest and best fishermen, Frank Nidever and Clarence Libbey, to San Nicolas Island, where they would fish for crawfish. These were "high men" in the fishing game, and Ira knew if he stayed around them very long he would learn a great deal about the different ways of making money. He had never been to San Nicolas himself, but they told him it would take twelve to fifteen hours to get there, for it was about a hundred miles from Santa Barbara. A hundred-mile trip in Ira's little boat seemed to me the equivalent of going to China or Japan.

Ira helped the men load their fishing and camping gear on the *Irene,* a job that took all day. They were taking plenty of supplies as they would be on the Island for several months. After supper Ira went aboard the boat to get some sleep, and they left about midnight.

Six days later he returned from San Nicolas and told me

all about the trip. Nearing the island, they had run into a
school of killer whales—every one of them dead. There was a
terrible stench from their decaying bodies. Frank and Clarence
said there must have been some volcanic disturbance or an
epidemic responsible for the death of so many; such a thing
didn't happen very often and might not be seen again for many
years.

Clarence built a fireplace and cooked supper while Frank
and Ira unloaded the boat and set up camp. They sat around
the fire and had Spanish beans, fried fish and good coffee. That
supper tasted so good to Ira, and he thought that life in the
open was so much better than living cooped up ashore. After
supper, Frank and Clarence talked about their experiences
while hunting seal and otter in Japanese waters. Frank also
told Ira about the lone Indian woman who had lived there on
San Nicolas Island for eighteen years. Frank's grandfather,
Captain George Nidever, had gone there in his schooner to
hunt otter, and had taken the woman off the island to Santa
Barbara. She had made her home with them for quite a while.

While out at the island, Ira helped the boys build two crawfish traps, ballast them, and bait them with abalone. They took
the traps out in the skiff and dropped them in the kelp. The
next morning at daybreak they pulled the pots in, full of crawfish. They had them fried with garlic, in chowder, and cooked
in many other ways, too. The boys gave Ira a dozen crawfish to
take home with him. In addition to the crawfish, Ira also
brought home a leg of good meat; he said the goats ran wild on
San Nicolas and didn't belong to anyone in particular.[1] I followed Frank's instructions for cooking it, and my, did that
meat taste good! It was so juicy.

Frank and Clarence intended to come back to Santa Barbara
for a week after crawfish season was over. Then they would
go up to San Miguel Island, where they would shoot the large
bull seal on the rookeries. The hides would be salted, the blubber boiled down, and the whiskers and trimmings sold to the
Chinamen who used them for medicinal purposes.

When Ira came home from what I called his "adventures,"

he would tell me that every minute of them was a pleasure to
him. He would hug and kiss me and say that all he wanted was
to get over his stomach trouble and make plenty of money for
the baby and me. I knew he was trying his best to prove to me
that he was right to leave his mill job and run the boat himself.

The *Irene* began to be chartered for fishing trips by various
parties of guests at the Potter Hotel. Sometimes the hotel
would put up their lunch and send along a waiter to serve it.
The people always enjoyed the trips, up the coast or to the
islands. One party gave Ira all the fish they had caught—
barracuda, yellow tail and bonita. He sold it at the market and
handed me the money, telling me to spend it on myself and the
baby.

In August, three men hired the *Irene* to make a trip to the
islands, fish on the way over and have lunch at Valdez Harbor.
They told Ira that they had heard so much about the Islands
and were anxious to make the trip. But on coming near Valdez,
they asked Ira to change his course and go around the west
end. They wanted to be taken ashore at Forney's Cove and, as
soon as Ira landed them safely, they threw back their coats and
showed him their badges. They were fish and game commis-
sioners, come to arrest the poor Chinese who had been picking
and drying abalones but were not throwing the undersized
ones away. The men explained that they had to pose as tour-
ists because the waterfronters were so clannish and would not
hire out their boats to the law. Ira felt terrible about the trick
that had been played on him, for he knew that all the waterfronters would think he was a stool pigeon.

By this time it was nearing the end of the passenger season
and getting close to crawfish season, and Ira started putting
out the first crawfish camps. The Lumber Company and
Dardi's Grocery Store advanced lumber and groceries to last
the fishermen for the whole season, which was about five
months. As each catch of fish was brought to market, weighed
and sold, Ira took out two cents a pound for hauling the fish
across the channel to town. He then made payments to the
Lumber Company and the Grocery until all the advance bills

were paid in full. This done, he took the balance of the cash back to the fishermen. They elected him their official banker, and anything they needed—from sou'westers to corn plasters —he bought, paid for, and delivered to them.

On his first trip Ira unloaded five men and equipment at Forney's Cove. There ahead of him were a bunch of Japanese fishermen and their equipment. He figured this was not so good for the white fishermen—he believed that if the Japanese were left alone, they would get a stronghold around the islands and prevent others from fishing there. But there was no use saying or doing anything to cause trouble, so he just let them fish. Later he stole their catch and sold it in town.

On one trip over to the island camps, Ira took along some men who wanted to camp on San Miguel. Unloading them, he decided to circle the whole island as he was anxious to know more about it. Coming down the north side, he looked ahead and saw a large ship, the *Colman,* aground on a reef. Coming near the ship, he and his helper, Danny, dropped the hook and shut off the engine, then rowed over in the skiff. The captain was in the pilot house studying his charts. He came out, leaned over the side of the ship, and asked where he was. Ira told him he was at San Miguel Island, about fifty miles from Santa Barbara. The captain invited Ira aboard and told him he had lost his course in the heavy fog. The first mate and four sailors had left the ship in a lifeboat and were rowing to the nearest coast to give news of the wreck. Ira said they would have a long trip ahead of them. The *Colman* was loaded with lumber, bound for San Pedro from Seattle, and the captain was concerned with saving his ship and cargo. Ira told him that would depend on the weather, and promised to keep an eye out for the lifeboat on the way back to town.

The mate and crew were picked up by a steamer and left off at San Pedro, and the next day they arrived in Santa Barbara and chartered the *Irene* to take supplies back out to the ship. When Ira went aboard the *Colman,* he found the captain very much upset. The second mate had dived down after a chest of gold that had sunk when the ship hit the reef, and he had never come to the surface again. They supposed he must have drowned. Ira said he was very sorry that had happened, and then, as there was nothing more he could do, went on his way. The steamer and wrecking crew did not reach the *Colman* in time, and she was pounded to pieces on the rocks by the heavy swell.

On October 17, 1905, Ira got an order for seals from Captain McGuire, so early in the morning he started for the islands, taking along Charley and Arturo Valdez and a man named Cooney as crew. On the fifth day he was back in town with the seals, which were shipped to London, England. He reported that he and the boys had discovered another entrance to the Painted Cave. This was the famous cave that the old-timers on the waterfront said was painted by the Indians, but Ira said he thought that nature made its beautiful colors. It had a high entrance and went way back into the mountain, no one knew how far. At low tide you could row in about two hundred yards to an inner chamber. Many of the old-timers thought that Painted Cave must have another opening, but no one could find it.

Ira and the boys drove all the seals out of the Painted Cave and set out the seal net across the opening so none could get back in. A few hundred feet up the coast they found another cave and another bunch of seals; one of these had unusual markings which would be easily recognized. These seals were chased into the second cave, and another seal net stretched across the opening. At low tide, the men rowed into this cave as far back as possible and could hear the sound of rushing water, but no seals came out. Then they rowed back to Painted Cave and there they found the same big bull seal with the funny markings—he had traveled through the underground watercourse and come out in Painted Cave. Ira thought the inner ends of the two caves were about three hundred yards apart. When he finished telling this story, I said that not so long ago he had been building his boat and wishing he could catch seal like Captain Vasquez; now he was in the business himself.

At the end of October Ira went to bring Clarence Libbey

and Frank Nidever back from San Nicolas Island. They had seventeen hundred pounds of crawfish, three tons of abalone and four tons of shell. They had also found some good pearls in the abalones which they could sell for two or three hundred dollars. Abalones brought a good price in the market; they were boiled, dried and sold to the Chinamen, who shipped them to China for food and medicinal purposes. The shells were shipped to Germany and made into jewelry and fancy articles.

One day in November, Ira told me he had a charter from an Englishman named Sir Reggie Boehan, a famous writer who was staying at the Potter Hotel. He wanted to hire the *Irene* for a five-day camping trip to the islands at twenty dollars a day. Ira was to do all the cooking and setting up of the camp, at a different harbor every night. Arturo Valdez, an Indian, would go along to help. Arturo knew everything about cooking, fishing, and boating, as he had been making camp for wealthy Montecito people for years. This was Ira's first camping party.

This Sir Reggie sported a light grey suit with a vest, spats, a monocle; he carried a silver-handled walking cane. When Ira came back after the trip, he had quite a story to tell. The Englishman had been too impatient to fish on the way over to the Island, so they went directly to Valdez Harbor, had breakfast and set up camp. In a couple of hours he wanted to move to another place, so they packed up again and went to Lady's Harbor, after having to go back once because he had forgotten his cane. That night he insisted the men give him their blankets or he would go back to town, as he was freezing cold in his silk pajamas. The next morning he had to shave and have his shredded wheat served warm, along with coddled eggs and bacon fried to a crisp. Then he wanted to see the Painted Cave, but was terrified when all the seals dove into the water next to the skiff and made a deafening noise with their barking in the dark inner chamber. After that he wanted to go to Anacapa Island, so they went some thirty miles down there and set up camp again. After supper, Sir Reggie let out a yell and said the island was infested with vermin—little field mice. He demanded they leave for Santa Barbara at once, although it was seven o'clock at night.

He had tried Ira and Arturo's patience for the last time. Once again they broke camp, and this time Ira made sure to pack all the blankets in first, under all the other equipment. A northwester had come up and the sea was very rough. On the way back to town, Ira went out of his way to hit every swell that came along. Arturo wouldn't pump out the two feet of bilge water from the hold where Sir Reggie was trying to sleep, and the blankets were inaccessible when he called for them. If Sir Reggie had never been seasick before, he surely learned what it was like on that trip. Finally they arrived at the buoy, and Ira stopped the boat and said he would collect his money now. Sir Reggie objected, saying he had not been treated like a gentleman. Ira said he had been hired as a boatman, not a valet, and they would stay out in the channel until he was paid. So Sir Reggie decided to pay.

Two years later Sir Reggie's book was published, and in it he said that the Californian boatmen were the most independent cusses he had ever met. Ira said that if the California boatmen never saw Sir Reggie again, it would be too soon.

My little girl had not been feeling well. She took a terrible cold and her milk did not seem to agree with her. All kinds of treatments were tried, but nothing helped. She continued to worsen and I was nearly insane when it became obvious she was going to die. She was buried the first of December, 1905, just eleven months and seven days old. For days at a time I did nothing but cry; I thought my heart would break. Finally I knew this would not bring her back, and I tried to direct my thoughts to the new little one that would be coming in just a few months. But for a long time afterwards when Ira came home and told me about his trips I was resentful, thinking he had the whole ocean to roam about in and forget his troubles, but I must stay home and live with mine.

One day Ira came home from the islands all excited about his first wild boar hunt. He and Frank and Clarence had been at Santa Rosa Island and the weather had been too bad to fish, so they walked up to the ranch house and asked the superintendent, Frank Pepper, if they could go shoot a wild hog. He was very hospitable and said, "Yes, shoot all the damned hogs you can hit—they are no good to the island. But please try not to frighten the cattle." So Clarence brought back a big boar, and that night for supper they had pig's liver fried with olive oil and wild mushrooms they had gathered. It was such good eating that Ira said he would hunt wild hogs any time he got a chance. He told me that Santa Rosa Island had rolling hills, not high mountains like Santa Cruz, and was easier to walk. The owners were noted for raising fine cattle; they also had a few sheep and goats, but only enough for their own use.

After one of the southeast storms that winter, we went down to the Boulevard where a forty-foot whale had been washed ashore at the foot of Chapala Street. The city authorities had driftwood piled around the carcass, oil poured over it and lit afire. All day long it burned, the blubber roasting in the flames, and it was still burning when night came. There was a continuous crowd of people on the beach watching it, in spite of the disagreeable odor.

About the middle of February 1906, Ira had another seal order from Captain McGuire. Taking Frank, Arturo, Charley and Cooney along as crew, Ira decided to catch the seals at Santa Barbara Island this time. The weather around our islands was very rough, and Frank said that the seas were always calmer around the islands to the south. After about five days Ira telephoned to let me know he was back with his seals and had also brought a large mess of red abalones which he would cook for our supper. I learned that red abalone is named for the color of the shell. The meat is white, and delicious dipped in egg and fried in olive oil.

Ira reported that they had no trouble catching their twelve seals by setting the net in front of a cave. Then they went ashore to have a look at the island. As they landed all they could see were little rabbit heads bobbing up and down from burrows. There must have been three or four hundred of them. They got their guns, and every shot hit one or two rabbits;

they quit shooting when they had four dozen. Ira said that Santa Barbara Island was just a rock sticking up out of the ocean, and the whole thing was full of rabbit holes. If these animals were not cleaned out soon, what little grass there was would be eaten up completely.

That afternoon Father Eaton and I went down to the wharf to look at the seals before they were shipped to London to be trained for the circus. Captain McGuire said that this species of seal (the California sea lion) was the most intelligent and best behaved. This group ranged in age from eight months to four years. Unlike most wild animals, these did not show much anxiety when captured and put into cages. They did not sulk but poked their noses through the wire trying to be friendly.

About the first of March when it was time for me to expect my baby, I moved over to Mother Eaton's house. She did not think it was good for me to be alone and Ira was away so much. I was feeling much happier now. All I thought of was my baby, and I prayed daily for strength to go through whatever was before me. I needed that little one so much. After twelve hours of labor, my second baby girl was born March 15, 1906. All the pain was forgotten when I hugged her to me, and I was the happiest woman in the world. Meantime, Ira was away on a fishing trip and the *Irene* developed engine trouble. He arrived home three days late, to discover he had a new daughter, whom we named Vera. In spite of the baby's bout with measles when she was only a week old, we both progressed nicely. I stayed at Mother Eaton's house for three weeks, then moved back home.

In April, Ira took the head gardener of the Potter Hotel over to Santa Cruz Island, along with a party of five. The purpose of their trip was to collect water birds and animals to add to the hotel menagerie. Ten days later they came back. While hunting they had discovered a bald eagle's nest with seven young eagles. They brought all of them back, as well as some island foxes, and ferns and other valuable plants. Ira said that a large school of porpoises had played around the boat on this trip and he wished I had been along to see it.

That summer flew by. I was busy and happy with my baby girl, and Ira was busy fishing and catering to parties who chartered the boat. One of these was the famous writer Joaquin Miller, the "Poet of the Sierra." He was staying at the Potter Hotel and took a party of his friends to the islands for the day. The hotel put up a fancy lunch with plenty of champagne in silver ice buckets, and a private waiter to serve. Mr. Miller invited Ira to eat with them, and of course he accepted. There was a whole roast turkey, and each person got half a fried chicken; also there were French rolls, cheese, potato salad, chocolate cake and ice cream. No expense had been spared to give them the best.

When the summer tourist season was over it was time to put out the crawfish camps again, and Ira was busy hauling and selling the catches. In December, he came back from one of these trips and said that all the boys who were camping at Forney's Cove had invited him and Frank to have Christmas dinner with them. There were eighteen of them living there in a large hay barn that belonged to the owners of the island. Each set of partners had their own space in the barn and their own gasoline stove, and they all got along fine together. Among those camped there were George Nidever and his brother Jake, Clarence Libbey, Wes Thompson, Big Jerry, Little Danny, Kangaroo Joe, Hard Working Tom, the Big Swede, our friends Arturo, Charley and Cooney, and several others. They were also expecting some of the other fishermen from the camps around the island to drop in.

When Ira returned after Christmas, he said that a good time was had by all. The men had captured two wild hogs and fattened them for Christmas dinner. Ira, Clarence, Big Jerry and Hard Working Tom had gone over to Santa Rosa Island and shot thirty-five wild geese, and brought back Frank Pepper, the superintendent, to be a guest of the fishermen for three days. The geese were stuffed with a dressing of celery, olives, raisins and oysters. The hogs were butchered, dressed, stuffed and roasted in the big stone oven next to the barn. It had been used to bake bread for the ranch hands in the early days.

Next to the barn stood two heavy manzanita posts with a crosspiece between them, from which hung a large copper dinner bell that had been used to call the ranch hands to their meals. When Christmas dinner was ready, Little Danny rang this bell until all were at their places at the big long table. It had been decorated with holly, and there was a whole roast goose on each wooden plate. There were also the two roast hogs, mashed potatoes, fresh green peas, a crate of celery, two gallons of olives, crawfish salad, French bread, and coffee. Big Jerry had made dozens of pumpkin and mince pies, enough for half a pie of each kind for each person. To drink there were five gallons of whiskey, twenty-five gallons of dago red, and a couple of barrels of beer.

The men had had a meeting beforehand and agreed that they were all sharing expenses and could drink as much as they wanted to, but anyone who got too boisterous would be taken outside and hobbled to one of the posts until he calmed down. Of all those men, the rule was put into action for only one. Big Jerry got funny and wanted to fight, so the whole crowd escorted him outside and chained his right foot to the post. The rest of the men went to their bunks for an afternoon rest, but outside Big Jerry kept singing very loudly and they couldn't shut him up. Finally they gave up and joined him, and sang all the old fishermen's songs. Then Jerry, still hobbled, danced a hornpipe and made so much noise with his chain they decided to let him loose. They all went back to the table, which had been left just the way it was, and finished the rest of the food for supper. After that, everyone got out musical instruments— fiddle, guitar, accordion, banjo, jew's-harp and mouth organs —and played. Big Jerry sang and jigged, and a dog that was there sang too. About ten o'clock they all turned in for the night after a fine day of good-natured revelry.

After the New Year, Ira left one Sunday morning to fish at the islands, even though a northwester was beginning to blow. He expected to be back in time for the Friday market. I worried about him going out in such weather, but figured he knew what he was doing.

Tuesday at noon he came into the yard. His cap was missing, his hair all ruffled, his face scratched and bruised, and his fingernails broken down to the quick. He threw his arms around my neck and said, "Oh, Margaret! My boat *Irene* is lost!" My heart sank, and suddenly the whole world seemed turned upside down. We clung to each other and I asked how it had happened.

He said that just outside Valdez Harbor Sunday night the engine had quit; he turned the wheel over to his helper Frank and worked on the engine for about an hour with no success. The storm was worsening and the boat drifted toward the rocks. When they saw there was no hope of saving her they jumped overboard. The icy raging sea dashed them against the rocks, and finally they made shore. They took off their freezing wet clothes and tried to dry them in the howling wind. When daybreak came they hiked about ten miles over the roughest part of the island to Forney's Cove, where the fishermen gave them a hot meal and a change of clothes. Big Jerry's blue jeans almost doubled around Ira's waist, and the seat hung down to his knees; he rolled up the long legs and tied them with fishline. Ira wore a number eight shoe, and Big Jerry's were a number twelve. Even though he had lost everything, Ira could see the humor in that. And at least he was warm and dry. The next morning a fishing boat brought him and Frank back to town.

After he had a hot bath and changed his clothes, I asked about the insurance policy on the boat. That was my one ray of hope. "Oh," said Ira, "I didn't tell you, but I have had a great deal of engine trouble lately and it has cost me quite a penny. There won't be much left when I pay all those bills." Then he kissed me and left for the wharf to arrange to work on shares on some other boat. I was stunned. We had gone without so much to make this business a success. There were many other bills still unpaid. What would happen to us? I had been trying to hold back the tears but now, kneeling beside the bed, I just let them fall. Why had this trouble come to us? I had always tried my best to do what I thought was right, but it had all been for nothing.

As I knelt there, I could hear the baby cooing and then felt two arms around my neck. Father Eaton was kneeling beside me; he had just seen Ira and knew how I felt. He told me to put my trust in God and everything would turn out for the best. After all, Ira could have been drowned, and that would have been much worse. He also said not to worry about the bills, that everyone knew Ira was honest and would do his best. Then Father Eaton and I said the Lord's Prayer together, and we both felt better. I made up my mind to take things as they came, and to try to make the best of everything.

Ira came home later and said that many of the boat owners had offered to let him work with them, just as other men had worked with him. He had made arrangements to work on the *Baltic*. When crawfish season was over, he brought all the fishermen and their equipment back from the islands. It would be a few months before the summer business began. I suggested that Ira go to work helping his father build the Gregson Hotel; Father Eaton had said he had a place for Ira any time.

So Ira went to work as a carpenter and I thought, now we can live just like ordinary people, with meals at regular hours and evenings at home. But the first week Ira was down at the wharf every evening after supper. I knew what that would lead to. To help save money, I rented out a room in our house and also boarded two of the men who worked on the Gregson job. I did ironing four hours a day for Mrs. Axtell, who ran the Bellevue boarding house next door, and instead of paying me she provided lunch and dinner (except for the meat) for all of us.

On Saturday of Ira's second week of his new job, he came home and put his arms around the baby and me and kissed us. He said, all in one breath, "Margaret, what would you think if I started another boat? Just a small one this time!" When I commented that I had known this would happen sooner or later, he continued, "You know that I love you and the baby

very much. You both come first with me, and then I love this
boating game. I don't want to be tied down to carpenter work
all my life. I have tried my best to settle down to it, but when I
can see the ocean I have the urge to drop my tools and go down
to the wharf and take the first boat over to the islands. I can't
help it. There is some fascination about the sea that holds me
—I miss it every moment I'm away from it. Can't you see my
side?"

I knew now that there was nothing I could do to change our
life, so I gave in gracefully and let Ira build his boat in our back
yard. Just as he had done with the *Irene,* he worked on the new
boat in the evenings and on Sundays. This boat was to be only
twenty-five feet long, ten feet less than the *Irene,* and it would
have a five horsepower engine. There was less lumber to buy,
and Ira was making four dollars a week more working for his
father than he had at the mill. The arrangements I had made
helped out too, so we managed better this time around. In four
or five months the second boat was finished and ready to go out
fishing for smelt. She was dubbed the *Sam Pan.* There would
be no more boats named after our babies.

CHAPTER III

My First Visit to Santa Cruz Island
Summary, 1908

Getting Ready — To Pelican Bay in the *Gussie M.* — First
Meal in Camp — Captain Nidever Comes to Visit — The Lone
Woman — View from the Hill — More Visitors — Back to
Town

IRA'S STORIES about the islands had always been fascinating
to me. Now and then I would ask him when he was going to
take me out there so I could see for myself the places he was
always talking about. After the *Sam Pan* was finished, he
promised to take me to Santa Cruz Island for a camping trip
sometime during the summer.

One day Ira came home from the wharf having just talked
to Captain Colís Vasquez, who was going to take a party over
to Fry's Harbor on his boat the *Gussie M.* Ira had made arrangements for me to go along. After the party had been left
off at Fry's I would be taken to a place called Pelican Bay,
where Ira camped when he was fishing at the island. He
would take my camping gear over on the *Sam Pan* when he
left on a fishing trip the following morning. Then after fishing
for a couple of days he would meet me in camp.

Ira would also take along someone to stay in camp and help
me. This man was Dicey Jones, and his people had a saloon on
State Street. Ira said that Dicey was a bit down and out, and
had been drinking heavily. They were both members of the
Eagles Lodge, and the Eagles had asked Ira to take Dicey to
the island to get him away from liquor so he could sober up.

35

He could be of help to me by gathering firewood and doing odd jobs.

We discussed what I would need for my two-week stay on the Island. "I am not taking a tent," said Ira, "because you won't need one this time of year. You will cook, eat, and sleep out in the open under the beautiful oak trees. Their branches spread out all over the place. I will take your double springs and mattress, bedding, and some cooking utensils—not many, just a couple of pots and a frying pan. And I have some heavy plates and white mugs with handles. Some yacht left quite a few of those dishes up at Fry's Harbor, and the captain said I could have them."

"I know the kind you mean, Ira. When you drink from them your mouth is full of china. How large is the cook stove? You haven't said anything about it."

Ira thought for a second and said, "Well, cooking for only about two weeks you won't need a stove, do you think? It won't be like keeping house, just camping. I've built a cobblestone fireplace on the edge of the creekbed and put some bars on top. It's a dandy stove. You'll like it. You may get your hands black and chapped from the smoke, but out camping you won't mind a little dirt, will you?"

"Don't worry and try to discourage me. Mrs. Axtell makes some wonderful cream with mutton tallow, lemon, and some other stuff, to use on her face and hands. I can get a jar of it from her and use it every night."

"Be sure to get a large hat for shade, too, because the sun beating down from the rocks and cobblestones can be very glaring."

I asked whether there were any flies and bees on the island. Ira said he had only seen kelp flies that bothered the yachtsmen, and yellowjackets. Reacting to the look on my face, he said, "Yes, they sting, but if you don't bother them they won't bother you. Just don't leave any sweet stuff open, and try to keep everything covered up."

So I planned to take along a dozen dish towels to cover the

table, as well as a large piece of mosquito netting to protect the baby while she was sleeping. Ira also told me to order plenty of groceries, because over on the island we would feel hungry all the time. He could bring us more of whatever we wanted when he went back to town with a load of fish.

"Can I get fresh milk for the baby at that wonderful ranch you have told me about, where they have horses, cows, chickens and turkeys? You said that every time you went ashore at Prisoners' Harbor, the French watchman always gave you a large cup of fresh milk. Can I wheel the baby's cart over to the ranch to get her milk? I would pay the Frenchman, or you could trade him smelt for it; you said he was very fond of fish."

Ira laughed. "Margaret, you don't know what the country is like over on the island. That ranch is about three and a half miles from where your camp will be. You couldn't walk or wheel the baby buggy because there are mountains to climb and steep canyons to walk down. Anyway, I don't want you going away from camp at all with the baby. I don't want you climbing the hill to the fishermen's shack behind the camp, because the baby might get away from you and go up there alone and fall off the cliff. Then what would you do? There's a smooth little beach near the camp that is safe, and you and the baby can have a salt water bath every day."

I answered, "Don't you worry one bit about the baby. If I can just get over to that island, I won't let her out of my sight. You know that here she is never one bit of trouble to me." But I agreed to stay near the camp. Condensed milk diluted with warm water would do for the baby while we were there.

I had no camping shoes, just house shoes with high heels. Ira told me to get a pair of heavy camping boots, because the beaches and canyons were full of rocks that were very hard on shoes, but I thought to myself that I would wear out the shoes I had before I bought another pair. Little did I realize just how worn out my shoes would be by the end of the trip!

"If you are a good camper this time at Pelican Bay," said

Ira, "I may take you and the baby over to Willow Canyon on the south side of the island for the winter. Frank Nidever and I are planning to camp ashore there and fish from the *Sam Pan*. We will haul our own fish back to town about every ten days to save freight charges, so we can bring out supplies for you."

I was delighted at this piece of news, and promised to keep everything in our camp just spic-and-span. In Pelican Bay I would be living in the open, but Ira told me that at Willow Canyon there was a cabin to stay in. It had been built by Frank Nidever's father and uncle from lumber that washed ashore on San Miguel Island when the sailing ship *Colman* was wrecked two years earlier. The cabin had no windows and only a dirt floor, but it had a fireplace and a lean-to kitchen with a wood stove. I thought it sounded just grand. Once I got over there, there would never be a grumble out of me, I said, and I would fix up the cabin and kitchen just dandy.

"Now I must hurry," said Ira. "I have stayed home longer than I expected. Whatever you do, don't keep Captain Vasquez waiting. His boat is to leave at nine o'clock sharp Monday morning. Order a cab from Sam Stanwood's stables, and ask for Wes Thompson to drive you to the wharf. He is about the best driver in town."

Putting his hand in his pocket, he gave me fifty cents for the cab. Then waving his hand he was off.

Monday morning at eight o'clock, Wes Thompson and the cab were at the gate. We arrived at the wharf in plenty of time so as not to keep Captain Vasquez waiting. As my suitcases were being put aboard the *Gussie M.*, two express wagons loaded with baggage and seven campers seated on top drove out onto the wharf. The four men in the party wore regular khaki outfits. The three woman had khaki divided skirts and shirt waists. They all wore red bandanna handkerchiefs tied around their necks, heavy-top hiking boots with hobnails, and canteens with khaki straps slung over their shoulders.

I was wearing a black alpaca dress, full skirt and blouse

with white collar and cuffs, and a black sailor hat with a white gauze veil tied around it and then under my chin. The ends acted as a shade for my baby's eyes. After all the baggage and camping gear was stored away and I was helped on board, I took my seat in the stern of the schooner and held the baby in my arms. The photographer in the party remarked that we looked just like the Madonna and Child.

Standing in the pilot-house door, Captain Vasquez took out his watch from his pants pocket and said, "We are leaving exactly on time: nine o'clock."

"Captain," I said, "this is my first trip to Santa Cruz Island, and I am so thrilled about it."

He replied, "Yes, once you go over to those islands, you will never be satisfied away from them. I have parties who have been going over there with me every summer for the last fifteen years, and they never miss a summer."

As we passed the whistling buoy, the Captain told us the joke about what happened when the government first installed it. A few days afterward came a heavy northwest wind and heavy swell. When the swells hit against the whistling buoy, it sent out a sound, just like the one we heard now. On shore— and especially up on the hill—this sound was just like the moo of a cow. Some of the people who lived there didn't know about the buoy and thought there were several cows somewhere that were being mistreated, so they rang up the humane society to complain. After some investigation, the humane society discovered that all that noise was caused by the new whistling buoy.

While Captain Vasquez was talking I noticed what a good-looking man he was. Tall and broad shouldered, he had dark wavy hair and laughing blue eyes, an olive complexion, a very fine set of pearly white teeth, and a drooping black moustache. On that morning he wore working clothes: a dark blue, heavy woolen sailor shirt with large pearl buttons, khaki trousers, a sailor's belt of crocheted white twine with a large silver buckle that had his initials engraved on it, and broad black working

snoes with low heels. I learned later that he was quite a ladies'
man in town and was always dressed in the height of fashion,
changing his clothes twice a day.

I found Captain Vasquez very interesting and entertaining.
He explained that most of his orders for seal had been taken
over by Ira and the *Irene*. Now in summertime he was kept
busy taking people from Santa Barbara to Santa Cruz Island.
There were many who were anxious to get away from town
and live outdoors, fish and hike, as this group would be doing
for the next two weeks.

The Captain told us how to dig abalones from the rocks at
low tide, and how to take the skiff out to the kelp beds and
catch fish for our breakfast. Crawfish were also abundant
there and could be easily seen in the beautiful colors of the
undersea growth. On the island there were wild hogs, he said;
in fact the whole back country was full of their tracks. The
hogs would lie around in the manzanita in the daytime, but
came out early in the morning to feed. He suggested that the
campers take a gun when hiking if they thought themselves
good hunters, because these hogs made very good eating.

Then the Captain told the campers of the other things they
should be sure to see on the island. He said that no trip was
complete without a visit to the Painted Cave. Then pointing
ahead of the boat, he said, "If you are very energetic and good
hikers you can climb to the top of Mt. Diablo, which is about
2400 feet high. Many people start to climb it but they don't
finish; halfway up they just quit and go back to camp. If you
want to try it, put up light lunches and start about daybreak.
You will find good sheep trails to follow up the mountain.
When you reach the top of Mt. Diablo, you have a wonderful
view of the island. Santa Cruz is formed something like my
hand—the fingers represent the mountains, and the spaces between them the canyons leading to the beaches. The long rows
of mountains are covered with wildflowers of every description.

"When you are on top, facing the channel, you will see the

whole of Santa Barbara, the Santa Ynez Mountains, and the surrounding country for miles around. To your left you will have a good view of San Miguel and Santa Rosa, and you will see Anacapa, Santa Barbara, San Nicolas, and Catalina Islands in the distance. When you reach the top, take a good long breath, for you seldom breathe such pure, fresh air. And you will think you are sitting on top of the world, lords of all you survey. To us who have nothing, that is a glorious feeling."

As we were crossing the channel, the island looked like a row of barren mountains and canyons, but when we neared Fry's Harbor the vision changed to one of extreme beauty. The harbor was surrounded by high rocky cliffs, which were covered with scrub oak, cactus, and many succulent plants. These were in full bloom, making masses of yellow, red, lavender and magenta color. Growing in wild profusion among those beautiful plants were ferns of the deepest green. Up the canyon was a dense growth of willow and live oak trees, which from the boat seemed much larger than those on the mainland. The water in the bay was so blue and so transparent that I could see the rocks on the sandy ocean bottom. Under the boat a school of fish swam lazily back and forth; they had large, strange-looking heads and thick bodies with a three-inch-wide red stripe around the middle. They were sheephead, said the Captain, and not good to eat.

All the hustle and bustle of unloading the camping equipment and taking the passengers ashore was accomplished without stopping the engine or dropping anchor. Amid hurried goodbyes and promises to call on me at Pelican Bay, the campers were left at Fry's, and we headed down the coast.

Captain Vasquez pointed out large openings in the cliffs called blowholes. At high tide, the sea fighting and raising battle against the cliffs would send the spray fifty or a hundred feet high, and the swells hitting the entrances of the blowholes would sound just like thunder. Then we passed Mussel Rock, from which our friends were expecting to get part of their food. It was a big rock, about a hundred and fifty feet long and a hundred feet wide, and was covered with a mass of mussels.

Soon we had reached Twin Harbors, and the hills behind the steep cliffs were covered with a vast forest of pine trees. According to the Captain, they were Torrey pines, which were found in only two other places.[2] There were also manzanita and scrub oak. Up on the flats we could see large flocks of sheep grazing.

Finally we reached our destination, Pelican Bay, and the Captain slowed his engine. The bay was wide and deep, protected on the west and east by high points of land, making an almost perfect U. There were thick kelp beds below the cliffs. Perched on a tiny rock sticking out of the kelp was the first heron I had ever seen, looking as if he owned the bay. Even when the whistle was blown, the heron never moved. The Captain told me that as long as he had been in the boating game, whenever he came to Pelican Bay there was always a heron on that very same rock.

There was an old, almost tumbled-down shack with a sagging door, perched on a shelf of solid rock about two hundred feet up from the ocean. It seemed to have been hewn out of the hill, and to me it looked as if it might fall into the sea at any moment. Then I realized what Ira had meant when he said the baby might stray away, and I felt a pang and wondered if I had done right to risk bringing my baby to this hilly country. But then I would have nothing else to do but take care of her.

We rounded the eastern point of land and entered a small cove called Little Pelican, where I was to camp. The beach was not more than two hundred feet wide, and the cliffs on either side of the canyon were high and straight and covered with cactus and wildflowers. Dicey, whom Ira had left in camp, was standing on the beach waiting for me.

The anchor was dropped and my suitcases and groceries loaded into the skiff. The Captain was in a hurry to unload me and my things so he could get back to Santa Barbara before dark. He took the baby in his arms and said, "Mrs. Eaton, I must land you two safely ashore, for I don't have the pleasure of carrying a Madonna and Child on my boat every day." Then we all got into the skiff, rowed to shore, and landed high on the sand. During the unloading, Dicey didn't make a move to help, for which Captain Vasquez chastised him.

Turning to me, the Captain said goodbye and I thanked him for all his kindness. He patted the baby on the cheek, and assured me that it was a pleasure to bring us over on our first trip to the Island. He would see us two weeks later when he came back to pick us up, if he didn't stop by before then. Back on the boat, he blew the whistle and waved his hat, then headed for Santa Barbara. I stood on the beach and thought what a wonderfully kind man he was.

Then I turned to Dicey and asked him to show me the camping place. He picked up my suitcases and I followed him up the canyon. About fifty feet up from the beach was a high rock with a large opening, which Dicey said was the cave where he slept. As we rounded this rock, the full view of the canyon was before me.

There was a level stretch of ground about two hundred and fifty feet wide and four hundred feet long, and in the center of it was the most beautiful oak tree I had ever seen. I had always thought that the oak trees in Hope Ranch were beautiful, but they could not begin to compare with this one. To the right was another clump of oak trees which seemed to tower halfway up to the sky. Their huge branches shot out in every direction, then came swooping down to the ground forming a natural arch. From Ira's description I knew this was our camping ground.

Back of the oak trees were five willows whose branches were entwined among the oaks and formed a dense canopy overhead. To the right of the natural arch was a high boulder covered with a dense growth of wild blackberry vines and poison oak. The ground and hills were covered with wild snapdragon and red Spanish dagger.

The double bed Ira had made before going fishing was raised from the ground on six orange boxes, one at each corner and two in the middle. My mattress, a pillow, and bedding were spread on top. The cobblestone fireplace that Ira had told me about was on the edge of the creek.

I longed to explore the place, but I had to think first of my baby, who was hungry after her hard day. Dicey started a fire and brought water in an old black lard pail while I unpacked the groceries. Hunting for a kettle, I discovered that all the camp cooking utensils from the last two days had been put away dirty. Apparently it had been too much trouble to wash them. So I washed the baby's bottle, made the tea, and boiled an egg all in the same kettle, and figured I was doing well right from the start. Then I toasted some bread in an old pie tin set on the iron grate over the fireplace. The baby was propped up on the bed with pillows, and her supper served to her from one of the thick white mugs.

I filled the water basin and pail from the spring, which was about seventy-five feet from the camp, and set the basin on the fire grate to warm for the baby's bath. After bathing her, I dressed her for bed and had her say her prayers. Tucked away under the bedclothes, she was soon fast asleep.

While more water was warming so I could wash too, I made a wash stand from an orange box some other camper had left there. When I had washed I put another basin-full on so Ira could have hot water to wash off the salt and grime when he came in. Then I found my bungalow apron in my suitcase. Being very anxious to get out of my black dress and not having a tent to change my clothes in, I asked Dicey if he would go and look to see how near the *Sam Pan* was. He walked up the hill toward the bluff, and when he was out of sight I rushed behind the willow branches and made a quick change into my bungalow apron.

When Dicey came back to say the *Sam Pan* was in sight, I was calmly peeling potatoes for supper. I put them on to fry with bacon grease and minced onion. Ira was fond of potatoes cooked that way. He had left some fileted smelt when he went out fishing, and when the potatoes were cooked I moved them to the back of the fireplace, rolled the fish in flour and began to cook it. I felt so happy there on the island, listening to the fish sizzle in the pan, that I began to sing. There was nothing to stop me from singing just as loud and long as I wanted to.

While the fish was cooking, I turned my attention to the table. It was a sorry mess, for Dicey had put the black pots and pans on it. I covered it with a clean dish towel, and then set it up with our dishes. With an empty tomato can cleaned up for a sugar bowl to replace the sugar sack Dicey had been using, the table didn't look half bad. An olive oil can split in half became two serving dishes. Then the lard pail was filled again and set to heat for tea.

By this time the *Sam Pan* was in the harbor, and Ira and the man who was helping him were pulling the skiff up high on the sand. Ira introduced his helper Frank, a heavy-set Italian man with a round face, small dark eyes, and straight black hair. I asked how the fishing had been, and they said they had caught a thousand pounds of fish, which they had sold to the market for three cents a pound. I figured quickly three times one thousand was thirty dollars; divided in half it would be fifteen dollars each. If the men could do that well every night, fishing would not be so bad.

Supper was all ready for the men, and the pots were set on the table on top of two of Dicey's dime novels so they wouldn't blacken the dishtowel tablecloth. The lantern was lighted, for by this time it was getting dark, and we pulled up the empty apple boxes we had brought from town to use as chairs. We sat down and had as good a supper as anyone could ask for.

Then Ira said to Frank, "How about a drink of wine?" Frank had carried a five-gallon jug of wine up the creekbed and set it down behind an oak tree. They agreed that they liked wine better than tea, especially since they had worked all day; tea was only good for ladies. While they drank their mugs of wine, I quietly enjoyed my tea, subtracted the cost of a jug of wine from the fifteen dollars, and frowned to myself. That would leave only twelve.

As we were eating, I told Ira about my trip over, how kind and entertaining Captain Vasquez was, and that I had invited the other passengers to come over and visit me from their camp at Fry's Harbor. Frank the Italian laughed and asked if I knew how far that was from Pelican Bay. It was about seven miles by boat, and he thought it unlikely that the people would want to row that far. By land it was about twelve miles over the hills, too far for the women to walk. I thought Captain Vasquez might pick them up on his way from San Miguel Island and bring them down for the ride, but Ira said the Captain preferred to spend his free time dressed up, hanging around Stearns Wharf in Santa Barbara.

When we had finished supper, it was time for Ira and Frank to go out fishing again. He was very tired, for they had worked the beaches all the previous night with only a little sleep on the way over to Santa Barbara and back. But the market expected him to bring in another load of smelt the next afternoon, so they had to go up to Lady's Harbor and set the smelt nets.

Ira kissed the baby, asleep in the bed, and told me to take good care of her. Then he put his arm around me and said, "Just come down to the beach with me, Margaret, I haven't seen you for two days and tomorrow will be three." So we walked down the creek, over the cobblestones to the beach. It was only a minute before they had shoved off in the skiff, calling goodbye and promising to be back as soon as they could. Then the *Sam Pan* was heading out of the bay and up the coast.

I hurried back to camp, for the baby had been left alone. Dicey said he would turn in now, for it was about seven o'clock, but if I needed anything in the night I should just call him, for he was a very light sleeper. Tidying up the camp, I covered the dishes with a towel and left them to be washed the next day.

Then I undressed and slipped into bed beside my baby, and lay there feeling so happy and contented. In the heavens above were millions of stars, and I felt childish enough to repeat, "Twinkle, twinkle, little star, how I wonder what you are, up above the world so high, like a diamond in the sky." As I lay in bed I could hear the soft rustling of the branches overhead and feel the light night air blowing on my face.

I thought I heard a noise—a man's voice down at the beach. I knew it wasn't Ira, because I hadn't heard the sound of the motor coming into the bay. I held my breath a minute, then pulled on my clothes as fast as I could. The voices got louder, and I heard a skiff being pulled up on the beach. Then I could see Dicey running up the creekbed as fast as he could, slipping over the cobblestones.

"Don't be frightened," he called. "The Captain of the schooner *Santa Cruz*, his brother, the crew, and the watchman from Prisoners' Harbor have come to serenade you, this being your first night on Santa Cruz Island." The moon was shining very brightly and I could see four figures coming up the creek. As they rounded the big rock, they pulled out musical instruments and began to play "La Paloma."

The baby had awakened and began to cry, but then she listened to the music and quieted down. I was so thrilled the tears rolled down my cheeks. I wiped my eyes with the baby's blankct, for I did not want these men to see me crying.

By this time they had reached the camp, and I made them welcome. The Captain introduced his brother Jake, the crewman Geronimo, and the watchman. They were dressed like the usual fishermen, in blue jeans, heavy shirts, caps and heavy boots, and each had a red bandanna handkerchief. Sitting down on the apple boxes, they played another tune. The baby was spellbound.

When they finished the Captain asked how I had enjoyed the trip across the channel and how long I planned to stay. I told him about Ira's idea to take me to another harbor to camp for the winter, for Ira expected to fish there with a man named Frank Nidever.

The Captain nodded and said, "Frank Nidever is my son, and Jake here is my brother." This was Captain Nidever, the son of George Nidever who was a famous sea otter hunter. Ira had spoken so much of him that I felt I knew him already.

After playing an old Spanish dance tune that had the baby

clapping her hands and feet to keep time to the music, the Captain asked me if I had ever heard about the woman on San Nicolas Island. "When we were coming up the creek playing and you were standing in the opening of this tree holding your baby, you reminded me of the woman in the story. Our father told us so many times when we were young about the lone woman who lived on San Nicolas Island for eighteen years."

Then he told the story just as he had heard his father tell it:

As you know, San Nicolas lies about eighty miles south of Santa Barbara and thirty miles from the nearest island, in the playground of the southwest trade winds and exposed to the open sea. The shape of the island is such that it affords no safe harbor, and it is seldom that a sailing vessel can land there safely.

Many years ago, Indian tribes lived on this island. Today many relics of their existence can be found—skeletons, arrowheads, and other things. These tribes were very peaceful, loving and contented people.

Later, Russian seal hunters came along southern California shores. They made raids on these island homes, killing the men and taking away the women and children. They wrought such havoc that the priests on the mainland made an effort to relieve those who were left. They engaged a small sailing vessel to bring those who remained on the island over to Santa Barbara.

In those days, sailing vessels were very scarce in those waters, and the captain was not familiar with the ocean currents and the sudden winds which blow furiously about San Nicolas. It was a terrible undertaking indeed to make the trip. The Indians were told that a ship was going to take them to the mainland, and while they were getting ready to leave a storm began to brew. The captain was desperate to get away from the island, or they might lose their ship and be marooned on the island with the Indians.

Everywhere there were Indians hurrying to load their belongings onto the ship. Some distance inland lived a woman named Juana María and her baby. In her hurry to get her belongings down to the beach, she thought someone else had taken her baby to the ship; but when she reached the shore she could not find her baby. Then it dawned on her that the baby had been left behind. In a frenzy, with a true mother's love, she rushed back to hunt for her baby.

The water about the island was getting rougher, and the captain could not wait for her. He put to sea at once, and they reached Santa Barbara safely. When Juana María went back to search for her baby, she discovered evidence of its clothing. The awful realization came to her that the wild dogs which roamed the island had killed her child while she was on the beach.

The captain intended to go back and get her, but for some reason never could, so poor Juana María was left alone on the island. Day after day she ran along the beach, looking for a sail, but none came. It is hard to understand how she survived alone, but somehow she did. Eighteen years passed, and all that time Juana María was the sole human inhabitant of San Nicolas Island.

Shortly after 1836, my father, Captain George Nidever, sailed his trim schooner down from San Francisco, and was successful in hunting otter and seal around the Santa Barbara islands. He heard the story of the Indian woman, and determined that at the first opportunity he would go to hunt for her.

He made the trip over to San Nicolas Island, and waited for favorable weather to land. On the island, he found the prints of a human foot. A storm began to blow and he had to put to sea again, but he waited near the island and when the weather was calm again he went ashore with some of his men to search.

Some distance from her sheltered home, they found her. She was clad in a wonderful gown made from feathers, a marvelous piece of work. When she saw the men she smiled, being pleased to see human beings again. She came to them and made signs, for she could speak only her own tongue. My father made signs to tell her that he had come to take her to Santa Barbara where her own people had been taken so many years before. She seemed delighted and happy to go, so her belongings were put aboard.

Juana María's manner was modest and gracious. She would accept food, but not until it was offered to her. My father brought her to his own home in Santa Barbara, and he and my mother took great pains to furnish her with every comfort. Father hunted around to find someone of her own tribe to come to see her and talk to her. Finally he heard of an old Indian at Santa Ynez and had him brought over. The two talked together and could understand each other.

She was very fond of us children, and by signs made us understand that she had had a little baby which had gone on before her. She took great interest in all that she saw, especially men riding on horseback, which seemed to delight her very much.

For eighteen years she had eaten only wild roots and herbs, and although my father and mother took great care that she should eat the best, our food still did not agree with her, and after six months in Santa Barbara she passed away. She is buried up at the Old Mission. Her grave is marked with a cross hewn in rock, just at the right as you come out of the Mission Fathers' Holy Garden. Her possessions—the fishbone needles and bones from birds that she used in various ways, and the wonderful feather robe—were sent to the Pope in Rome and are on exhibit in the Vatican.[3]

When the Captain had finished telling his story, Dicey

started the fire again and made coffee. The men all stood up, raised their mugs and bowed, and drank to my and the baby's health. Then they had to take their leave, for it would take them twenty-five minutes to row back to the ship.

I followed them down to the beach and stood listening to the sound of their oars. The moon was shining brightly, and soon the men started singing. When they rounded the point and were out of sight, I turned to Dicey and said, "This has been a day I will remember all my life. Everyone has been so kind to me. It was very thoughtful of the Captain and his crew to come and pass the evening with me."

Then I hastened up the creek and put the baby to bed again. Undressing for the second time, I crawled into bed beside her, and it was not long before I was fast asleep. I had had quite a first day on Santa Cruz Island. I didn't get up until ten the next morning.

The next two days I spent very lazily, just cooking for the three of us, washing up, and resting. I knew the men must have caught a load of fish and taken them to Santa Barbara; otherwise they would have returned. On the third day, Dicey saw the *Sam Pan* coming across the channel.

Soon the men came ashore, spread their nets to dry, and went to rest for they had been up all night. The weather was turning windy, with whitecaps outside the bay and quite a ground swell on the beach. It would be too rough for fishing, and Ira could stay in camp with me for a day or two.

After Ira had slept we had a supper of fried smelt, boiled potatoes, bread and butter, tea for myself and wine for the men. Then, carrying the baby, we walked up the trail to the hill to look the place over. It was the first time I had been out of camp. At the top of the hill was a set of stone steps, and below them a space about ninety feet long and twenty-five feet wide. The Japanese had built a crawfish cannery there some years earlier, Ira told me, and when they were making the excavation they had found eighteen Indian skeletons. All the old-timers believed this to be an Indian burial ground. To the right of the flat was the old shack I had seen from the boat.

As we stood on top of the bank, beautiful Pelican Bay lay below us, with its clear blue, still water. Across the windy channel, Santa Barbara, Montecito, Summerland, and Carpinteria were clearly visible. Ira pointed out a cut in the mountain ranges over on the coast behind Santa Barbara which the fishermen called "the Saddleback," or "Larco's Dip." In the early days, fishing boats often lacked compasses, and when it was clear weather they would steer their course by that dip.

"There is the watchman of Pelican Bay," said Ira, pointing to the heron. As he spoke, the bird spread its wings and left its perch, flying in a circle of the bay and then back to the rock again. Near the heron's perch, hundreds of seagulls and pelicans rested at the foot of the high, straight bank. When the heron landed, they all rose overhead and made the same circle. Ira said that all the fishermen thought a great deal of the heron and would never let anyone harm either it or the pelicans, though they would occasionally shoot at the seagulls, which were noisy pests.

Down the Island coast to the east was Prisoners' Harbor, where the owners of the island spent their summers. The rest of the year they lived in San Francisco. Beyond the harbor was a little rock where Ira said the leopard seal roosted. They were not any good for the market, but had a pretty, spotted skin which gave them their name. Then past that rock, about six miles away from us, was China Harbor or China Bay. An old Spanish man named Joe lived there alone in a little shack, fishing in the winter and working for the Island Company rounding up sheep in the springtime. Further down were the huge dark cliffs of Black Point, where there was a large seal rookery. Sometimes in the breeding season, Ira said, there would be two or three hundred seal, which at the approach of a boat would dive off the rock into the ocean, barking incessantly and creating a deafening noise. Ira had caught many seal there to fill orders for Captain McGuire. At the end of the island, as far as we could see, was a chalky white cliff. In that area was Potato Harbor, which had brackish water in the canyon; a lone fisherman named Kangaroo Dick lived

there in a shack perched on a rock shelf. Then, my scenic tour
of the island complete, we returned to our camp.

The following day was very windy, with whitecaps all over
the ocean. Every time a gust of wind blew down the canyon,
it raised clouds of dust and blew the fireplace ashes all over
the place. Dicey was kept busy running to the spring and
sprinkling the ground to keep the dust down.

Early the next morning, even though it was still storming
out in the channel, Ira decided to take the *Sam Pan* up the
coast to Lady's Harbor to wait for the wind to die down. The
beaches to the west were better for fishing, too. With the boat
gone, the camp seemed very quiet that day.

By six o'clock, supper was over and the dishes washed, and
I lay on the bed thinking how happy I had been living here on
the island. Then I thought I heard a noise up the hill—it was
the sound of tramping feet and many happy voices.

Dicey went up the hill to look, was there a few minutes, and
came running back all out of breath. "Mrs. Eaton," he said,
"your friends from Fry's Harbor have come to call on you."
For a moment I didn't understand him; how could they have
walked all that distance? My next thought was: seven people
and only three sets of dishes! But they were coming down the
trail and I must make them welcome. I was very pleased to
think they had walked that twelve miles to call on me.

They arrived, and after greetings were exchanged, they
admitted that they were very hungry after their long hike up
and down the mountains. So the ladies sat on my three apple-
box chairs while I fried fish and potatoes for my visitors' supper. Understanding my short supply of dishes, the men ate
their fish between pieces of bread and drank their coffee from
empty tomato cans; the ladies got the mugs and plates. I kept
cooking fish until everyone was satisfied.

After cleaning up, I prepared beds for my guests by spreading plenty of gunny sacks on the ground to cushion them from
the rocks. We all shared my blankets and a heavy tarpaulin,
and the campers removed their coats and folded them up for
pillows. Leaving the lantern lit and hanging in the oak tree,

about eight o'clock we turned in for the night.

We were all settled when we heard three blasts of a boat whistle. Dicey and two of the boys went up the narrow trail to see who could be in the bay. Then they came running back, laughing and talking, to the opening of the oak tree and asked, "Mrs. Eaton, who do you suppose has come to call on you? It's Captain Vasquez of the *Gussie M.*, the boat that brought us to the island!"

So we all got up, and with great rejoicing made the Captain welcome. I asked if he and his son had had their supper, and he answered, "I never eat my own cooking when there are so many good cooks on the island."

Again I started frying fish. The third supper of the evening was served to the Captain and his son, and while they ate we all sat around and talked. Then, at the Captain's suggestion, we all went up the trail to the top of the hill, carrying the baby who was fast asleep. In a large open space, we built a bonfire and sat and talked some more.

Captain Vasquez told us about a shipwreck over at San Miguel Island. The boat, the *Anubis,* had become lost in the fog on her way from San Francisco to Mexico and run aground on the rocks. The crew were throwing the cargo, big sacks of flour, overboard to lighten the ship so she could be towed off the rocks. There were about a dozen boats over there now, despite high winds and swells. Captain Vasquez thought that Ira could do better by salvaging the flour than by fishing, but that he personally thought it was too much work.

Then the Captain asked the campers what they had done to amuse themselves during the past week. They said it had been so windy they couldn't get their skiff off the beach, and so had had none of the mussels, abalones, or fish they had planned to eat. The fish I had cooked for their supper that day was the first they had eaten since coming to the island; they had spent every day on long hikes and finally decided to come and visit me. They had left all their groceries packed away in boxes at their camp so the wild hogs wouldn't get them. And they had had a taste of wild hog meat: they had shot a mother hog, which got away, but they caught the four little piglets which weighed about fifteen pounds each.

After leaving me at Pelican Bay, Captain Vasquez had made a trip from Santa Barbara to San Miguel Island, taking over four Chinamen who were going to pick, boil, and dry abalones for the market. He told us about another Chinaman who had once drowned picking abalones at San Miguel; the man had got his hand caught under the shell of a big red abalone he had mistakenly thought was loose from the rocks, and the tide came in.

We begged Captain Vasquez for more stories, and he kept us entertained for hours. Finally he had to take his leave, as he was leaving early for Santa Barbara. We started back to camp. The light of the full moon made Pelican Bay look like a silver sheet, and the *Gussie M.*, tiny in the distance, rolled gently in the light swells. Out in the channel, freighters and brightly lit passenger ships traveled up and down the coast.

Reaching camp, we said goodbye to the Captain and tumbled into bed. It was now three o'clock in the morning. We had no sooner fallen asleep than we were awakened by two blasts from the whistle of another boat in Little Pelican. It was Ira, signaling Dicey that he had arrived with a load of groceries from town and a supply of fresh fish for the camp.

When he found out that the campers had walked over from Fry's Harbor to visit us, Ira decided to stay for breakfast and then take them back to their camp on his way up the coast fishing. Hearing the story about the *Anubis,* he decided to try his luck salvaging the flour to make some extra money.

Soon breakfast was over, and we all walked down to the beach. Goodbyes were said, and my visitors got aboard the *Sam Pan* and went on their way back up the coast. I went back to camp, crawled into bed beside my still-sleeping baby, and slept until almost noon.

Every morning since I had come to Pelican Bay I had awakened to hear the birds singing and calling to their mates. The doves would coo nearly all morning, and there were also some blue jays that came around the camp. I saved crumbs and scraps to feed them, and they also seemed to enjoy oatmeal. The first day there were two birds; by the end of the week there were a dozen, all screeching until they were fed. They kept the baby amused with their antics.

Everything went along merrily, and too soon the morning came when I was to return to town. I was up early to pack, and told Dicey, "Whatever you do, don't forget to feed those darling little birds, because if you don't, I know they will miss me."

After two weeks on Santa Cruz Island my shoes were about ready to fall apart, and Dicey had to find some twine to tie the soles up around my instep, for they were completely loose. My suitcase was quickly packed since I wasn't taking back my camp outfit, only myself and my baby. I climbed the steps to watch for the boat and soon saw it rounding the point from Fry's Harbor.

By the time I got down to the beach, Captain Vasquez was waiting for me in the skiff, and then I was back on board the *Gussie M*. My friends the campers reported that the weather had improved after their visit with me, and they had been fishing almost continuously ever since, rowing their skiff up and down the coast.

When we reached the wharf at Santa Barbara, a down and out feeling came over me, and I couldn't decide whether I wanted to go home or turn right around and go back to the island where I had spent such a wonderful time. Captain Vasquez had warned me about that feeling. But then I remembered that it would not be long before I would be going to Willow Canyon, and I must get ready.

CHAPTER IV

Roughing It at Willow Canyon

Winter, 1908–1909

The *Anubis* — The *Sam Pan* Aground — Aboard the *Baltic* —
We arrive at last — Setting up Camp — Our First Day at
Willows — The Spanish Beans — Woodgathering and Garden-
ing — Homemade bread — Moving Into the Cabin — Wild
Hog — *Sam Pan* Back in Action — A Visit to the Linscows —
The Cobblestone Fireplace — Abalones — A Trip to Town —
Christmas 1908 — Rain and Storms — Time to Leave

WHEN I RETURNED from my two weeks at Pelican Bay, Ira
was in the midst of salvaging the flour cargo from the *Anubis*,
which had run aground on Flea Island off of San Miguel. The
captain and crew were still there waiting for the wrecking
boats to come and try to save the ship. The sea was white with
flour that had been thrown overboard, Ira told me later. He
made several trips, taking mail out to the captain and bringing
sacks of flour back to Dardi's store, where they gave him credit
on groceries. At about fifteen dollars a load, this helped our
finances quite a bit. The *Sam Pan* was small and maneuverable
so could pull up right alongside the wreck even in rough seas.
There were about ten other boats there too, and Ira helped load
them full of flour—sometimes as many as eighteen hundred
sacks each—to sell at San Pedro. He also set aside quite a supply of it for our own use.

Before he went out to the *Anubis* for the last time, Ira told
me we would soon be leaving for our new camping place at
Willow Canyon on the south side of Santa Cruz Island.

"You'll just love this place, Margaret. It has a wide sandy

57

beach where you can sit and watch the baby play. There is plenty of good water and a large plot of ground where we can raise all of our vegetables. The main ranch is about nine miles away, so we won't be able to rely on it for supplies. You will have to learn to make your own bread, and condensed milk will have to do for the baby just as it did at Pelican Bay. Frank Nidever and I will be busy building our crawfish traps and I won't be coming back to town for about three weeks, so you may have to work more than you did at Pelican Bay. I'll take over a good supply of groceries when I go. We expect to fish and gather abalones for about six months and haul our own fish back to town, so there will not be many boats calling at this camp."

The first thing I did to get ready for this trip was to buy a pair of boy's high-top boots and have hobnails put in them. I was not making the mistake of taking any more high-heeled shoes camping with me! And I got a recipe for homemade bread from my neighbor Mrs. Axtell.

Leaving me with my preparations, Ira and his partner Frank took the *Sam Pan* to Santa Cruz Island to move our stuff from Pelican Bay to the new camp at Willow Canyon. They would spend the night ashore there. The next day, Dicey would be left to unpack while Ira and Frank went out to San Miguel for the load of flour. Then they would return to Santa Barbara and pick up our camping gear, baby Vera, and myself on the way back to Willow Canyon. This was Saturday.

Sunday morning there was a change in plans. When Ira awoke about five o'clock and went down to the beach, the *Sam Pan* had disappeared. He and Frank launched the skiff and rowed outside the bay; still nowhere in sight. So following the current, they rowed down the coast, and there sitting on a reef of mussel rocks, sat the *Sam Pan* just as saucy as could be. She seemed to be saying, "Here I am—just try to get me!"

Nothing could be done until the tide came in, so they beached the skiff and assessed the damage. The planking on the sides would have to be torn off and the whole bottom replanked. Ira and Frank rowed the mile and a half back to Willows, got some rope, and rowed back again to the *Sam Pan*. At high tide, they attached the rope to her bow, and with the two men at the oars of the skiff they managed to haul her off the rocks and back to Willow Canyon, which was no easy matter as she was almost full of water. They anchored her in the harbor and went ashore.

To get the *Sam Pan* out of the water so they could work on her was quite a task. They dug a large hole in the sand and put down logs to be used as deadmen; the tow lines, with a block and tackle, were wound around these. Then they laid their skiff rollers down on the beach at the water's edge and started hauling her in. When the *Sam Pan* hit the rollers, she could be rolled up on the beach. That made the work easier, but it still took them three days to haul her up into the canyon and jack her up.

Then they had to find a way to get back to Santa Barbara. Leaving Dicey in camp, Ira and Frank hiked the nine miles from Willows to the main ranch and another three and a half miles down to Prisoners' Harbor. They arrived about one o'clock, exhausted, and discovered that the company schooner, the *Santa Cruz*, was leaving for Santa Barbara the following morning. Geronimo the French watchman let them sleep in the hay barn for the night and gave them mutton chops and coffee for breakfast, and they came back to town.

When Ira arrived home he had already made arrangements for us all to go over to the island together on the *Baltic* if I could get my stuff ready. She was leaving at ten o'clock the following night for San Miguel to haul flour to Santa Barbara, and would drop us at Willows on her way out. Ira told me what had happened to the *Sam Pan*, and I knew it could not be helped; but I was glad it had not spoiled my camping trip, for I did not want to stay in town for the winter.

Ever since I had come back from Pelican Bay, I had been so restless. I always had the feeling that I wanted to start right back to the islands—something over there just drew me to them. So I hurried all the more with my packing, and by three-thirty the following afternoon everything was down on the wharf ready to be loaded onto the boat.

At eight, Ira's father drove us in his horse-drawn buggy to the wharf, where the *Baltic* lay waiting, and I was introduced to the Captain and crew. The Captain lisped in talking and walked with a heavy limp. He was Norwegian. His helper was a Dane named Charlie, who had laughing blue eyes, a sandy moustache, fine teeth and a jolly disposition. In later years I came to know Charlie very well.

The gear had already been loaded, so we went aboard and soon were underway. It was a full moon and I sat on the deck, holding the baby and thinking of the two wonderful trips I had had on the *Gussic M.* and watching the boat nose her way from the wharf out into the channel. The whistling buoy was mooing like a cow. The boat rose and fell on the large swells, and I was in a happy mood, knowing that all my worries were nearly over. This new camping place would be paradise to me. I would have enough to eat, and I would sleep in a tent while Ira was fixing up the inside of that lovely little cabin with the cobblestone fireplace. I had visions of the wonderful time I would have keeping the fire burning in the fireplace on cold winter nights.

After awhile I noticed that the boat had changed course and the swells were hitting her broadside. That did not feel so good to me, and I was afraid I would slip from my place on top of the cabin. I braced myself against the railing, but my feet and knees began to tire. Just as I was about ready to take my feet down from the rail, a big swell hit the boat broadside and something near me slid from the top of the cabin, under the rail, and into the ocean. I thought my baby had fallen overboard and yelled to Ira, who came running to help. The baby was safe, but frightened, and crying as loudly as she could.

Ira and Charlie helped the baby and me down into the hold and closed the hatch. It was no fun down there—the boat was pitching and tossing with no one steering her. Ira ran back to the wheel and we were left to try to make ourselves comfortable. Frank was asleep, sprawled all over the floor. So that Vera would not roll over, I pulled out pillows and put one on each side of her, and blankets underneath and on top of her. She stopped crying and was soon fast asleep.

I tried to go to sleep myself but could not. The only light in the hold was the dim lantern that hung from the beam, and it pitched and tossed along with the boat. I looked over to where Frank lay, and his body hadn't moved, but his hands were going in all directions around his face, as if to shoo flies away. Then he would turn his head toward his shoulder, as if he were trying to hide his face. Poor man, I thought, he must be very tired to be so restless. I knew he had worked very hard.

First he moved one leg and then the other, then he shifted from his right side to his left. Now I was beginning to get frightened. I wondered if the baby and I were really safe down here in the hold with this man. But I did not have time to think further. Little Vera began to whine pitifully. I gave all my attention to her, talking to her and trying to soothe her. Then she gave out a screech, and I thought that everything she had eaten for weeks came up.

Just then the hatch cover was lifted, letting in some fresh air and spray at the same time, and Ira's voice asked, "How are you getting along, Margaret?" I just had time to tell him to bring down a bucket when a big swell hit the boat, sending me sprawling against Frank. The hatch being open, we got the benefit of a shower bath. Ira jumped down into the hold and helped me up, propped me up with my blanket roll, handed me a pail, and jumping back up on deck shut the hatch as fast as he could.

Now I noticed that the baby was going through the same movements that Frank was. She waved her hands upwards and passed them over her face. I cooed and sang to her. She lay still for awhile, then was seasick again, and her little legs would double up; I just could not imagine what was the matter with her. I thanked my stars that I had not been seasick so far, but soon the effect of that stuffy hold began to tell on me and I began to feel rather funny myself. My first thought was, if I get seasick, what about my baby?

I found myself using my hands to ward off what felt like fleas and more fleas. I knew that was why Frank and Vera had been acting so funny—this boat must be full of fleas! Frank must have packed them from San Miguel on his clothes, and they had left him and come to torment the baby and me.

I reached for the pail, but couldn't find it, and didn't care either. So I decided just to be sick in the blankets or towels or pillows or whatever was handy. I wondered, will this trip ever end? Ira had said it would take us about five hours from Santa Barbara around to Willow Canyon which was in about the center of the south side of the island, but to me the time seemed endless. I vowed that if I ever put foot on the island ground again, I would never leave it or move to another camp.

Finally, after what seemed an eternity, I heard the boat's engine slowing down and knew that at least we were at our new home, Willow Canyon. I listened, heard feet hurrying up forward to the bow, the anchor chain rattling, and voices talking as if there were an argument. The heavy anchor was heaved overboard and I heard the splash of the water as it hit and the chain being played out, making such a noise I thought you could hear it for miles around. Everything was quiet aboard for about a minute, then Ira raised the hatch and called, "How about coming up on deck, Margaret? The fresh air will do you good, don't you think?"

I felt as if I never wanted to move again; I would just as soon have died right then. Frank revived and started to move around, stood up, and raised himself from the hold to the deck. I thought, well, he is pretty spry for all the contortions he has been through.

Ira hopped down into the hold saying, "We are up at San Miguel Island. I will help you up on deck to see the big ship *Anubis* that I have been telling you so much about."

In what must have been a very pitiful voice I asked, "Ira,

how come we are up here? I thought we were going to Willow Canyon."

"I thought so too, Margaret," he answered, "but at the last moment on the wharf, some important mail came for the captain of the *Anubis,* and since the boys here on the *Baltic* are not charging anything to take us over, I thought we should come here first. It is just about six o'clock now, and we have been running for eight hours, but the worst of the trip is over now. From now on it will be fine. How do you and the baby feel?"

I told him the boat must be full of fleas. He took Vera in his arms and looked at her closely, then started picking something out of her hair. He said, "They are not fleas but bedbugs. They are in the baby's hair and her face is covered with their bites. While the hold was dark they worked on her face, but when I raised the hatch they ran for cover in her beautiful hair."

Ira and Charlie helped us from the hold up to the deck. How good that fresh air felt! I still felt wobbly, but Ira made me comfortable with some canvas on the stern of the boat and handed me the baby. She snuggled close to me and gave many long sighs, as babies have a habit of doing after a crying spell.

Ira, Charlie and Frank got into the skiff and took the mail over to the *Anubis* while our Captain cooked breakfast over the charcoal fire. I managed to eat my egg even though it had sand in it. The men told me that after I had been over there awhile, I wouldn't mind a little thing like grit in my food.

After breakfast the men slept until about two o'clock and then started loading the *Baltic* with flour from the wreck. When that was done and mail taken aboard, it was ten o'clock at night and the boat was again on her way to Willow Canyon. I fell asleep and did not awaken until I heard Ira saying, "Margaret, we are at our new home at last!" It was about four-thirty in the morning.

I sat up and noticed the south side of this island, which I had not seen before. There were steep rocky cliffs and very little vegetation; as it was late in the season, everything looked

dried up. I thought, this place is going to be my home for the
next six months, and I am going to make it just as comfortable
as I can for Ira and Frank.

Ahead of the boat I could see a wide sandy beach about three
hundred feet long. The ground swells were pounding on the
shore, breaking in one mass of foam. There seemed to be from
one to six rows of breakers, one trying to beat the other to the
shore, and when they hit those large rocks, the noise sounded
like a peal of thunder. Past the mass of foam, on the beach was
our skiff, stern pointing toward the bay. Sitting on the stern
with his feet hanging over was Dicey. He was expected to be
there when we arrived and bring out the skiff to meet the boat,
as the *Baltic* had not brought a skiff with her.

The morning was cold and grey and it was not quite light
yet. Ira called to Dicey but he did not answer or make a move
to take the skiff off the beach and come out to help. If he were
deaf, dumb and blind he could not have made a better job of
just sitting there. Ira, Charlie, Frank and the Captain all yelled
to him together, but still there was no response from Dicey.

Finally Ira decided he would have to strip, put on a life preserver and jump overboard, and swim ashore in that heavy
swell to bring the skiff and that dumbell out to the boat. The
water must have been very cold—I heard an "Ah!" when Ira
surfaced after diving in. The three men on board were saying,
"Well, I'm sure glad Ike went overboard instead of me," and
"If he doesn't get a cramp before he gets ashore, he'll be a
lucky fellow."

I sat in the stern and watched Ira swim through each of the
four rows of breakers, his head bobbing up and shaking the
water off his face like a seal. The fourth breaker took him high
on the beach, and I saw him walk over to the skiff, take off his
life preserver, and talk to Dicey. Then Dicey turned around
in the skiff, and Ira shoved it off the beach and rowed
back out to the *Baltic*. As Ira climbed aboard I got him some
bath towels to dry off with. He changed into some of Frank's
clean underclothes, and then said to me, "That was a wonder-

ful swim and bath, all in one." I thought, how brave Ira is to talk that way!

Then the unloading began. Bedding, cooking gear, tent poles, suitcases, all the gear for the crawfish equipment, bunches of lath, kegs of nails, lumber to repair the *Sam Pan,* piles of gunny sacks and walnut sacks rolled into bundles and tied with wire, and two or three crates of chickens were all unloaded onto the beach. We had brought quite a variety of chickens—Black Minorcas, Plymouth Rocks and Blue Andalusians. They all looked half drowned. When the coop was opened they did not stir, but at last the rooster started to strut around and pick sand fleas off the beach, and then the others all began trying to dry their feathers.

With all four men helping, it did not take long to get the equipment ashore. Before they made the last trip back to the *Baltic,* Ira told Dicey to pack his suitcase, get aboard and go back to town. Ira was through trying to help him when he wouldn't help himself. He would be just another mouth to feed, which we couldn't afford to do.

The baby and I were the last ones to leave the boat. The swells were pounding on the beach and it was no easy matter to land us ashore, but we made it without trouble. I knew when I set my feet on that beach that I was not in a hurry to leave it again. While I sat on the sand, Ira went to make coffee for the men. They did not stay long, for they had important mail to deliver in town. Goodbyes and thanks were said, and Ira rowed them out to the *Baltic.* They pulled anchor, waved to us, and sailed out of the bay toward the west end of the island for home.

We went over to look at the *Sam Pan* braced up on blocks about twenty feet from the beach and to the right of the canyon. Her side planks were torn off, but her bow and stern were in good condition. It would not take Ira long to get her in running order again.

Then we walked on up the creek toward the cabin Ira had talked so much about. I did not take much interest in it because

I was very tired, hungry, and not quite over my seasick spell yet. Frank and Ira spread out our tent under some willow trees, and I laid Vera down on top of it and covered her with blankets that had not seen use in the hold of the boat. I lay down beside her and it was not long before we were both fast asleep.

The men fixed themselves some breakfast and ate while I rested. Then Ira came back and awakened me, saying he had my breakfast ready—boiled egg, toast, and best of all, a pot of tea. He served it to me on a tray made from a round barrel top, set down on an orange-box table. How I did enjoy that food! The baby was allowed to sleep as she had put in two horrible nights.

I knew the boys would have plenty of work to do, so I offered to wash the dishes and clean up the kitchen. Ira was well pleased at this suggestion and said that would be helpful, if I felt up to it. He and Frank went off to carry our camping equipment up to the cabin. They would work on the crawfish traps and the *Sam Pan* down on the beach.

My breakfast finished, I took my tray and dishes over to the little lean-to kitchen. Built on the left side of the cabin, it was about eight feet long and six feet wide. At one time it had been covered with tarpaper, but it had not been lived in for a couple of years and the wind had raised cane with it. There were strips of tarpaper left hanging from the roof like ribbons. As you entered, to the left side of the lean-to was a table made of two heavy planks about five feet long and three feet wide, with a bench nailed to it. To the right was the wall of the one-room cabin. At the end of the kitchen was a tiny wood stove set up so the oven door faced you as you entered. There was just enough room to squirm your way between the end of the table and the stove to clean out the ash box. This stove looked more like a plaything than a stove to cook on. I opened the oven door and wondered how I was going to cook more than one loaf of bread at a time; but Ira would help me manage that part.

The little stove had a wonderful coat of red rust, but that did not worry me any; I only longed to tackle the job of removing it. Ashes? There were enough piled in and around the stove to fertilize the garden. The whole place looked very greasy, but it wouldn't take me long to straighten it up, I thought to myself. It would even be a pleasure to do it. I had done wonders at Pelican Bay, and this place was a little palace compared to that.

I started right in to clean up, and then heard a little voice calling. The baby was awake. Ira had left a coal oil can filled with water set on the stove, and by this time it was quite warm. I used it to give the baby a good sponge bath and dressed her in her overalls. Her little face and the top of her head were just one mass of bedbug bites, so I put some condensed milk on her face to soothe it. Meanwhile Ira had come in, and he made her some breakfast. After we had fed her she still did not look too spry, and Ira thought she needed some more rest.

I suggested that we should set up Vera's crib before setting up our own bed. So Ira brought up the crib from the beach and set it on two wide boards, taking out the casters which were of no earthly use over here. Then he nailed the four posts of the wooden crib to the boards so that it would be level and the legs would not sink in the soft dirt. The mattress for the crib had been lost overboard. Frank spoke up and said he had brought over about twenty-five walnut sacks. We could fill two of them with wild oats and put them crosswise in the crib for a mattress. Then we could use more of the sacks for a pad so the wild oats would not work through. Since Frank had slept out a great deal while camping on the islands and knew a great deal about camping, I thought that was a good idea.

I noticed that Frank saved the wire that was around the rolls of sacks. He told me that we would be out here on the island for six months or more and everything must count; nothing should be wasted. He and Ira would use this wire for their bait baskets.

By this time Ira had hunted all over for the spring that belonged to the baby's crib, but could not find it anywhere. Frank suggested they take a piece of wire from the garden fence and fix a spring for the crib. The garden fence was patched up with old boards, laths and gunny sacks, all tied together with baling wire. Ira measured the crib and went to the further end of the garden patch to cut a piece of chicken wire to fit. When he brought it back I could have just cried, the wire was so rusted and bent. He asked me to go down to the beach and bring the sack of staples from the nail keg, as they would do better than nails for holding the wire.

I had been standing there with the baby in my arms; when I started off still carrying her, Frank said he could hold her until I came back. He put out his arms to reach for her, and Vera at the same time put out her arms and held on around his neck. He seemed so pleased to think she was not afraid of him, and from then on they were very good friends.

I went down to the beach and, beginning to feel thankful for that old piece of rusty chicken wire, returned with the staples for Ira. He and Frank nailed the wire to the crib, stretching it to take the kinks out. Next, they took two large walnut sacks from the pile and went over to the side of the hill, where they pulled up wild oat hay to fill the sacks. Then Ira found a sacking needle and some twine and sewed up the ends of the sacks, just like flour sacks. He put them down on the ground and stamped on them to level them out, and then put them in the crib crosswise. About five more sacks were put on top of this mat, and I put the baby's pads and then her little pillow on top of them. Her bed was now ready.

Ira picked Vera up and kissed her, and laid her in the crib. I found her quilt, and snuggling her down, told her I would sing her to sleep. Frank said she should be covered with mosquito netting if she were to sleep out in the open, so I took out the mosquito netting from her suitcase and covered her crib with it. As she was very tired, it was not long before she was in slumberland.

Next Ira made a shelf in the kitchen from the end of an apple box sawn diagonally, and put our clock up on the shelf. Instantly our kitchen took on such a homey look. It was exactly nine o'clock.

I asked where the spring was; I would like to be introduced to it. While Ira unpacked for me, Frank walked over to the

middle of the creekbed and lifted a large white top like the top
of a barrel, with a handle on top. There was a barrel—I think
it was a sugar barrel—with both the ends knocked out and set
into a large hole in the creek. The barrel prevented the gravel
from falling into the hole and filling it up. This was to be our
water supply.

For carrying the water from the spring to the kitchen,
which was about fifty feet away, Frank made pails from two
oil cans with a short piece of rope for a handle. Kneeling, he
raised the lid from the barrel, dropped the cans into the spring,
and brought them up full. Then he covered the spring again.
If left open it might get some dirt in it, or someone might walk
right into the hole sometime. I would have to be careful to
cover the spring because I had my baby to look out for; I didn't
want her falling in and getting drowned.

Then from two apple boxes we made a stool by the kitchen
door for the two cans of water, because if they were left on
the dirt floor the dirt would blow in, and then the water could
not be used for drinking purposes. Barrel ends would be set on
top of the cans for a lid and covered with a dish towel. Then I
put our washbasin upside down on the top shelf of the stand
and placed a dish towel in front to prevent the dirt from blowing into it.

By this time Ira had all my dishes unpacked. He hammered
a nail over the water pail for the large tin dipper so we could
bail the water out of the cans instead of plunging the kettle or
pans into them. He also hung up a tin cup to be used for drinking purposes for all four of us. I don't think there were paper
drinking cups in those days. If there were, we could not afford
them.

Next Ira unpacked the pots and pans, handed them to me,
and I hung them on the nails back of the little stove. I brought
out our dishes, put them on the clean table, and covered them
with a clean dish towel.

With all the hammering of nails I had not heard little Vera
calling, "Mamma, mamma!" I rushed over to her, lifted her
in my arms and hugged and kissed her. She laid her head on

my shoulder, both arms around my neck, just as if she were afraid I would take her back to that boat. I said, "Mamma's baby is not going on that boat again—she is going back to sleep for mamma," and laid her down again. As she was still very tired, she was soon asleep.

The men were very tired too. Although they had a nap on the boat, they said they could stand another one. I suggested to Ira that we lie down on the tent and cover ourselves over with some of our blankets. When we woke up we could set up our tent and make our beds. That suited the men fine. Frank went beyond the lean-to kitchen where he had a little shack and closed his door. That was all we saw of him until about three o'clock.

I surely enjoyed my sleep out in the wide open spaces. I woke up first, at about twelve o'clock. Ira was still snoring. He was so tired from the boat trip, having been up all night. I lay there for quite awhile, thanking the Lord above; although that trip had been so terrible, I was here, and no matter what hardships I had before me, I would not grumble, but make the best of everything. I was also thankful that Ira was so considerate of the baby and myself, and although we had no money we had our health, and that meant more than all earthly goods.

Finally Ira awoke and wanted to get up, put up our tent and fix our bed. Everything was so peaceful and restful, I suggested that he lie there until the heat of the day passed, and he agreed. It was so pleasant to watch the limbs of those willow trees sway back and forth with the breeze and to hear the wind play through their branches. You could see the swallows, meadowlarks, linnets and mockingbirds overhead and hear them singing and warbling, and the old black ravens cawing. I saw the bluejays flying from branch to branch. They were too smart and would not come down on the ground. I told Ira how over at Pelican I had fed them oatmeal and table scraps, and they had destroyed my food and soap for me in return. I vowed I would not pay any attention to them here but would make them keep their distance.

As I lay there thinking I had not a care in the world, Ira

raised his arms above his head, gave out a big yawn, and then, sitting on the edge of the tent, said that this would never do— there was still plenty of work ahead of us. Taking my two hands he helped me to my feet, and we went over to the kitchen and had a drink of water from our new water cans. Emerging from his bunkhouse, as he called the little shack that was not more than seven feet long and five feet wide, Frank joined us.

As they had not had anything to eat since five o'clock that morning, Ira said that he and Frank would put up our tent while I got them some lunch. We could live in the tent for about a month yet before we would need to move into the cabin. Ira started the fire in the little wood stove for me. Frank went down to the beach and was gone for a few minutes; then he came back and surprised us with a large bass that weighed about eight pounds. One of the fishermen on the wharf in Santa Barbara had given it to him and he had put it in a gunny sack in the stern of the *Baltic*. When we came ashore that morning, he had dug a hole in the sand on the beach just above where the swells rolled in, put in the fish, and covered it with gravel. It would keep better there than hanging in the sun where the blowflies would get at it. He took the fish outside again and scaled it and fileted it, leaving nothing to do but fry it. Ira told me to put the potatoes on to boil with their jackets, and when they were done to call him and he would fry the fish.

Ira and Frank set up the tent in a shady spot under the willow trees. Then they carried the mattress and bedspring up from the beach and into the tent, setting them up on four pieces of two-by-four. A wide board about three feet long was nailed on for a head rest for the pillows. The mattress was made of excelsior on one side and cotton on the other, and on it I placed my bed pad, an old quilt covered with flour sacks, to cover the many hard lumps. There was only one blanket left—the others were in a terrible condition—so we put some of Frank's walnut sacks crosswise on the bed between two sheets. You would never know but that we had the best bed on the island; and I don't doubt that, at that time, we had.

Frank was already settled in his bunkhouse with a bed of

wild oat hay stuffed into walnut sacks. He had no bedspring but slept down on the floor, "just like a Chinaman," he said.

By this time the potatoes were nearly done and Ira went to cook the fish. He put some driftwood into the stove to make a hotter fire. Then he opened a can of olive oil by punching two small holes in the top, and showed me how to plug the holes with sharpened matchsticks to keep dust, flies, and ants from falling in. Although olive oil is more expensive than cottonseed oil, Ira explained to me, it is much better for your stomach. That is why the Italian fishermen are so healthy: they use olive oil for all their cooking.

Frank helped me by draining the heavy pot of potatoes outside. I made milk gravy by mixing flour with cold water and adding it to milk and bacon grease in a pan, and stirring it while it came to a boil. Lunch was ready. The pans were set on apple-box ends right on the table, as the food would keep warm longer and it would save washing serving dishes. I set the table and cut the bread.

Then I heard a little voice calling, "Mamma!" I dropped everything and ran to the willows, and there was Vera with her bedclothes thrown off, her two feet sticking up in the air, playing. Putting her little shoes, stockings and jacket on her, I carried her to the kitchen. Ira took her and kissed her, and sat her in her high chair at the further end of the kitchen.

The food was put on the table and we all seated ourselves: Frank to the left of the kitchen, Ira next, then me. Since the bench was nailed to the table, we just climbed over and sat down. There was just enough room for us to sit comfortably. We were all very hungry and did justice to the meal. That whole fish just disappeared! There was one thing I did not like: the flies and yellow jackets. No sooner did you set your food on the table than there were swarms and swarms of them around. How we did not eat them with our food, I never could figure. It was not their fault if we did not.

When we finished eating, Ira suggested we take the baby, walk to the beach, and sort out some of the fishing gear, as early the next day the boys would have to start making their traps for crawfishing. I declined the invitation and said I would clean up the dishes and straighten the kitchen instead. I set my dishpan on the kitchen table, which served as a dining table, work table and sideboard, and scalded the dishes in a colander set into a half-gallon coal oil can. Then I dried them, set them on the end of the table, and covered them with a clean dishtowel. I poured the fish grease over the stove while it was still hot, and rubbed it hard with a rolled-up gunny sack to help take the rusty stains off. I dumped the dishwater out some distance from the house where there was a shell mound, wiped out my dishpan, and hung it on a nail outside the door. I was all set until the next meal.

My work finished, I walked down to the beach to join Frank, Ira and the baby, and asked what the program was for the morrow. Ira told me not to get up in the morning but to rest, as I had put in a couple of hard days. The men would just fix themselves some coffee before starting to work early.

We all walked back to the camp. Bidding Frank goodnight, we went into our tent. I undressed Vera and handed her over to her father, who kissed her on the cheek and laid her in the crib. Then he got into bed and asked, "How do you like camping so far, Margaret?" I replied that it was just wonderful.

"Not counting the trip over," he commented.

"I don't know how the baby feels, Ira, but for myself I have forgotten all about that trip. I am not thinking about it at all, for I don't want to spoil my good time here. I don't care if I never see the mainland again." A goodnight kiss, and we were soon fast asleep.

The following morning I did not awaken until about eight o'clock. The sun was shining through the tent. The baby and I had slept since seven o'clock the night before—thirteen hours. The first sound I heard on awakening was the hammering of nails; the sound of Frank's hammer was not in rhythm, but Ira's had the sound of a trained mechanic. I thought how wonderful it was to lie here and not worry about anything. Then I heard a chorus of birds, singing what sounded like their morning prayers, and I slipped out of bed, knelt, and offered up my morning prayer too, thanking Him above for all He had done for us. Then a little hand reached out through the side of the crib to my neck, and a little voice said, "Mamma, what are you doing?"

"Mamma is saying her prayers."

"I want to, too, Mamma." So right then I began teaching her. I knew then that the baby's experience of the two days before was all forgotten.

I got up, dressed myself and the baby, and we had breakfast. I cleaned up the kitchen and raked the dirt floor, put some deadwood in the stove and closed the dampers. That way the fire would be ready when it was needed. The morning's work was done. I went back to the tent and made the beds. Then I fashioned a dressing table from two boxes set one on top of the other, with a sugar sack tacked in front to form a curtain and my hand mirror tied to the tent post. I put my washbasin on the shelf underneath and my work basket on top.

Then Ira came up and told me to put some Spanish beans on to cook for dinner, as Frank was very fond of them. In the kitchen I found the pink beans, spread a newspaper over the table, and cleaned them, because in those days you paid for just as many small rocks as beans. Then I washed them and put them on to cook; the pot was almost full. I added a good-sized piece of salt pork, a sliced onion, and a couple of cloves of garlic.

While the beans were cooking I packed rocks from the creek over to the garden, where I piled them on top of one another in a double row to make a pit for my washtub, and carried water over from the spring.

Then I went into see how my beans were getting along. My stove was covered with them! I thought the grocery man had given us jumping beans by mistake. I ran out to the edge of the creek and called Ira. He came up, took one look, and said I had put too many in the pot at one time. They had swelled up and were running out over the top of the pot. He told me I should just get another pot and divide them. Soon they were done, and we had Spanish beans, bread and tea—a meal fit for anyone.

I had kept the fire going to heat wash water while we were eating. After dinner, while I cleared off the table and washed the dishes, Ira and Frank washed and rinsed my four blankets and spread them out on the fence to dry. Then Ira explained that I would have to take them off just as soon as they were dry, as the tops of the laths might wear into the blankets and make holes in them. If they were not dry by four o'clock I should take them in anyway, or else the "four o'clocks," a sort of sticker, would dig into them and I would have a terrible time getting them out.

At about one o'clock the men went back to the beach to keep on building their traps. They had just about ten days to get ready before the season opened, and usually the fishermen liked to put their pots in the water early and get them well soaked up. If you dropped them in new, the lath did not absorb the water, little bubbles came up to the surface, and the crawfish would not crawl into the pot. So, by putting them in ahead of the season, you had a better chance of making good.

While the baby was having her nap, I took two gunny sacks up the canyon, filled them with deadwood, and tried to drag them both home. But dragging them over the rocks would damage the sacks, and each one cost five cents. So I struggled back to camp carrying one sack at a time on my shoulder. Well, I surely knew now it was no easy job, but I was very much pleased with myself. I was thinking how lucky it was that I had those heavy boy's shoes—I could walk so much better than with high-heeled shoes.

When I got back to the kitchen I emptied my two sacks and sorted the long pieces of wood out from the short ones. Then I went down to the beach and asked the men for a hand ax so I could split some of those large pieces. Ira did not want me to split them and told me to stack what was too large for the stove and he would chop them when he came up for supper. I wanted to try it anyhow, so I took the hand ax and went back and started chopping. I did so well that I finished the whole pile. Of course, some of the wood flew over my head and all around the place, but I did not knock an eye out, and that was something.

I went to the tent and found Vera awake, so taking her by the hand, I got my two sacks and we went up the canyon again. She picked up quite a few pieces which would help for kindling. I picked the large pieces and filled my sack again. Back at the kitchen I emptied my sacks, chopped what was too large for the stove, and made quite a neat pile of wood. Then I heard Ira say, "Where is my hand ax?" When he saw what I had done, he complimented me, saying he knew I would be of great help to them.

It was time to think of supper, because working all day, men get hungry. Knowing Ira was a regular Chinaman for rice, I measured out two cups of rice and washed it in my dishpan, throwing the water out on the vegetable garden. Then I put four cups of boiling water in the pot with the rice and one full teaspoon of rock salt, which we used for cooking to save money. I covered the pot and let it boil for about twenty minutes, then moved it to the back of the stove to let it steam. I made our toast and tea, and supper was ready. I sent little Vera down to the beach to call her daddy. Ira lifted her on his shoulder, carried her up to the kitchen and set her in her high chair. I put the rice, toast and tea on the table and diluted the condensed milk for Vera.

After supper Ira and Frank went to the garden, which was a space about fifty feet square, about twenty-five feet from the front of the kitchen. Frank's father and uncle had put in the garden years before and raised all the vegetables they needed during the winter fishing season. We all three decided we would raise peas, lettuce, cabbage, young onions, radishes, and kale for the chickens. Ira chopped the weeds, of which the garden was full, and Frank spaded. They extended the fence to take in more ground, as we were three to eat from the garden now. The two men worked until about eight o'clock at night and then put up their tools and made ready for bed.

Frank went off to his bunkhouse. Ira took Vera by the hand and put his other arm around my waist, and we walked to our tent and turned in for the night. This was our third day at Willow Canyon, and I had been busy every minute. I was also very happy, and I did not regret one minute of my trip over.

The following morning about four o'clock the men made their coffee, and then worked in the garden until six. Between the two of them they got it almost all spaded and raked over. The ground was very rich; part of it was old shells from mounds, left from when the Indians had occupied the island, and there was quite a bit of dirt washed down from the hills.

While the men were working in the garden, I got dressed, made myself a cup of tea and a slice of toast, and walked up the creek to gather more wood so I could do my family washing before the hot sun came up. I found some hard knots of dead wood that would burn slowly and filled two sacks with them; the men would haul these back for me. A third sack I filled up halfway and brought it down to the kitchen myself, noticing that my arm was not as tired as it had been the day before. I was getting used to my exercise already. Next I made eight trips carrying water from the spring to fill my twenty-gallon washtub, eight more for rinse water in a second tub, and another trip to fill the dishpan for bluing the clothes. Then I went down to the beach and gathered two more sacks full of kindling wood and started the fire.

Into the washtub went my sheets and pillowcases and towels that had been used on that wonderful boat trip. I let them boil for awhile, but not too long as carrying all that water was a problem. After the clothes had boiled I took them to the kitchen and rinsed them, carried them in the dishpan over to the garden fence, and hung them to dry. While the second batch of clothes was boiling I went back to the spring and carried more water to replace all the drinking water that had been used in washing, in case the boys came back thirsty. They were still busy building their traps—sounds of hammering and sawing came from the direction of the beach. I hung the rest of the wash to dry on the lath fence. Some of the clothes looked as if they might blow onto the freshly spaded garden soil, so I spread out the handkerchiefs and the baby's and my things on the wild oats over by the hillside.

It was time to think of dinner. I put on a piece of salt pork that I had soaked the night before, three small cabbages from the garden, and some onions and potatoes we had brought from town. We had to plan differently here on the island; it was not like town where you could run to the corner grocery store. We had not brought canned goods because we could not afford them, but expected to live on wild hogs, fresh fish, salt pork, vegetables from the garden, and the eighty sacks of flour off the *Anubis* that we had stored in Frank's bunkhouse.

While dinner was cooking I went up the creek and gathered more wood to replace what had been used in washing. Then I sent Vera down to call the men to eat. All morning she had been amusing herself with her little dolly and had been no trouble to me at all.

After lunch, Vera went to bed for her nap and I brought the washing into the kitchen. I folded the sheets, pillowcases and towels, and put them away in an old trunk Frank loaned me from his bunkhouse. Then I mended socks and sewed buttons on Ira's blue shirts. Knowing I had accomplished quite a bit of work, I stretched out on my bed, thought how grand everything had been so far, and fell asleep.

At four o'clock I awakened, much refreshed and ready to tackle anything that came along. Vera was already awake and playing with her doll. We got up and walked down to the beach, and I sat on the sand while she played. Ira came over and asked what the idea was of letting the baby run around without shoes and stockings. I told him that there was no fear of her taking cold until the rainy season and that we might as well start hardening her feet now while the weather was warm.

I mentioned that I wished we had brought over a chair from town as I had nothing to rest my back against, and Frank promised to make me one by cutting down an old sugar barrel. With a seat put on it and padded with a cushion, it would serve the purpose. After talking for awhile longer, I took the baby and went back to prepare supper, picking up driftwood on the way. We all enjoyed our warmed beans, bread and tea.

After eating, Ira suggested that, as our bread supply was getting low, it was time for me to try making a batch of homemade bread. I put my cake of Magic Yeast to soak—we were not acquainted with Fleischmann's then—and boiled two potatoes. I added sugar to the yeast and transferred it to the potato water, put in half a sifter of flour, and beat it all very hard. Then I set it on the end of the bench nearest the stove to rise, covered with an old cotton blanket. I was sure I would have great success making my first batch of bread.

Meanwhile the men had gone to work in the garden. They made straight rows with stakes and string, and planted lettuce, carrots, turnips, beets, radishes, young onions and a patch of garlic.

A lot had been accomplished that day—not a minute had been wasted. We bid Frank goodnight and went to bed, ready for a good night's sleep. It was so good to lie there talking and planning what to do the next day. Everything so far had been wonderful, and I had managed very well in spite of all the inconveniences. Ira kissed me goodnight, and we were soon fast asleep.

Toward midnight we were awakened by the sound of cats meowing. I thought that was funny, for I had never seen any cats around the camp. Ira explained that they were tame cats gone wild. All the fishermen brought cats to the island with them, and most of them left the cats behind when they returned to the mainland. I worried that the cats might come into the tent and bother the baby, but Ira said there was no danger of that, and finally I fell asleep again.

In the morning after the men had finished their coffee I went to the kitchen to check on my bread. The yeast had risen! I was so happy I could have screeched and yelled, but I didn't want to wake the baby. I measured in flour, salt, lard, sugar, and water—for I could not afford to use milk—and stirred until all the flour was absorbed. Then I kneaded the dough on a board set on the end of the table, put it back in the dishpan, and set it, covered, by the stove again.

Then I started up the canyon to gather more wood, for I knew I would need plenty for the baking. In the canyon I discovered an old sugar barrel. This would do nicely to hold all the old dishwater, which could then be used to water the garden.

By the time I got back, the baby was awake and calling from the tent. I brought her over to the kitchen, washed her and gave her breakfast. While waiting for the bread to rise, I brought out Ira's underwear and cut up one set to mend the other three. They were pretty thin around the knees. As he would have to kneel on the seat of the skiff to pull up his crawfish traps, I patched the full length of the legs. This would keep the wind from penetrating them during the four miles of rowing up to Gull Rock. When I was through with the legs, I patched under the arms where they were very thin. When the two suits of underwear were put together they made a very heavy set, which I thought would be good. Then I took two pairs of khaki overalls and applied the same method, patching the whole front of the legs, and then put two good patches in the seat of the jeans.

Now my bread was ready to put in pans to bake and the thought dawned on me that I couldn't bake all five loaves at one time in that tiny oven. I walked down to the beach and asked Ira what he thought I should do. Frank said he would show me how to bake bread outside in a Dutch oven. I followed him back to camp, and from his bunkhouse he brought out two heavy iron pots with heavy iron covers and handles. Then he dug a hole in the ground and built a fire, and from the way he used the wood, I had visions of packing wood down from the canyon for some time to come. He told me to mold the loaves, not too large, and put them in the Dutch ovens, as he called the iron pots. When the fire got down to coals, I was to put the Dutch ovens with their lids on tight in the hole and shovel live coals on top of them, and leave them there for an hour and a half. Then he went back to the beach.

For the whole hour and a half I wondered how the bread would bake, sure that it would burn. When the time was up, I raked the coals away, and taking my potholder, raised the lid off. You should have seen that bread! It had a wonderful brown crust and had risen clear to the top of the pot. Was I proud? I was willing to pack wood twice daily if I could bake bread as good as that batch every time. When I set the bread on the table that night for supper it was enjoyed by us all. Ira was so pleased. He said that when fishermen were out of bread, they usually made a stack of hotcakes and ate them cold three times a day with their meals.

The time was nearing for the crawfish season to open. The traps were made, baited and ballasted, and put in the water to soak. On opening day, September 15, the boys were up at four in the morning to pull their traps. If you leave the traps down too long, the sheephead and eel get into them and make a sorry mess of your catch. They attack the legs first, biting them off next to the body, and that ends your crawfish. After they have worked for a couple of hours there is nothing left but shell. After the season began, the men were up every morning before daylight, had coffee, and then rowed the skiff up to Gull Rock to check their traps. Sometimes their catch was good, sometimes poor.

The skies were beginning to cloud, and there would be rain before long. Soon we would have to leave our tent and move into the one-room shack, but first I wanted to wallpaper it and have it look a little cleaner inside. When the boat arrived to pick up the crawfish catch, we sent in an order for some groceries and lumber. I also sent Mrs. Axtell a letter asking her to send me the roll of wallpaper from our shed at home, and a dozen new dishtowels at fifty cents a dozen. These arrived the following week.

Now I could paper the cabin. I tacked the dishtowels all over the wall, and where they didn't come together over a joist I

sewed them together with a sacking needle. To make the wallpaper paste I mixed together flour and cold water so it wouldn't
get lumpy, added rock salt, and poured in boiling water until
it was the right consistency. Not having a brush, I made one
by tearing a piece off one of my dishtowels and tying it tightly
onto the end of a piece of lath. I spread the wallpaper on the
kitchen table, figures down, and piled the paste on. Then I carried it into the shack and put it up over the cloth lining. Well,
it wrinkled and stuck in the wrong places. Carefully I pulled
it off, daubed some paste on the lining, and put it up again.
That seemed to work better. I decided to start papering from
the top down because if I ran out of wallpaper I could use
newspapers on my side. The bed would be next to the wall and
cover that part. I would not do the ceiling since that would
make it seem too low, and anyway I was beginning to think if
I got all four walls done, I'd be doing well.

When Ira and Frank returned at noontime from fishing,
the kitchen was cleaned of all evidence of my morning's work,
and their dinner was waiting for them. Ira was surprised and
pleased that I had done the work so nicely. It was just in time,
too, because that night there were light showers, and the next
day we moved from the tent into the little shack.

I was thrilled about our little shack, even if it had only a
dirt floor. The dust could be kept down by sprinkling the floor
with water every day, just as I had been doing in the kitchen.
Ira moved the double bed into the far corner of the room, right
up against the wall. At the foot of the bed there was just room
for the baby's crib. The only other furniture in the room was
the old trunk that held our extra bedding and clothes. Ira laid
down a long board by his side of the bed, which would feel
better to his feet on cold mornings than the dirt floor. My side
of the bed was next to the wall. The only thing I did not like
about our cabin was that it had no windows. The door would
have to be kept open in all kinds of weather for ventilation.

I told Ira that we had some extra firewood and I thought it
would be nice to build a fire in our cobblestone fireplace, but
he thought we should wait until the fire was really needed.

That seemed sensible. I put the baby in the crib, and when she knelt to say her prayers, I had her thank God for our little home. Climbing over Ira into bed, I told him I was so happy doing this work that I could do it without asking any help.

About nine o'clock, a very late hour for us, I fell asleep. Later in the night, I awoke to a faint noise like something scratching. Could it be a mouse in the baby's bed? My first thoughts were always of the baby. I listened again. The sounds came from somewhere near me; perhaps mice were trying to tear the wallpaper apart, after all my work. I felt chills creeping up my back. What if they were bats? Frank said that if bats got in your hair they clung there, and you had to have your hair shaved off. I hopped out of bed, went to the crib, and pulled back the bedclothes. There was nothing there. I went back to bed; still there was that creeping, creeping noise. Finally I nudged Ira and whispered to him, "Listen! What is making that noise?" He asked very sleepily what I wanted. I poked him in the ribs. "What is that noise? Listen, Ira!"

Awake now, he listened for a few minutes and said, "Oh, Margaret, that noise is only stinkbugs coming out of the dirt floor and crawling up behind your wallpaper. They hide in the daytime and come out at night."

It made me sick at my stomach to think I might have slept in this cabin without papering the walls—the stinkbugs would have crawled all over us. I tried to go to sleep again, reminding myself that the wallpaper was between me and the stinkbugs, but still it was not very pleasant to have that scratching going on all night. There was a new job ahead of me: taking off all the bedding and putting it out to air every morning.

When they were fishing, the men did not have much time in camp. As soon as they left early in the morning, I would go to the spring and pack water back to the garden. The vegetables were nicely started and I did my best to take care of them. I would make five or sometimes ten trips to get the garden watered, depending on how moist or dry the ground was. After a week or so the ground was well soaked and did not need so much water. The men carried water Chinaman style, using a wooden yoke curved to fit the neck, padded with a gunny sack, a pail hanging from each end. I preferred to make more trips and carry less each time, but I had to do it early in the morning before the baby woke. I did not want her getting acquainted with the spring and perhaps falling in when no one was around.

In the afternoons and evenings Ira worked on the *Sam Pan*. When she was back in the water, he planned to dig abalones, boil and dry them, and save the shells, as there was a market for them in town. The men were working very hard, so I did everything I could around the camp to make things easier for them. I brought in all the wood and water for cooking, washing and the garden. Every day the camp was looking better and better.

One day a heavy nor'west storm sent clouds of dust flying all around. Frank let me have some of his walnut sacks to cover our lean-to kitchen so some of the dust could be kept out. I tackled the job myself, and between hammering the nails on the head and the nails on my fingers, I got it all finished, even to covering the door. This would help to keep the flies and yellowjackets out of our food.

After supper that evening, while Ira was working on his boat, Frank took his gun and said he was going to see about getting a wild hog. "I hear them prowling around here every night. The other night I got up about midnight, and there was one by the garden fence, trying to get our green vegetables." My heart almost stopped beating. I had been sleeping in the cabin with the door open all night for air. I thought, what next? In about an hour Frank was back in camp with a young, sixty-pound hog thrown over his shoulder, handling it as though it did not weigh more than five pounds. He hung it under the willow tree, where the tent had been, and cleaned it.

Frank said the heart and liver could be fried to make a good dish for dinner the next day, and asked if I had ever eaten wild hog. I hadn't, so he told me how to prepare it. You take a leg, cut some holes in it with a small potato knife, put some cloves of garlic in the cuts, and roast it in the Dutch oven on top of the stove. An older animal should be cooked for a longer time.

These wild hogs feed on manzanita berries, cactus, oak galls, wild cherries, and all kinds of wild roots. Their fat is not as white as that of domestic hogs, and the meat is very tender, but with a wild taste.

There is no part of the hog that you should throw away. Take the head and four shanks, throw in some whole spices, boil them all together until the meat falls from the bone, then dice the meat in small pieces, and you have head cheese. Frank took the hide and tacked it up on the back of his bunkhouse to sun-dry. When cured it would make a good rug to set on his floor. I was beginning to realize that nothing should be thrown away—there was a use for everything around this island.

A day or two later the *Sam Pan* was nearly ready to launch, and Ira and Frank invited two other fishermen, Big Jerry and Louie, to come and help. I was on the beach with the baby when they arrived. Big Jerry was a husky fellow about six feet tall, broad-shouldered, with brown eyes and brown hair and moustache. He wore ordinary work clothes and high rubber boots. He was very good-natured and always had a joke to tell about some other fisherman. His camp was up at El Pozo, toward the western end of the island. Louie was an Italian, short, stocky and dark, wearing light blue overalls and work shirt, dark blue tasseled cap and a matching wide wool scarf that fit tightly about his waist, and high rubber boots. He was about the cleanest and neatest fisherman I had ever seen, not that our men were not clean, but Louie was different —he had a crease in his overalls, as if they had just come from the laundry.

Dinner was ready and I invited them all up to the camp. I served roast pork, Spanish beans, brown potatoes, head cheese, rice pudding with raisins, and hot coffee. Then Big Jerry said, "Folks, I brought some good old dago red. You cannot launch a boat without some good drink." No doubt dinner tasted a hundred percent better to the men with wine instead of water. Big Jerry offered me some wine. I told him I didn't drink, but then I decided to try some anyway. Tasting it, I found it very sour, so Ira put some sugar and water in it for me. Sure enough, if I thought the dinner tasted good with tea, it tasted much better with wine. Big Jerry gave some to the baby too, and she drank it all down and held out her cup for more. He laughed and said she would grow up to be a good sport, just like her dad.

Then Big Jerry told us about an accident that had recently happened up at the next harbor, Laguna. Three men had chartered a boat, the *Real* from San Pedro, to go hog hunting. They dropped anchor at Laguna and started to row ashore in the skiff. Laguna beach is very treacherous, as the local fishermen knew; only an experienced surf man could land there, and even he must know his stuff. The swells had been high that day, and the skiff upset. Seeing the men in trouble, the captain jumped overboard and managed to pull one man to safety on the beach, but the other, a policeman, drowned. It had taken several people, including Big Jerry and his partner who had happened to be in the area, to form a human chain in the surf to retrieve the drowned man's body. The other man they found wandering up the canyon with no clothes on, half-crazy. In trying to get the body back to the boat they had upset the skiff again, and Big Jerry had found himself in the ocean with the body around his neck. Finally they got it aboard and took it back to Venice for burial.

Big Jerry knew from experience that they were lucky to have gotten off the beach at all, having once been marooned at Laguna himself. He said, "We ran short of redwood buoys for our crawfish traps, and knowing no one ever went ashore at Laguna, we figured that those good redwood posts there would do just fine. So we went ashore one morning and started pulling up some of the posts. When we thought we had enough, we took them down to the beach to put them in the skiff, but the swells were so high we could not get off the beach. We had to stay in the canyon for two days with nothing to eat. Our boat was moored out in the bay, and we thought we would never get aboard her again, or that she would come ashore with the swell. Finally on the third day, toward sundown we shoved off the beach, made our boat, pulled our anchor, and we've never been back to that harbor until last week when the policeman drowned, and I would advise everybody to keep away from it." In answer to my question about what happened to the posts, he said they had to leave them there. "We thought afterward that the swell was sent as a just punishment for us, for trying to take what did not belong to us in the first place."

By now it was getting close to high tide, just the right time to launch the *Sam Pan*. With block and tackle and dead men sunk into the beach, Ira and Frank hauled the *Sam Pan* to the water's edge, and Jerry in his boat pulled her into the water. Ira was aboard, and he took her out to her mooring and anchored her safely. We said goodbye to Jerry and his partner and they were on their way. There was much happiness in our camp that night. No longer would the men have to row the distance up to Gull Rock and back—the little *Sam Pan* would do the work.

The following morning I was up just as early as the men and went down to the beach to see them off. Going back to the kitchen, I thought I would try to make jelly from the cactus pears. The hills in Willow Canyon were covered with cactus, and Ira had helped me gather the fruit. Holding the fruit in a newspaper, we cut it off with a sharp knife. When we had gathered enough, we peeled them with a knife while holding them speared on a fork in the left hand. The stickers came off at the same time. I covered the fruit and seeds with water and boiled it just like jelly, then strained out the pulp through mosquito netting. I added a cup of sugar for each cup of juice and boiled it and boiled it. It refused to jell. It tasted good, though, and made a good substitute for golden syrup at a dollar and a quarter a gallon.

One morning I noticed my Blue Andalusian hen was missing. I found her clucking and fussing near the cabin, shooed her out, and forgot all about her. That night when I put the baby to bed, there at the foot of the crib was one egg. Ira said to let her go ahead and lay, because later she might want to set. After that, every morning about eleven o'clock, the Blue Andalusian hen left an egg in the baby's crib. There were no lice on the hen, and every morning I put a double newspaper down on the crib, so everything was clean enough.

Soon it was time for the boat *Charm* to stop at our camp to pick up our fish, for we had quite a catch. Frank decided to go into town to get a roll of 16-gauge wire to weave bait baskets for the crawfish traps. Something was needed to keep out the sheephead, eels, and devilfish, and we couldn't afford chicken wire.

The next morning, Vera and I dressed very warmly and went out in the *Sam Pan* to watch Ira pull his traps. He anchored the boat off the Laguna beach, and as he rowed us toward the rock warned us to be careful not to get wet when the fish started flopping around in the skiff. Kneeling in the stern, he pulled up the traps, opened the doors, took out the fish and put them in sacks. When we got to the last trap and he pulled it in and opened it up, he said, "Look at the size of this one!" Sitting Vera on the seat and telling her not to move, I went to the stern and looked into the trap at the largest crawfish the boys had caught that season. Pulled out by the feelers, he flapped his tail as if he wanted to go back to his ocean home where he belonged. Ira said he must weigh at least twenty-six pounds. Vera and I must have brought him good luck that morning.

Then we started for home and I realized how hungry I was. It was a good thing I always had a hot dinner ready for the men when they came home, for I no sooner hit the beach than I made for the kitchen to find something to eat. Vera and I each ate a piece of bread to hold us until dinner was ready. Hot boiled fish, a couple of sliced onions, and boiled potatoes with their jackets on, all mixed together with a dressing of oil and vinegar, made a wonderful meal.

The following week Frank returned, glad to be back at the camp again; one day in town was enough for him. He brought news that the *Anubis* was to be saved after all. A tug had been sent to the wreck and they patched her bottom with canvas, floated her on pontoons, and towed her to San Francisco to be repaired. Of all the boats that had been wrecked around these islands, she was the first to be saved.

Talking of shipwrecks, Frank said his father told him about a ship that had gone on the rocks at San Miguel in the early days. Divers were hired, as her cargo was very valuable. One morning a diver went down in forty feet of water to work on the wreck. Suddenly a great tentacle, about four inches in diameter, grabbed his leg. Before he realized what had happened, another one had encircled his thigh. He began to chop at them and at the same time signaled to be pulled up. When he was brought to the surface, he was in a fainting condition and almost crushed to death. They thought the devilfish must have gotten into the hull the night before. Frank added that maybe that was what had happened to the mate on the *Colman* who had drowned diving after the chest of gold.

Ira said to Frank, "A boat called the *California,* shaped just like a barracuda, called here yesterday afternoon. I told the fellows that I knew what they came for and they had better not fool with our receiver, as we had a gatling gun set on a hair trigger, to go off as an alarm if anyone meddled with our fish. They went on their way. I slept aboard the *Sam Pan* with my gun last night, watching for them, but they did not come back."

Frank asked if Ira knew about another large boat anchored behind Gull Rock. Ira answered, "They have their fish traps just inside and outside our string. I talked with them this morning, but I didn't say much, only that they were fishing on our grounds. The Santa Barbara fishermen never throw traps in the water when another fellow is there ahead of them. We should show those San Pedro fishermen what we do when another boat hijacks our fishing grounds."

At eleven o'clock that night, Ira and Frank left the camp and did not get back until four o'clock the following morning. Ira came into the bedroom with quite a pile of short pieces of new rope, which he threw under the bed. Then he went to the kitchen, made coffee, and he and Frank went out as usual in the *Sam Pan* to pull their traps.

The next day, Big Jerry dropped anchor in the bay. He had brought us a young, red-haired pig, weighing fifteen pounds or more, that he had caught alive on Santa Rosa Island. Ira told Jerry about the boat out by Gull Rock. "They had their fish traps strung alongside ours, so at two o'clock in the morning Frank and I rowed up there, pulled every trap they had, took their fish, and cut the ropes and buoys off their traps. We left them ten out of their seventy-five traps. We were back in camp at four o'clock, made coffee, and started back up the line in the *Sam Pan*. We knew they could see us leave at our usual time, and they wouldn't have any idea it was us who cut their traps loose. When we got abreast of their boat and were pulling our own traps, they asked us if we knew who had cut theirs loose. We answered, no, we didn't. They said they guessed they were not wanted around here, pulled the ten traps we had left them, and went down towards Louie's camp. That night Louie cut the other ten traps loose, and this morning the boat left for San Pedro where she belongs."

"So that is where you got all the rope you threw under the bed this morning!" I said.

"Yes," said Ira, "we are entitled to it because those men were fishing in our grounds."

Slapping Ira on the shoulder, Big Jerry said, "That's the way to do it, kid. Don't ever let an outsider pull one over on you."

Louie the Italian visited us every week to get all the news the boat brought from town. On one trip, he brought a bulldog for Vera to play with. I let her take the dog down to the beach, where they played together for some time. Back in the kitchen I told Louie that he always looked so neat, and asked him how he took such good care of his overalls. He said, "I take the overalls, fold them and set them on a board. I rub on lye soap, scrub them first on one side, then on the other, and rinse them good. Then I hang them, bottom side up, so they will dry with the crease in them. Then I put newspapers on my bedspring, lay the overalls down, and set the mattress on top of them. When I need them, they look as if they came from the

French laundry." Later, when Louie had left, I took Ira's good trousers, put them on the bedspring, and Ira slept on them for a month without knowing it.

After we had been talking for awhile, I heard the baby, screeching at the top of her voice. Running down to the beach, I saw the bulldog pulling her back and forth on the sand by the back of her skirt. Her father got there ahead of me, picked her up, and carried her back to the kitchen. I washed her face and put salve on the bruises. Ira patted her on the back, saying, "Vera, you're a big girl now, and big girls don't cry. Mamma, we won't call her 'baby' any more." From then on we both called her Vera. Louie did not stay at our camp that night, but took himself and his bulldog home.

About a week later the men went to take their fish to Santa Barbara in the *Sam Pan* and stayed in town for three days. I was left alone in the canyon with the baby. It was a relief to be alone, and it gave me a rest. I spent the time taking care of the garden, watering and hoeing to keep down the weeds.

The boys came back from town having forgotten the potatoes in my grocery order. When Ira came in from fishing that noon, I had just finished baking five loaves of bread. I suggested we go up to see the Linscows, a father and son from Lompoc who were fishing at Johnson Canyon, to the west of us, and trade some homemade bread for a mess of potatoes. Ira agreed that we could start out early the following morning, pull the traps, call on the Linscows, and come home before the wind started to blow.

So it was arranged. Vera and I were all ready when Ira and his helper Danny were on the beach to go fishing. Frank stayed in camp. This was the first time I had left the camp since coming to Willows, and I was looking forward to seeing more of the island. Also, Ira had told me that old man Linscow was a very good cook. I thought it would be grand to have a change from my own cooking.

Aboard the little *Sam Pan* we started up the island. Laguna beach, the first canyon to the west, looked very pretty—something like Fry's Harbor, with plenty of shrubbery and green trees that looked like oaks and willows, but oh, what a beach! Ira said it was the freakiest beach on this side of the island. Our beach at Willows was very smooth and gave us no trouble getting off and on, but this beach was one mass of breakers. After Laguna there was not much beach, just high cliffs, the ocean washing right up to them, with no anchorages for boats. We saw a large rock out in the ocean, which was Gull Rock, where our string of traps ended and Linscow's began. The rock was a large rookery for seals and seagulls. There was a thick patch of kelp all the way between it and the island, and we went around the outside of it. When we rounded the kelp, I could see a little shack perched high on a bluff at Johnson's. I wondered how you could get up there, but as we neared the shore I could make out a narrow trail.

We dropped anchor in the large bay. There was not much scenery here, just bare plains covered with wild oats. At the foot of the bluff, a reef of rock extended out into the ocean. It was low tide, and on the reef I could see two men picking abalones, which Ira said were used as bait for the crawfish traps. The men kept right on working, and Ira said, "I expect they are bashful because a woman and a baby have come to call on them. We'll go ashore, I'll take you and Vera up to the shack, and Danny and I will wait here for them."

We climbed the narrow trail single file. As we went into the house, the first thing I noticed was that there was a floor in it. You could stand in the middle of the floor, stretch your arms out, and touch both sides of the shack at the same time. There were no chairs, only short benches. There were two narrow bunks on one side of the shack, and at the end was a table and a stove the same size as ours, and in the same condition. There was a window facing the bay. Ira opened it and left the door open for air, for I began to feel rather squirmish from the different odors.

There were ashes all over the floor, overalls left on the floor just as the men had stepped out of them, socks that could stand up alone and keep the overalls company, boots thrown here and there, dirty red bandanna handkerchiefs scattered all over.

The table was covered with dirty dishes from the night before, their coffee had boiled over, and the coffee grounds were all over the stove. Groceries were stored under the unmade bunks. The smell would knock you down. I thought, what a difference there is between men batching for themselves and having someone to keep house for them. I stepped outside the shack and walked around. Outside the kitchen door was a washbasin. The water in it had probably been left there a couple of days and had been used again and again.

The two men came up the trail, and the old man was making excuses for the condition of the shack. "It won't take me but a few minutes, and I'll have this mess straightened out," he said, and did so by throwing the soiled clothes under the bunk with the groceries. Then he started a fire and called me in.

Ira told him that we were short of potatoes, and that I had baked some bread and had suggested trading it for potatoes. Mr. Linscow said that he was just cooking the last of his potatoes for our dinner now, and he would not get any more for ten days. But we would have a nice visit anyway. Watching him get the meal ready, I figured that my husband and Frank were very lucky to have me in camp to fix all their meals and clean the place up. Mr. Linscow must have thought so too, because he said, "If my old woman were here she would keep things clean, but she is too old to come out camping."

My auburn hair was hanging down in two long braids, Mr. Linscow said, "Ira, you have a wonderful-looking young woman, with such beautiful hair. Aren't you afraid to have her out on this island among these roughneck fishermen?" Ira said he wasn't, and I told Mr. Linscow I had had a wonderful time and everyone had been so kind to me.

The boy took the abalones outside and pounded them for steaks. Ira sat down on the bunk and the three men started to talk. Mr. Linscow said that Big Jerry had been there the night before and told him about the policeman drowning at Laguna. Then Ira talked about how we had launched the *Sam Pan* and what a great help it was to him in his fishing. The old man said he had seen Ira and Frank row up this far every morning, pulling their traps, but since they had never stopped to see him he thought they were sore about something. Ira answered no; when they were through pulling pots they were tired and hungry, and were always in a hurry to get back to camp. They knew what good meals I had ready for them.

I began to smell the food cooking while they were talking, and realized I was very hungry. We all sat down at the table, which Mr. Linscow had pulled out from beside the wall. He and his son sat at each end, Ira and Danny on the inside, and Vera and I on the outside of the table on a bench. I thought, if I can ever go anywhere again where I can sit in a chair and rest my back, I don't think I'll ever want to get up. For dinner, we had fried abalone steaks, boiled potatoes with their jackets on, fried young pig chops and gravy, tea for me and coffee for the men, and my homemade bread. How we did eat! I don't think there ever was a meal that tasted as good as that one. No one wanted to get up from that table in a hurry.

When the meal was all through, Vera went to sleep on a bunk, and the men got out their pipes and smoked and talked until about three o'clock that afternoon. They talked about everything that had happened on the island since the men had come here to fish, and how much fish each camp had sent in. Ira said he did not expect to make much money, because he had the extra expense of buying the lumber for the *Sam Pan* and had not finished paying the local market for outfitting him. He was satisfied with how he was doing so far, though. Then they talked about how wonderful it was out here away from town and all its worries, especially bills which you expected to pay sometime in the future, but just now could not.

I asked Mr. Linscow if he was going to spend Christmas in Lompoc, and he said no, he didn't expect to go into town until the season was over about the middle of March. If they went in now, they would spend too much of their money, and he wanted to give his earnings to his old lady all at once. I thought this old man had some nerve to call his wife "old lady" since he was pretty old himself.

I invited him and his son to have Christmas dinner with us

down at Willow Canyon; Christmas was four weeks away. Ira said to save them rowing all the way down to our camp, he would come and get them in the *Sam Pan* when he had pulled his traps on the morning of Christmas Eve. They would stay the night with us, but would have to bring their own blankets, as we had just enough for ourselves. I wondered where I would put them to sleep—every space was already taken.

Then, bidding them goodbye until Christmas, we went home minus our potatoes and five loaves of bread. Our camp certainly looked good to me, and I prided myself on how clean our kitchen was. I would have to set my yeast again, for we were out of bread as well as potatoes. On arriving we found that the *Charm* had stopped that same afternoon and Frank, hearing of a chance to buy a sailboat, had gone to town.

We had not much for supper that night, just tea and a bowl of rice, as we had eaten so much at noon. I had been gadding about all day, and I felt as if I did not want to move again for awhile. We all piled into bed, and it was not long before we were all pounding our pillows.

In a couple of days Frank was back with the new boat; it was not large, only about twenty-five feet long. He wanted to go abalone picking, so he and Ira divided up all the gear. Ira bought the little stove from him. Then Frank bade us goodbye and sailed to Santa Rosa Island to fish for himself, leaving Danny with us.

One morning when Ira and Danny had gone out in the *Sam Pan* fishing, Louie came to camp. His hand was wrapped up, and I asked him what was the matter. He told me a crawfish had bitten him two days before, and his hand was hurting him badly. I unwrapped the bandage, bathed his hand in warm water with plenty of bluestone in it, and wrapped it up again. Then I asked him if he had had any breakfast; he said he could not eat, but I made him drink some strong coffee and lay down to rest in Frank's bunkhouse for awhile. Ira and Danny would be back as soon as they gathered their fish, I said, and then told him all the news about going visiting at the Linscows' and about Frank getting another boat. Then I said

I was going up the canyon to bring some wood for my fireplace, as we were planning to have a fire in it for the first time
that night.

Taking Vera by the hand, I got an old piece of rope and
walked way up to the waterfalls, farther away from camp
than I had ever been before. I thought how beautiful, how
restful it was on this island. There was hardly a sound, only
the rustling of the trees in the soft, mild wind blowing down
the canyon. I stood there awhile thinking: here I am at last,
free from all cares and worries. I have no fear of anything,
and I'm living a life worth living. Even if we do not have much
of this world's goods, we have happiness, which is worth
everything. Ira and Vera and I are always together now. I
looked up toward the waterfall and saw how beautiful the
scenery was all around, and I felt oh, so happy. How wonderful it was to wake up in the morning and hear a chorus of song-
birds lifting their voices to heaven, offering their morning
prayer. Then I thought, Margaret, why don't you offer one
too? And as I was piling my wood, I started to sing the hymn
I had heard my mother sing so often when we were children:
"As the mariner turns to the star of the north, so Mary, my
soul turns to thee. For naught are the storms that toss my
frail bark, as she sails o'er life's changeable sea."

I tied my old piece of rope to a thick log and started hauling
it down over those cobblestones, but the rotten rope broke.
Vera was just behind me and I fell backward over her, but she
did not cry—she just picked herself up. The log was too heavy
to carry, so I doubled the rope and tied it around the center of
the log. That way it was easier to haul, and finally I got it down
in front of the shack. That thick log would burn all night in
our fireplace.

The skies overhead were cloudy, and I was sure it would
rain. I packed sack after sack of wood for the stove and the
fireplace that I had planned about so long. The next thing to
do was get the fire ready, so Ira would only have to strike a
match. Then we would watch the flames roar up the chimney.

What a good idea Captain Nidever had, building this cobble-stone fireplace. I thought, it must have given him and his brother Jake much comfort on cold, rainy nights to watch that fire burn. Every day I would make a couple of trips up the canyon to bring down big wood; I must not use my stove wood in the fireplace. I would not mind the cold or the rain now—I could keep the two fires burning, and the heat from the fire-place would keep the dampness out of our little cabin.

While I'd been up the canyon getting wood, Louie, restless, had walked up the thirty-foot hill to the right of the canyon to see whether the *Sam Pan* was in sight. She was not. I got dinner as usual, but no one showed up. Suppertime came; still no boat. About seven o'clock it started raining. At eight, I heard the exhaust of the *Sam Pan* and went down to the beach to see what had kept her so late. As soon as Ira saw my light on the beach, he hollered out, "Is supper ready?"

"It's been ready since noon!" I answered.

Ashore, he said that the *Sam Pan*'s propeller had dropped off in about eight fathoms of water. He had to row the four and a half miles up to El Pozo to ask Big Jerry and Arturo for help. They all went back to the boat, and Arturo dove down, brought up the propeller, they put it in place, and the *Sam Pan* was on her way again.

As the boys were eating supper, I hung their wet clothes on nails around the kitchen, saying that the next day I would keep the fire going in the fireplace and dry all their clothes. After supper I said, "Come and start the fire, Ira. Vera is sitting in her crib waiting to see it."

"All right, Margaret," said Ira, coming into the room. He kissed the baby. "Vera, watch Daddy light the fire." He struck the match on a cobblestone and stooped to light the paper. "Margaret, you surely set this fire right."

Grabbing Ira by the arm and dancing up and down, I said, "Let's go out and watch the smoke curl up the chimney!" Tak-ing Vera along wrapped in her blanket, we went and stood outside for a few minutes, but no smoke came out. Ira was just

going to investigate when clouds of smoke poured out the
door. Both of us started to go in, but Ira told me to stay outside as the smoke was not good for Vera.

Well, Ira fussed and fussed with that fire, but still the
smoke came out the door in clouds. We had to wait in the
kitchen until all the smoke was out of the room. The wind-up
of that fireplace was, it wouldn't draw, so Ira had to make a
Portuguese stove to set inside it. He took one of my water
cans, cut out three sides of a square hole and bent the metal
down on the fourth side to make a damper near the bottom.
Then he built a fire in it with stove wood. At least we could
keep the room warm, which was what counted most, but that
was the end of all my dreams of having a fireplace.

We had rain that evening. It rained and stormed for about
ten days, with a heavy southwest ground swell. Danny knew
I was afraid something would happen to our little *Sam Pan*.
Early one morning he came up from the beach and said to me,
"What do you know? The *Sam Pan* isn't in the harbor. The
ground swells are so high, she must have broken from her
mooring."

I dropped the eggs I was cooking for breakfast. "Oh, no,
Danny, nothing like that could happen."

He said, "Come along, have a look." I ran to the edge of the
cliff and the swells were so high I could not see the boat. Then
I ran down to the beach. Large combers had broken in on the
sand, and there was our little boat, bobbing up and down like
a duck. What a pretty sight, to watch her climb those large
swells! Danny was standing on the beach, thinking he had
played a good joke on me. But he had really frightened me. I
had thought she was gone. Ira came along and assured me the
boat would sink before she would part from her mooring.

After the storm it was the light of the moon and the crawfish wouldn't bite much, so the men only had to pull their traps
about every third day. During this time they decided to take
the *Sam Pan* over to Anacapa Island and get a load of abalones. There was money in drying them for the market. Ira
said he would not leave me alone in camp if he thought I would

be afraid, but I assured him I would be fine. I put up boxes and boxes of cooked food and made a special batch of bread, for if men must work they must also eat.

I asked Ira how far it was to Anacapa. He told me, "It is twelve miles from here to the east end of Santa Cruz Island, or Hungryman Gulch. There is a fisherman living there, and we'll stop and see him. Then it is six miles from there across the channel to the extreme end of Anacapa where the Big Swede is. We won't get back for three days, but when we do, we'll be loaded down."

I helped them take their stuff down to the beach. Aboard the *Sam Pan,* they got that little five horsepower motor going and pulled anchor. They honked the boat horn while Vera and I stood on the beach waving our hands and hollering goodbye, watching the boat disappear around the next point.

I realized that I was alone in this canyon, the only woman on the island. I thought of the story Captain Nidever told about the lone woman on San Nicolas Island, and how her baby was devoured by wild dogs. I looked down at my little girl and thought of the wild hogs that are on this island. What if something happened to my little girl? What if something happened to the boat and it did not come back?

I must try not to get down-hearted. I planned to mark the days off on the calendar the first thing when I got up each morning, so I would not forget. I took Vera back to the kitchen and got her breakfast, then worked in the garden all day. I was just killing time. On toward evening I went to bed early. When the sun set and it began to grow dark, I began to think that maybe I really was afraid after all. Such a funny feeling came over me, one that I could not explain. I left the lantern burning all night. I heard every little noise that other nights I would sleep right through: the usual chorus of the stinkbugs, the fighting of the cats, the barking of the foxes, and the odor of the civet cats.

Daylight finally came. Throughout the day I walked to the beach and back perhaps a dozen times. I knew that the boat was not coming until at least the following day, but I had the thought that perhaps they would come home sooner than they expected. They didn't.

Toward the morning of the third day, there was a heavy mist. I went up the canyon and gathered wood, so that I could look down from there and see if the boat was coming. Then the rain began to come down heavily, and I thought of all the water I had wasted, packing it to the garden.

The fourth day came; there was no boat. I went to bed and lay there listening for the sound of the exhaust. I looked at the wall next to my bed and wondered why no one had ever put a window there. The first money we have to spare, I thought, I will have Ira buy a window and put it in the wall facing the ocean. Then I can look out from my bed.

Well, I might just as well count all the sheep on this island and try to sleep. I looked at my clock: it was eight o'clock. I thought I heard the sound of an engine. I was rigid for a minute, listening. Yes, it was the old familiar put-put of the *Sam Pan*. I heard Ira saying, "All right, Danny, let her go!" and the anchor being lowered overboard.

In the space of a second, everything changed. The cobwebs were brushed away from my brain. I hopped out of bed, rushed into my clothes, flew out the door down to the beach, and waved my lantern to let Ira know I had heard them. I heard Ira holler, "Supper ready, Margaret? Awful hungry!"

I hurried back to the kitchen, lit the stove, and put on some rice, cold roast pig and Spanish beans. There was a new batch of homemade bread. It was not long before the men were in the kitchen with their slickers and southwesters on. Ira said they had not eaten for two days. I asked what they had done with all the food I had given them.

"When we stopped at Hungryman Gulch," Ira said, "Kangaroo Dick wanted us to stop and visit. Then Hard Working Tom and Skinny came down from Smugglers'. We stayed there until about eleven o'clock that night. The following morning we were up at daylight and went on to Anacapa. The fisherman there called Jimmy the Flea came out and invited us ashore, so I took some of our food. Your homemade bread disappeared in a hurry, as those fisherman were almost all living on hardtack and flapjacks."

I asked if they had gotten any abalones. Danny spoke up. "If we put another sackful on the *Sam Pan* I think she would sink. Just wait until you see her in the morning—you'll say we have been working."

Then Ira said, "My, but it seems good to get back to camp again! When you came down on the beach swinging your lantern, that was the first light we had seen since we left Anacapa. Every one of those fishermen must go to bed before sundown. I'm ready for bed right now myself." Was I happy to have Ira home again! He came into the bedroom and kissed the baby. After I had told him what all I did while he was gone, we went to sleep.

The men were up again at daylight. Now that Frank was not in the camp, I felt I could get up and go to the kitchen without being in the way. That morning I made the coffee and heated some leftover rice in a frying pan with olive oil. Then I broke two large raw eggs in the rice, stirred it around and let it fry for a few minutes. With that and toast we had a fine breakfast.

Ira and Danny went down to the beach to start preparing their abalones. They dug a hole six feet long and four feet wide, about fifty feet above high tide. Ira put six iron bars across it, then built a tank to fit over the hole. The sides were redwood, three feet high and two inches thick. Both sides were curved upwards towards the ends. The bottom was galvanized iron with the edges clipped to fit the curve of the sides so the redwood wouldn't burn when set over the open fire. Then Ira banked dirt on both sides of the tank so no fire would come out the sides; the back and front were left open. With the ends of the tank built so they curved up, you could fire the pit from both ends. Danny filled the tank with salt water. A wooden cover was made to fit the tank, the fire was built in the pit, and the water heated until it was boiling hot.

While the water was heating they got their abalones ready. Ira took a large tree stump and nailed two abalone bars on it.

Then he sat on a box—covered with sacks to make a cushion—
and put cotton gloves on, as this work was very messy. He
took an abalone, placed it under the bar, pressed hard, and the
meat came loose from the shell. He dropped it in a can to his
right, and Danny took the abalone, removed the innards, and
threw it into the tub in front of him. When the tub was full,
they dumped it into the boiling water. Then when the tank
was filled, they covered it with gunny sacks to keep the steam
in and put on the long wooden cover. After the abalones had
boiled for four hours they were ready to come out, but someone must stay to feed the fire all the time they were cooking.

After the four hours were up, the boiler was opened. Ira
used a dip net with a long wooden handle to scoop the abalones
up, held them for a few minutes to let them drain, and then
dumped them on gunny sacks spread out by the side of the
boiler. The men worked this way for two days, and I watched
the whole process carefully in case they ever needed me to help.
I knew they had about three tons to clean and boil, and were
up to their necks in work. Ira asked me to spread the abalones
out on the sand to dry while he was getting the next batch
ready to boil. I finished that job quickly.

It was getting near dinnertime. Ira had cleaned, sliced, and
pounded five large white abalones, which I fried and served
with a pot of Spanish beans. Vera went to call the men for
dinner. I had plenty of hot water ready for them, for they were
covered with slime. After eating, the men put their second
batch of abalones on to boil. I soaked Ira's clothes to get the
salt water out, then washed them and hung them on the garden fence to dry. The rest of the afternoon I spent up the
canyon gathering wood for my stove.

The following morning, the men left for Laguna beach to
get more abalones and a load of wood. I gave them a box of
lunch, in case they got hungry before they came back. I had
plenty of work to do. As usual, my wood was about used up
and I had to go further for it every time. I had the canyon
cleaned out clear up to the waterfalls, about a mile away. I
picked and sacked ten sacks of wood and carried them back

one at a time before the sun came up, as it would be very warm working in the sun. Then I had the three tons of abalones that must be turned, and that took the balance of the day, with Vera helping. I talked to her just as if she were a grown person— she was so much company to me.

At suppertime, no boat had shown up yet. Well, I thought, they probably want to put in a good day's work. By eight o'clock it was dark and they could not work any longer. I kept their supper warm, for surely they would be back any moment. Then I thought about what had happened to the policeman at Laguna. I got Vera and myself ready for bed and listened again to the song of the stinkbugs, field mice chasing one another, and cats fighting. I dozed off and on, listening for the sound of the boat, and finally fell into a restless sleep.

I awoke early the next morning. I thought I heard the sound of an engine and got out of bed, not even taking time to dress. I went around the side of the house to look; there was nothing in the bay. My whole world was upside down again. Could anything have happened? Ira did say he would be back last night. I thought I could go and look from the top of the hill, but decided the best thing to do was stay in camp. It was six o'clock. I dressed, started my fire in the kitchen, got my cup of tea, and listened. The air was so still these mornings. There was the put-put of an engine. I took my cup of tea and walked down to the beach.

The boat coming around the point was not the *Sam Pan*. It was Frank in his little boat, no bigger than ours. He waved, knowing I was all alone in camp since there was no other boat in the harbor. Coming ashore, he said he had been over to Santa Rosa Island and picked a load of abalones. He asked me if he could clean and boil them in our tank. I said sure, just make himself to home, and offered him hot coffee and mush. He sat down at his old place in the lean-to and ate. I did not want him to think I was worrying about the boys, but I asked him if he had seen the *Sam Pan*. He said no, he had come down the island just outside the kelp beds and had seen nothing. Well, I could not imagine what could have happened. Frank finished his breakfast and walked down to the abalone boiler. I had visions of him using up all my wood. I think he read my thoughts because he said he would go up the canyon and get some wood to start the fire.

Just as Frank was going aboard his boat to bring in a load of abalones, the *Sam Pan* came around the bend. I waved, jumping up and down at the same time. I was so glad to see them! Ira and Danny waved back. When I saw that everything aboard the boat was all right, I rushed to the kitchen and put on another pot of fresh coffee and mush, as Frank had finished what I had cooked before. I knew the men would be hungry.

While they washed the salt water off, I made the toast. We all sat down and I asked Ira why he had not come home sooner. Unconcerned, he said, "Oh, we stopped at Laguna and picked abalones until we had almost as large a load as we got at Anacapa Island, working both low tides. When we had all the *Sam Pan* would carry, we figured we must have wood to cook them, so we took a chance and went ashore."

I said, "Ira, you didn't go ashore on that beach after what happened to the policeman, did you?" He said sure, they just watched for a chance and only got dumped a couple of times coming out with a load of wood. They picked it all up and tried again. They had both had a good salt water bath, but that did not worry them when they had such a load of abalones on the *Sam Pan*. She had been anchored in the far corner of the beach and was so tiny that Frank had passed by without seeing her.

While Frank worked on his batch of abalones, Ira and Danny unloaded the *Sam Pan*. The wood was brought ashore; it was manzanita and oak about two feet thick. I hated to see all that good wood burned under the tank when I could make use of it in my little stove; but the boys were expecting to make quite a sum of money with the abalones, so it all went for a good cause. Ira saw me looking at the wood and said he would go back to Laguna and bring me another load of it when he was through boiling these abalones. It would burn more slowly and put out more heat than what I gathered up in Willow Canyon.

Frank talked of making a trip to town the next day, and I suggested that I go along, as we were very low on groceries. I got my few things together and was ready early the following morning. Ira sent Danny along as a helper; he was staying in camp to tend the abalones. There was a light sailing breeze outside, and we got aboard at seven o'clock to get ahead of the wind. Waving goodbye from the boat to Ira, standing on the beach, we were on our way.

We left the bay, rounded the point, then continued on up, passing Laguna. It didn't look so smooth that morning—there were rows and rows of breakers pounding on the beach. We were skimming along nicely, and I was enjoying myself. Vera was asleep in my arms. Next we passed Gull Rock and saw hundreds of seagulls flying around and perched on the rock. We came to Johnson's where, Frank said, the wind blows every day, all day and way into the night. There were the Linscows out in their skiff pulling their fish traps. We waved to them and they waved back. As the son waved, he let the crawfish trap fall back into the water, and the old man hit him a good one across the shoulder. We were amused at those two getting an unexpected shower bath so early in the morning.

Then we hit the breeze. Let me tell you, it was some breeze, but Frank's little sailboat skimmed right along. Next, Frank pointed out the Christy ranch house. It looked so home-like with its coat of whitewash, nestled among the tall eucalyptus trees. I asked if any of the fishermen camped there, but Frank said no, that beach was a terrible one to get on and off, just as bad as Laguna. The company that owned the island had a crew of men working at that ranch all the time. I thought that place looked just like the farms back in Quebec, and commented that everything about farm life was so peaceful. Frank answered that he thought farm life came right after fishing.

"We are nearing Forney's Cove," he said, "and as we pass it we will get a stronger wind. The old-timers claim that at

low tide there is a reef that runs from Forney's Cove clear
over to Santa Rosa Island, and there is only about three
fathoms of water. No matter how smooth the ocean is, if any
ground swell is running at all you will see the breakers loom
up along this part of the channel. There is no danger though,
as there is an inside and an outside passage."

As he talked a squall hit the boat, and she seemed to stand
on her stern for a minute, then her bow went down under. I
just cannot describe it, except to say it was like the boat made
a porpoise dive. Frank hollered "Duck down!" A large comber
broke over the bow, then swept on over the little boat. For a
second I felt as if we were going with it—I thought we were
washed overboard. I held on to Vera just as tightly as I could.
When the comber had passed on, Frank said he had not seen
that one coming; he hadn't realized we were so close to shore.
We were all wet, not a dry stitch on any of us.

Frank went down below and found the boat had sprung a
bad leak. I heard him say to Danny, "We're in a very bad mess
—almost sinking. The mainsail is torn and the staysails brok-
en. The only thing to do is make the nearest beach before the
weather gets any worse." That beach was Christy, which we
had just passed. Frank turned the boat around, and Danny
started bailing. It seemed that the faster he bailed out, the
more water poured in.

"This weather is what I call a dirty sou'wester," said Frank.
"There is no chance of the wind letting up until after sundown." The little boat was floundering about. The ocean was
covered with whitecaps that broke and sent spray all over us.
All this time the wind was getting fresher and the seas higher.

Finally we reached Christy Beach. The men helped Vera and
me into the skiff and got us ashore, then went back to manage
the boat. I gathered driftwood, built a fire on the beach, and
dried my clothes as best I could. I wrapped Vera in a blanket
and dried her clothes around the fire. She could not understand
what had happened and cried for her daddy. I soothed her and
told her we would be home in a little while.

Frank and Danny had some time beaching the little boat.

They towed her in as far as they could with the skiff, then tied a tow line to her bow, and the next big comber put her up on the sand. Then they walked over to the ranch house and were gone about an hour. They came back with their arms loaded with mutton tallow candles that the men at the ranch made, and also a leg of mutton. Danny brought a pail from the boat, and melted the candles in it over the fire. Then they started filling the leak next to the keel, mended the sail and spliced the staysails. Before long they had the boat in shape again.

Frank decided there was no use trying to cross the channel that afternoon. He cut the leg of mutton in strips and roasted it over the fire. With a loaf of hard dry French bread, the meat and coffee, we made a meal. Then Frank brought more blankets from the boat and made a bed on the lee side of a large rock. Vera and I slept there nicely that night, while the men slept on the boat.

Early the following morning at high tide, they got the boat off the beach, and Frank asked me if I wanted to go back to camp. I asked him, "Are we halfway on our trip?" He said we were. "If it suits you, Frank," I replied, "we may just as well keep on toward town." So we did. It took us several hours to cross the channel, and I am here to tell you it was some trip. Every moment the little boat climbed over swells that I thought would turn her over backwards and spill us all out. I figured, if I ever get back to camp I am riveted to the ground—no more boat rides for me.

We finally reached Santa Barbara. Frank told me he wanted to leave again at three o'clock the following morning so he could work the low tides toward evening. Leaving Vera with a friend, I flew around town. I bought whatever was needed at Dardi's grocery store and had them send it down to the wharf. They were very accommodating. The next morning I got a cab and was on the dock at three o'clock. Frank and Danny were there waiting. I did not want to think of the trip across.

Frank made a bed in the cockpit with a couple of extra blankets I had brought, and Vera and I were very comfortable. There was just a light wind at that hour of the morning, enough to keep us traveling along. I was so worn out. Vera and I fell asleep, and did not awaken until we had rounded the west end of Santa Cruz Island. The mutton tallow had the desired effect, and there were no leaks in the boat on the way back.

Maybe you don't think I was happy to see the old camping grounds again! Ira met us on the beach. When we told him the story of the trip, he said, "Why didn't you ask Frank to bring you back?" I told him I had all the confidence in the world in Frank and Danny; but I did not leave camp again in a hurry.

Ira made wire trays for the abalones to dry on and moved them up near the kitchen. This made it easier for me to turn them every day and saved me from working on the cold ground at the beach. After ten or fifteen days they were pretty dry and ready for market. Ira had only been pulling his crawfish traps about twice a week, and boats did not stop very often at our camp now that the *Sam Pan* was in commission.

It was getting pretty close to Christmas. I started preparing a butterless, eggless, milkless cake, with plenty of spices and raisins. I set the yeast for two batches of bread, one white and one raisin. I made mince pies with wild hog meat and plenty of brandy, and you would not know but that the meat was beef. I spent days getting the Christmas dinner ready, singing Christmas hymns, and thinking how pleased the Linscows would be to visit us.

On the twenty-third of December, our pig was killed, scalded, cleaned and stuffed. While Ira and Danny dug the hole for the pig by the vegetable garden and started the fire, I spread a couple of layers of willow leaves all around the pig, wrapped him in heavy paper and then in gunny sacks, then tied it all with baling wire. Ira raked out the coals, cut four oil cans and fit them together, set the pig in, heaped the coals on top, and left the pig there from two o'clock Christmas Eve until the following morning.

Then Ira, Danny and Vera went up the canyon and came back with armfuls of Christmas holly. Vera handed me some, saying, "A Christmas present for Mamma." I thanked her and gave her a big kiss. The men left to pick up the Linscows.

I walked out to the creekbed several times looking toward the ocean, thinking that my invited guests would be along soon. Shortly the little *Sam Pan* rounded the point to her mooring, dropped anchor, and the two men were rowed ashore. Vera and I were on the beach to welcome them and make them feel at home. They were all dressed up in their best clothes, white shirts with stiff collars. They knew they had looked so terrible the morning we called on them, they wanted me to know they could dress up once in awhile.

I suggested they might be more comfortable if they changed into their work clothes, so they did. When they came up to the kitchen, they looked more like human beings. Their blue work-shirt collars were open at the throat, and their black cotton trousers had a crease in the back and front of the legs, just like Louie's. I told them that Danny would sleep aboard the boat that night and they could sleep in the bunkhouse. Ira took them all through our camp as they had never been here before. They complimented me on the vegetable garden and on how clean everything looked, and said it really seemed like Christmas with all the holly hanging around. I was glad we had invited them.

For supper that night we had cold head cheese, Spanish beans, tea, and French toast. All through supper there was the same line of conversation as when we had called to visit them —about the different camps, who camped, what price fish was, who caught the most, and our last trip to town.

When everyone was asleep in bed and the camp was quiet, I crawled out of bed and pulled out a box from under Vera's crib. In it were four of Ira's white wool socks with red and green tops, that he wore with his rubber hip boots. I filled them with apples, oranges, mixed nuts, and assorted Christmas candy, and put a long, red and white striped candy cane in each one. I hung two socks on the bunkhouse door, where I had pounded nails that afternoon when the men were gone. Our socks were hung from the cobblestone fireplace. For Vera, I had made a rag doll, and I also had two pieces of checked gingham for dresses.

Ira was the first one awake in the morning. He woke Vera and me and wished us a Merry Christmas. "Santa Claus came to see Vera," he said, and carried her to the fireplace. "Oh my! Santa came to see Papa and Mamma too!" He gave Vera her sock and she pulled out her rag doll first thing. She was delighted. Then Ira emptied his sock on the bed and said, "Margaret, I didn't expect anything like this!"

"Why do you think I made that terrible trip to Santa Barbara?" I replied. "Just to get wire and groceries? No, I had Christmas in mind. Frank hid everything aboard his boat for me until he left to spend Christmas with his parents."

Ira kissed me and thanked me for my thoughtfulness. Then we hurried to dress and get breakfast, as our guests were early risers too. It was an ideal Christmas morning. The weather was cold and clear, and the birds were singing in chorus. A very happy feeling came over me; I imagine it was the Christmas Spirit.

I called out, "Merry Christmas to you!" toward the bunkhouse. The Linscows opened the door and returned the greeting. They had awakened earlier but had not wanted to disturb us. Then they saw the red and green socks hanging on the door. "Jiminy Christmas, are these for us?" They were so pleased. The father commented on how nice it was to wake up to the birds singing. There were no trees around the Linscows' place for birds to nest in, just wild oats all around, and the men were out working before daylight every day, so they seldom heard birds. I was so grateful to be living in a beautiful spot like this.

Then I went into the kitchen to get breakfast. We had stewed prunes, coddled eggs, and hotcakes with cactus pear syrup. The Linscows had not tasted this before; they did not know the prickly pear cactus was good for anything other than feeding island sheep and wild hogs. Mr. Linscow said he would have to write to his old woman and tell her how well we had treated them, with such good cooking and even Christmas socks on their door. After breakfast the men went for a walk up the canyon, and Ira worked in the garden most of the morning.

I cooked potatoes, green peas, string beans and cauliflower from the garden on a fire outside, using my stove for a work table. Since we had no pan or platter large enough, the pig was carved on my bread board, laths tacked on the four sides so the juice would not run out. The stuffing in the pig was just wonderful; the long, slow cooking had brought out all the flavor. I surprised everyone with a gallon of good dago red, which Dardi's grocery store had sent over with me as a Christmas present. We had just a grand feast. Almost everything we had for Christmas dinner was out of our garden: the lettuce and tomatoes, the onions for the dressing, homemade bread, and mince pie made from the hog fat.

Ira persuaded the Linscows to stay another night; he would take them back when he went to pull his traps the following morning. I was so glad they decided to stay for supper because I wanted them to enjoy my butterless, eggless, milkless cake, which I served along with the cold hog, raisin and white bread, and more dago red.

After supper Ira built a fire out in the open, and we sat around the fire and popped corn until about eight o'clock, which was quite a late hour on this island. Before retiring for the night, we sang "The Lord was Born on Christmas Day" and "Holy Night." So passed our first Christmas on Santa Cruz Island, and I hoped we would pass a good many more as happy as this one had been.

In the morning I gave my guests a good hot breakfast and wrapped up an extra spice cake and mince pie for them to take as a remembrance from us. I told them I hoped they could visit us again. Then Ira took them up the eight-mile run in the *Sam Pan*.

Time passed quickly, and then it was New Year's Day. I hoped someone would drop in to visit. Ira made me some hairpins from the heavy bait-basket wire, so I could put my hair up. My long braids hung down in the front and got in the way when I spread and turned the abalones. He also made new boot laces of fish twine for both Vera and me. I felt all dressed up for New Year's.

We heard the sound of an engine; it was the boat *Peerless,* which belonged to some Japanese fishermen who were working up by El Pozo near Big Jerry. Ira went down to the beach and waved to them. They waved back, knowing they were welcome. He talked to them for quite awhile and then they left for their own camp. At lunch Ira told me they just stopped to say hello and to ask about our abalones. They had been discussing Big Jerry, who in a friendly way often pulled the Japs' crawfish traps and took their fish. Jerry thought that was only fair since they were fishing in his area. The Japs knew he was doing it, though they wouldn't admit it. They got along with him just fine.

In the afternoon Big Jerry dropped anchor in the bay and we were all pleased to see him. He brought Vera a blue hair ribbon, a small set of china dishes, and a real doll, a little larger than my rag one. She was so pleased with her presents, but the rag doll had been mothered for a week already, and it had preference.

While I was cooking supper, Big Jerry noticed my braids wound around my head and said, "Well, Ike, I notice your old woman put her auburn hair up."

At that expression, I almost exploded. "If you and I are going to stay friends, Jerry, don't call me 'old woman.' I consider that an insult. Mr. Linscow calls his wife 'old lady' and 'old woman,' and I don't like it a bit."

Big Jerry bowed almost to the dirt floor. "Beg your pardon, ma'am, I meant no offense. That is an expression all us deep-sea sailors have for our wives, no matter if they are young brides or old women. I will not call you that again." Peace was restored. We all sat down to a supper of fried bass with garlic sauce, green peas, lettuce and tomatoes out of the garden.

Jerry said he had stopped at the Linscows' camp a day or so after Christmas. "They could not say enough about the good time you showed them on their visit. And Linscow said, 'Jerry, when you have your old woman with you' (here Jerry looked at me and smiled) 'it makes all the difference in the world. They keep everything in order and have your meals ready.' All us fishermen know you have the best camp on this island."

Ira said I had made the camp seem just like home. "Well," I said, "at first it was a bit hard for me to do this work, but there isn't anything in the world you can't get used to if you make up your mind to do it. I was so anxious to get away from town and come to this beautiful island that I made up my mind. No matter what came along, I was willing to do my share."

I asked Jerry how he had spent Christmas, and why he hadn't come to call on us. He said, "Well, I was in no shape to pay a visit where ladies were, and I know a good woman like you will think I'm a terrible man if I tell you. I bought me a five-gallon keg of good old dago red and another one of beer. I set one on the right side of me and the other on the left, and got two short pieces of rubber hose and stuck one in each barrel. Then I got me a pillow and laid down and drank first from one keg, then from the other. That saved me the effort of having to pour. I just laid there and drank and amused myself by singing every old-fashioned song I ever knew—'After the Ball Was Over,' 'Sidewalks of New York,' 'Old Black Joe,' 'East Side, West Side,' 'Nellie Grey,' 'Put on Your Old Grey Bonnet,' and 'Yankee Doodle.' The other songs I sang, I just don't remember. I think I must have fell asleep." I said I guessed he had.

With supper over, it was time for Big Jerry to get aboard his boat. We all walked down to the beach, wished him a Happy New Year, and he rowed out to his boat singing "Goodnight Ladies, We're Going to Leave You Now." We could still hear him singing as he rounded the point. Ira, Vera and I went back to camp and got ready for bed. As Ira kissed us goodnight, he said, "We surely have lots to be thankful for, don't we?" Thus began 1909.

In the new year, life went on the same as in the old—the men fishing and preparing their abalones between tides. Ira said he must get the abalones to town before it started to get rainy, as damp weather is not good for the meat. He had about four tons of meat, and as the shell weighs double what the meat does, that was twelve tons all told. So he and Danny loaded the little *Sam Pan* until she looked as if she would sink. As usual, I packed a couple of boxes of food for them, and at the grey light of dawn the men got aboard for their nine-hour trip.

I told Ira I didn't want him visiting all the camps along the island on his way over to Santa Barbara and back. I knew Big Jerry would show them a good time if they stopped there, and they might forget to move on for some time. Ira said he would be back in four days at the most, and right there I figured it wouldn't be less than six. Kissing me goodbye, he jumped aboard the load of shells in the skiff, and Danny rowed out to the *Sam Pan*. She looked as if she had all she could do to carry that load and tow the two eighteen-foot skiffs loaded with shells. Waving, they were on their way.

It looked as if the rain would come at any moment. There was a job waiting for me. The boys had washed out the abalone tank and set it up by the lean-to. It would hold quite a lot of extra water, which we would need when the stream came up and covered the spring. While the boys were gone, every morning and night I carried about ten gallons of water until I had the tank filled. Then I put the board top on and covered it with gunny sacks to keep the water clean for drinking.

There was also plenty of wood hauling to be done. I carried fifteen sacks of wood and piled it in the kitchen, leaving just enough room to walk between the bench and the wall. Then I filled the bedroom. Every space was taken up with sacks and sacks of wood. Then I piled more wood around the house and Frank's bunkhouse. When it rained, I would be prepared. I kept a fire burning in the kitchen and the Portuguese stove in the bedroom.

When I had finished, it rained that same night, but I lay in bed with Vera beside me and knew I had plenty of wood and water. This rain would fill the canyon with knots and dead wood, and I would have a new supply. It was nice to lie in bed and listen to the raindrops hit the roof. I listened for awhile.

The rain was coming faster and harder, and I could hear the breakers pounding on the beach. I figured Ira had got his load of abalones to Santa Barbara just in time.

Up the next morning early, I wrapped myself well, put on my rubber boots, and went down to the beach. There were large ground swells in our little harbor, the water was muddy, and the ocean outside very rough. Back in the kitchen I started the fire, got breakfast and cleaned up, then sat Vera at the table and gave her the dolls and china set. There she played all day. I sat on the bench and started knitting a pair of light grey wool socks for Ira. And as I knitted and mended our clothes, I thought of my beautiful mother, sitting in her rocking chair and knitting or mending for her large family. This beautiful island would be a wonderful place to raise a family, but I only had one child. We could not even afford to buy me a rocking chair to sit in while I mended, so I did not long for a large family. The rain came down heavier and heavier, but the baby and I were very comfortable.

The day arrived when the men were to return; no boat came. I went to the calendar to see if I had made a mistake in counting the days. Ira had left early Sunday, January the seventeenth. This was Sunday the twenty-fourth and he should be here. I wondered if I was going to be left on the island for good this time. Well, Ira always showed up sooner or later. Now the rain was coming in torrents. The creek was roaring, and I knew the spring had been buried by now. I was glad I had every tin can and pot filled with water.

Toward late afternoon the storm slackened for awhile and then set in anew. The creek was running from bank to bank, and I thought that any minute everything on the flat would be swept away. The water was rushing around the little kitchen, my one-room shack, and Frank's bunkhouse.

That night there was a cloudburst in the mountains back of the canyon with lightning—the great blue double kind—which nearly rocked the mountains. The noise of the thunder was so loud I could not hear the roaring stream that was flooding my cabin. Vera lay beside me asleep as I sat on the bed praying that my one-room cabin would be spared. I stayed awake waiting for morning to come. When it did, I could see that the dirt floor of the cabin was covered with rocks and small tree branches, and the opening of the door was blocked with large trees. It was a good idea not to have closed my door after all or I could not have gotten out. When this wood had dried I could make good use of it. I picked my way from the bedroom to the lean-to six feet away, up to my knees in muck and brush. I started a fire in the little stove to dry the walnut-sack walls and get the dampness out of the kitchen before bringing Vera out of her warm bed.

On the ninth day the storm was over, and there were hundreds of angleworms all over the ground. My chickens surely feasted for days afterwards. I cleaned up the camp as best I could, and at noon on the tenth day the little *Sam Pan* rounded the point. The men dropped anchor and rowed ashore, and Vera and I met them on the beach. Then we went back up to the kitchen, and while getting supper I asked Ira if he had stopped at Big Jerry's camp, he was away so long.

"No," said Ira, "we went straight to Santa Barbara. It took me two days to sell and unload the abalone meat and shells. Mr. McGuire shipped them to San Francisco. The fourth day I paid some bills and bought groceries. The next day we left town. Coming around the east end we hit a southeaster at Smugglers' Cove, turned back, and ran up the Island as far as China Bay. The *Gussie M., Charm,* and *Baltic* were anchored there too, and Frank's little boat the *Marghareta,* which he named after you because you were so kind to him when he was here. The first night we all went aboard the *Gussie M.* and had a big mulligan for supper. Colis Vasquez told us he had just taken six fishermen to Santa Barbara from San Clemente Island, where they had been living on fish alone for fourteen days. They all had terrible colds, and did not give a damn if they never saw another fish again. You know, it's a good thing I left here when I did, or our whole load of abalone meat would have been spoiled."

At the end of January there was more rain, with a southeast

wind and heavy ground swell. The men couldn't go out to pull
their string of traps and they began to get restless, wondering
if the traps would survive the storm. I made sure the men always got a good meal in the bad weather; that does make a
man feel better. I was glad we had our garden so we could pick
vegetables as we needed them. One day I fixed wild hog, cabbage, potatoes and gravy; another day, creamed salt fish, potatoes and carrots. I hoped the rain would stop soon, because
our quarters were a little cramped for all of us and the piles
of wood too. At least the wood was dry.

Vera was happy as a clam. She sat on the table in the kitchen
and played with her dolls all day; there was no room for her
anywhere else. At mealtime she sat in her high chair. The
walnut sack walls were dripping wet and the water was running down onto the dirt floor. We were just thankful we had
a roof over our heads.

One morning after it had rained all night, I heard Ira putter-
ing around in the lean-to and called out to ask what he was
doing. "Breakfast is ready, come and get it!" he answered. It
did not take me long to get Vera and me into the kitchen,
where Ira had the stove going full-blast. I ate my sourdough
hotcakes with cactus syrup and drank my tea. Everything
tasted so good, the more so because he had fixed it for me.

Then I offered to make a batch of doughnuts, as something
sweet would taste good in this sort of weather. Ira set down a
board on the floor so I wouldn't have to stand in the puddle of
water in front of the stove while I cooked. Then he said, "I
just wish I could afford to buy lumber for a floor in this
kitchen, Margaret. I hate to see you living this way. No matter what happens, you never complain."

"Ira, I just love it here every moment," I told him. "To me
this life is a regular paradise, so don't you worry. When you
can get out to pull your traps again, you will forget all about
this rain."

On towards evening, the wind began to blow down the canyon. We went to bed at seven o'clock and slept until nine, when
there was a terrible noise. Ira jumped out of bed, put on some

clothes and went outside, then came right back telling me to come and look. By this time Danny was also dressed. We stood in the doorway and heard a deafening roar. The boys hollered to one another: "There must be a cloudburst up the canyon!"

The lightning flashed in long, vivid streaks, and the thunder started, peal after peal of it. You could almost feel the earth tremble, and the noise sounded like the surf dashing on the rocks. A mass of water rushed down the creek, and great clouds of dust, leaves, and driftwood traveled past the side of the little cabin. Large trees swirled around and around in the river of water and waves of mud followed one another. I hoped all that driftwood would pile up on the beach. That would save me walking way up the creek to haul it down. Ira worried that our spring was stopped up with all that mud; it would be some job to clean it out. But, as there was nothing we could do at that hour of the night, we all decided to go back to bed again.

The next morning after the storm, the boys had a good catch of fish at Gull Rock. Ira said the water along the shore was very muddy from the storm, and that was why the fish were biting better. In the evening it started to rain again, and it continued to rain off and on every day for awhile. The men kept working, rain or shine. I kept the fires going all day so they could change to dry clothes as soon as they came in.

We did not need any newspaper, because whenever anything important happened in town, someone would always come and give us all the news. On January 28 the *Gussie M.* dropped anchor in the bay, and Captain Vasquez told us that two ships, the *Sibyl Marston* and the *Ensign,* had gone ashore on the coast. The next day, Big Jerry called on us. He had just come from town and said there had been a big landslide at Punta Gorda, burying an engine and four men under tons of rock and mud, and also doing great damage to the fishing camps there. Big Jerry said he was blessing his lucky stars that he was fishing the island instead of the mainland coast as he had first intended. On the 30th, the *Baltic* came to take our fish to town, but Ira decided to make the trip himself in the *Sam Pan* and save the three cents per pound freight. While ashore, the men from the *Baltic* said the mountains behind Santa Barbara were covered with snow. It had been cold here on the island too; I had been keeping my kitchen stove going all day and the Portuguese stove all night.

In early February Ira went to town with our load of fish and came back with a white and brown spotted fox terrier. He had got it from a woman who worked all day and left the dog locked in the house. Its barking annoyed the neighbors, and the woman, not wanting to send it to the pound because it would cost her a dollar, had asked Ira to put it in a sack and drop it in the channel on his way back to the Island. When Ira went to get the dog, really only a puppy, it had jumped up on his legs and licked his hand. That settled the question. He told the woman that the pup had a home—he had a little girl and the pup would be great company for her.

While Ira was gone, one morning I heard noises like shooting or explosions. When he returned I asked him about it, and he said it was the war boats outside at target practice. I guessed they couldn't have been very far away, for the noise had been very loud. It was a good thing we had no windows in our cabin or lean-to kitchen, or they would have broken.

Later in the month the *Baltic* came by and we invited the crew to supper. We had rock cod chowder, Spanish beans, hot homemade bread and coffee. "My," the two boys said, "you live like princes. There's not another camp on the island that has the homey feeling this one does. All the boys just love to stop here because there is always a welcome for them and a good bite to eat." One of them added, "We just picked up a load of crawfish from the Linscows over at Johnson Canyon, and they are still talking about the wonderful time they had here at Christmas. I tried to talk the old man out of one of the candy canes you gave him, but he almost got sore about it. He has them hung up over the little window in their bunkhouse with a piece of fish twine tied in a bow. Let me tell you, those candy canes are covered with plenty of fly specks, but the old man is taking them home to his 'old woman,' fly specks or not."

Then they told us the news about the boat *Charm* getting her anchor line fouled in kelp; when the tide came in she drifted up the coast and went ashore two and a half miles above Goleta. The *Baltic* had hauled her off the beach and she was taken back to Santa Barbara. After supper, the boys left our camp for the next harbor.

About the end of March, Ira mentioned that soon we would have to move from Willows, for the summer season would be upon us. There was no way of making a living on this side of the island, but on the north side he could work the beaches for smelt and also have a chance to cater to some of the campers.

I was almost sick at heart. I had never stopped to think that this life could not go on forever. "Ira, I don't want to go back to town. I am so happy here on this island. Isn't there another harbor we could camp in?"

He thought a moment and said, "We could camp in Dick's Harbor. There's no house there and no space for a vegetable garden. Everything will have to come from town. We'll have to sleep in a tent again and cook out in the open, like you did at Pelican."

I said, "Any place will do, just so we don't have to go back to town."

Three weeks later, we had everything down on the beach ready to move, including our chickens, which had increased to fifty. There was quite a lot of stuff, and all of it taken together was probably not worth ten dollars; but to us it was worth plenty, as it was all we possessed. In this game, if you threw anything away today, tomorrow you might need it. Just then Big Jerry came by and asked where we were going.

"We are moving to Dick's Harbor," Ira said. "I'll fish the beaches for smelt to make enough money to tide us over the summer months. Then next winter I'll fish at Scorpion Anchorage. I don't want to move there yet because there is no shade up there on the bluff; the north side of the island will be much better for now. My wife, as you know, is very much in love with this island and she doesn't want to go back to town."

"I don't blame her at all," said Jerry. "By the way, I'm passing by Dick's this afternoon. I can take a load of your stuff over there and leave it on the beach for you. There won't be many boats around now and I think it will be all right." That was very helpful to us.

Before he left, Jerry said to me, "My, your little girl has grown since she came here. The first time I saw her, she was puny and pale, but now she has such rosy cheeks and her auburn hair is beginning to look like gold. She is a fine young-'un."

I answered, "We have plenty of good plain food, and there's no germs around here, so there's nothing to prevent her from going ahead." Then I told him that he and all the boys had been so kind to us, and I would feel slighted if they didn't drop in and see us at Dick's. We bade him goodbye until we would see him again.

Making the rounds of the camp and finishing up in my little lean-to kitchen, I thought what wonderful times I'd had here. This little shack had made such a comfortable home for us. Then I heard Ira say, "Margaret, you could help a bit on the beach." So I took Vera by the hand and went down to help load up the skiff. Soon we were aboard the *Sam Pan*, the anchor was up, and we were underway. I looked back until we rounded the point, and Willow Canyon was out of sight.

CHAPTER V

Camping at Dick's Harbor

Summer, 1909

I MOVED to a new island home without having to return to
town at all. From Willows we went along the south side of the
island, around the west end, then back along the north side
until we came to our new camping place at Dick's Harbor. On
the way I recognized the places I had seen on my terrible trip
to Santa Barbara before Christmas—Gull Rock, Johnson Canyon with the Lincows' little shack up on the hill, Christy
Beach where Frank had repaired his boat with mutton tallow,
and Forney's Cove. Rounding the west point, we started down
the north side, passing Painted Cave, Valdez Harbor where
the *Irene* had been wrecked, and Lady's Harbor. Next we
came to Fry's, where the party of campers had stayed the previous summer when I was at Pelican. With all its green trees
and shrubs, it reminds you of the tropics. Ira said if we
camped there we would have no privacy at all. People came
from all over the country to camp there and they did not clean
up when they left, so the place was always filthy. Then we
passed the Fern Grotto and rounded the next point to our
camping place, Dick's Harbor.

After we landed, I didn't have much time to admire the
canyon or the scenery, as it was five o'clock and we had to set
up camp. The tent was put up to the right of the canyon by

the running spring, and my bed moved in. I put Ira's best suit of clothes under the mattress for future use. My best was a bungalow apron and heavy coat. Our stove was set outside, as here we would cook and eat in the open. Some campers had left a table in a cave; this became our dining room. Apple and orange boxes served as a dressing table and bureau. When camp was set up, it was my job again to furnish wood; I found there was plenty on the beach.

During the first couple of weeks while Ira was out fishing, two different groups of people came ashore at Dick's to hunt wild hogs. Both met with varying degrees of disaster. In the first group, two of the hunters got lost; one of them fell down a cliff in the dark, but was not badly injured. They had to wait for their partners to come and rescue them the next day, and came back to camp bruised and exhausted. After a good supper of fish, bacon and eggs cooked on my stove, they headed south for home—minus a good rifle smashed to pieces at the bottom of a cliff.

The second ill-fated party were Austrians who went out without guns, only a dog. Late in the afternoon they came back limping and cut up, reporting that the hog had almost had them for fresh meat. The dog, terrified, had run off and didn't come back. I gave them first aid and they went aboard their boat for the night. A terrible ground swell started pounding on the beach, and their boat, not securely anchored, was dashed on the rocks. The two men were lucky to get ashore with their lives before it sank. They lost everything they had, but were very brave about it. I made them as comfortable as possible, then Big Jerry took them into town the following night. Their boat provided me with plenty of driftwood, and I made good use of it. When I told Ira the story he said it was too bad, but the outsiders did not understand anchoring around the islands. They figured they were in Pedro, where they only needed a fishline and hook to anchor with.

One day when I was sitting on the beach with Vera, the *Charm* dropped anchor in the bay and the captain rowed three gentlemen ashore: Mr. Cameron Rogers, Mr. C. C. Felton, and Mr. Reggie Fernald. Mr. Rogers wanted to bring his family over to the islands for a three-week outing and was looking for a camp site. They had been up to Valdez Harbor, but the heavy swell and wind there would make it unpleasant getting on and off the beach. Then they went to Fry's Harbor where three different parties were camped, but the canyon was very dirty and messy, with tin cans and garbage all over the place. So the captain had suggested they try Dick's Harbor.

I gave them a tour of the camp and showed them how I kept my food fresh in an apple box covered with mosquito netting, up by the spring. All my fish bones and papers were burned in the stove, and Mr. Rogers told me the camp was very clean. Then he said that he would be back in a week with the camping gear, and that Mr. Whitney, the Mayor of Santa Barbara, had a camping permit from the owners of the island. I thought how wonderful it was that these people had a permit to camp; we had been on this island for so long, and nothing had been said about our camping without a permit.

The following morning, Ira came back from town with the great news that Mr. Rogers had chartered the *Sam Pan* to cater to his party while they were on the island. Ira was to take them fishing and show them the caves on the north side of the island, and Mr. Rogers would pay him ten dollars a day for the three weeks. That seemed a huge sum for our little boat, but it was what Mr. Rogers had offered to pay. We could still camp right where we were.

This was the same Mr. Cameron Rogers who wrote that beautiful poem, "The Rosary"; he had also chartered the *Irene* some years earlier, as I found by checking my diary. On the way home to Santa Barbara they had sighted a fight between a whale and a swordfish out in the channel, but the party had some important engagement that evening and did not stop to watch the fight.

I told Ira it would be grand having a great man like Mr. Rogers coming here to camp, and we would have the honor to say we had catered to him with our little boat. We must do all we could to please him. Ira said I would have to stay over here at our tent most of the time and not let Vera go near their camp, because those wealthy people wouldn't want to be bothered with someone else's child.

Now I got sore. "Goodnight, Ira! Do you suppose that because I've been camping on this island for more than a year and have met only fishermen, that I've forgotten how to act? Don't you forget for one moment that I've waited on some of the best people the Potter Hotel catered to, and I certainly want you to understand that I know my place!"

Ira answered, "I didn't mean it that way. It's just that these people have a permit from the owners to camp on the island and we don't, so they come first. Anyway, they're bringing plenty of their own help—Spanish and American cooks, and also a man to clean up the beach and amuse the children."

I set to cleaning up and washed everything in sight. I even starched and ironed my bungalow aprons that had not seen starch or a hand iron in a year.

In a week the *Charm* arrived with Mr. Rogers and everything you could imagine for the campers' comfort. He directed the men where to place things, and before long we had a regular city of red-and-white and blue-and-white striped tents. They all had porches in front, brightly colored grass rugs and lounging chairs, and two white iron single cots in each one. Nearer the beach, tents were set up with card tables and chairs. I figured, now we'll have some real life—their manner of living will be so different from mine since I came to this island. Ira and I helped them set up camp, and when the rest of their help arrived I went to my own quarters and stayed there. Mr. Rogers sent over a large basket of fresh fruit with his thanks for our assistance.

The rest of the party arrived the following day: Mrs. Rogers, Miss Fernald, the two children, Cameron and Sherman, and others. This camp was run on schedule. Breakfast was at eight, after which Ira was waiting on the beach for any of the party who cared to go out fishing with Mr. Rogers. As a rule, the ladies climbed the hills for exercise until about eleven. When the boat was seen coming into the harbor, that was a sign to get ready for the morning swim. At twelve thirty luncheon was served, and then everyone went to their tents to rest or lounge as they pleased. At three o'clock anyone who cared to could go fishing as Mr. Rogers went out in the boat again to catch enough fish for supper. The rule was to catch just enough fish for one meal at a time, and Mr. Rogers always made sure we had enough for our family too. That showed how kind a man he was.

Mr. Rogers was simply wonderful. If there is such a thing as loving someone mentally, that is how I felt about him. No matter what he wanted, you felt you could do it willingly. Some days he would go into town to look after business connected with the *Morning Press*, of which he was owner, and the camp just seemed dead without him around. But when the boat was sighted out in the channel on his return, there would be great excitement around the camp. All the party would wait on the beach to greet him, even though he had been gone only a short time. He always remembered to bring some toy for Vera; he loved children and always thought of everyone.

One day Mr. Rogers went down to Prisoners' Harbor in the morning and ordered five gallons of riesling, for which the island was famous. This was a refined party, not a drinking one, but they did like a little wine with their meals. In the afternoon when Ira was to go and call for the wine, Mr. Rogers suggested that the cook and his wife, the Spanish cook and I go along for the ride. It would be a little outing for us.

While Ira was talking to Mr. Rogers on the beach, the cook rowed the rest of us out to the *Sam Pan*. When we came alongside the boat, he said that since I was a fisherman's wife I should hold the skiff while he helped his wife into the boat. Not knowing as much about a skiff as he did but not wanting to show my ignorance, I held onto the side of the *Sam Pan*. Before I knew what had happened, the skiff moved away from the boat and I went overboard and down to the bottom. When I came up, the cook had the presence of mind to grab me by the hair, and his wife held me by the shoulder while I reached the side of the boat. Meanwhile, Ira threw off his coat and boots, jumped in and swam out. Between all four of them they got me aboard. I'll bet I weighed a ton in my boy's boots and heavy coat, and I felt as clumsy as a cow. They dragged me in head-first, and my feet stuck straight up in the air for a few minutes. From the beach, Reggie Fernald took a snapshot of the boat and me, two feet in mid-air. Through all this commotion I could hear Vera on the beach screeching "Mamma! Mamma!" Finally things quieted down and I went back ashore to change my clothes. The whole crowd had a good laugh at the ducking I got.

Aboard again and underway, we passed Orizaba Flat and then saw the arch under the long point of land that divided Twin Harbors. At Pelican Bay, the blue heron was perched on his tiny rock in the corner and never budged as we passed. I pointed out the old, almost tumbled-down shack on the hill. The cook's wife turned up her nose and said, "You like it here in this wilderness? I wouldn't live like you, not for the whole island. If my husband couldn't give me better than yours does, I'd certainly leave him for someone who could." Well, I figured there was no use trying to explain anything to her.

Passing the marine gardens, we reached Prisoners' Harbor, which I had not seen before. There was a very long sandy beach, shaded with tall pines that Ira said had been imported from Italy in the very early days. Huddled under some gum trees in the right-hand corner was a one-room fisherman's shack. At about the center of the beach was a long wharf extending out into the ocean. Between the wharf and the point of land on the west side of the harbor was the sixty-foot schooner *Santa Cruz* lying at anchor. She was used for hauling the Island Company's sheep, wool and wine; the wine especially was always in great demand. We all waved our hands American style and yelled. Captain Nidever and the crew raised their caps in the old Spanish manner, bowed low, and shouted, "Salud, Señor and Señora!" I told the party about Captain Nidever and his crew rowing up to Pelican Bay to serenade me on my first visit to the island, and how he had told me the story of the woman who had lived alone on San Nicolas Island.

The watchman met us at the wharf and handed down the five-gallon demijohn of wine. With a flourish of his hand he said, "Adiós, Señor and Señora." That meant "No hanging around, this is strictly business." We trolled all the way back to camp and caught enough fish for supper. Our employer was a good sportsman, and we tried to be the same.

Arriving on the beach, we were all happy with our outing. Mr. Rogers said that in a day or so he would put the boat at our disposal and we could go to some other harbor for the day. He asked me to go along as his guest, as I had been so kind to his two sons and had hardly been away from camp since they had been there. He would have the cook make up lunch for all of us, and he would pay Ira for the *Sam Pan* that day too. He was such a thoughtful and generous man.

That night in bed, I heard footsteps back and forth to the spring, and whispering. The kitchen help were sampling the wine. I thought, how terrible of them to play a dirty trick like that when Mr. Rogers was so kind. They were drinking so much of that wine that I knew there would not be much work done the following day.

Morning came, and I heard Mr. Rogers' cheerful voice saying his usual "Good morning" to the help in the kitchen. I did not hear any answer. Looking in that direction, I saw there was a little fuss at the breakfast table; things were not running so smoothly. Mr. Rogers seemed to have a worried look on his face, and I heard him asking, "Is the omelet ready?" Then someone else said, "May we have a little toast?" Well, surely there was something wrong. The cook and his wife waiting table seemed to be acting confused and in each other's way. Then I paid no more attention to that part of the camp, for I didn't want anyone to think I was snooping.

Just as I was starting my fire for lunch I heard a lisping voice call, "Mrs. Eaton! Oh, Mrs. Eaton!" My tent flap faced the ocean, and fifteen feet straight below me was the tent where the cook and his wife slept. I turned and saw that Maud, the cook's wife, had slashed open the back of her tent in the shape of the letter L. Her head and hand poked out of the hole, and in her hand she held an old-fashioned straight razor, the blade hanging down. Her long black hair was loose around her face and shoulders, and she had a terrible look of despair on her face. I was dumbfounded; I could not begin to write all the thoughts that ran through my mind. "Mrs. Eaton, I'm going to kill myself! Come here quick!"

I shoved Vera into my tent, saying "Don't come out until I get back. The lady is sick, and Mamma will go stay with her and see that nothing happens to her."

I went to the kitchen and told the cook that his wife was sick, and would he please go to her tent. All the answer I got was, "Ah, she's not sick, just plain drunk."

"But she has a razor in her hand and says she will kill herself!"

Said he, "If she does, I can't help it."

Well, there was no help from him, so I went over to that tent and sat on the edge of the bed, and talked to Maud in a kind way and at the same time took the razor from her, telling her she had better rest and I would take her place waiting table. Then I went back to the kitchen and had the cook make up a strong pot of tea. I had Maud drink it, straightened the bedding for her, and left her to sleep. I borrowed her clean uniform and waited table at lunch.

Early the following morning Maud and her husband were sent to town on the *Sam Pan*. For two weeks I helped in every way I could, and was happy to do something in return for Mr. and Mrs. Rogers' kindness to us. The two children would come to the kitchen between meals and tell Vera and me all about their life at home and the fancy parties they went to; Vera would listen, spellbound. I made lemon pies, and Mr. Rogers remarked, "As long as the flour, eggs, lemons and fish last, I am good for a couple more weeks of camping." He had originally intended to stay only three weeks, but they ended up staying for five. The whole time the weather was the best you could want—no swell, fog, or nor'wester, just the usual trade winds. The people said they could not wish for anything more pleasant.

I found Mr. Rogers very interesting. He would stroll up to the kitchen as Roberta and I were getting the meals ready and talk to us. He noticed I was at ease with the work in camp and asked me about our life at Willow Canyon last winter. I told him a little about it, and he commented that I seemed to enjoy this outdoor life. I said I did, and wished that we had a few acres here so we could farm, because I didn't want to go back to Santa Barbara. I loved the island. Mr. Rogers said, "Don't you realize that your husband *is* a farmer, Mrs. Eaton? He farms the sea." I had never looked at the fishing game in that light before.

Then Mr. Rogers asked me if we were going to camp on the island for the winter, and I told him that we expected to move to Scorpion Anchorage. "When the crawfish season opens," he said, "I'll come over sometime and bring my tent and blankets. I can sit in the skiff all day and catch enough sheephead to keep all Ira's traps baited. And I'll be looking for some of those fat lemon pies like you've been making for us here."

Just then we heard an engine; a large boat was passing the bay, heading north. Mr. Rogers asked me if I knew what the boat was. "Yes," I said, "they are Japs with a diving outfit. They dive for abalone, not like the white fishermen who wait for low tides and then gather the abalone. We are helpless to do anything about it."

He thought for a few minutes. "I see a way to protect the fishermen. When I go to town next, I'll take the matter up with the Supervisors, because if this keeps up there won't be an abalone left in the ocean!" That afternoon he went out in the boat and watched the divers at work.

A few days later he returned from a trip to town having attended the Supervisors' meeting. He had called their attention to the fact that Japanese fishermen were using diving outfits to get the abalone at Santa Cruz Island, and if allowed to continue, this practice would result in the complete extermination of the abalone. The Santa Barbara County Board of Supervisors adopted a resolution to use means within their power to make diving for abalone unlawful. I thanked Mr. Rogers for his interest in this matter which was so important to us.

The day came when the camp broke up, and the *Charm* arrived to take all the camping equipment back to Santa Barbara. Mr. Rogers decided to take the ladies back in the *Sam Pan,* for he had great confidence in Ira. There were fond adieus, and Mr. Rogers said, "Don't forget, I'm coming to visit your next camp sometime this winter when the crawfish season is open!" He was very fond of crawfish, but he would not catch them out of season; he said laws were made to protect the fish and should be obeyed.

(It turned out he was unable to visit us as he expected. He was taken ill and passed away April 20, 1912. When his ashes were thrown to the four winds out in mid-channel, it was Ira in the little *Sam Pan* that carried them out. We considered that quite an honor. In all the years that I catered to the public, both before and after, Mr. Cameron Rogers was the most human and thoughtful man I ever had the pleasure of serving. I still have a photo of him sitting, holding a book and supposed to be reading, which I will always treasure.)

Vera and I were alone in the canyon the night the Rogers party left, and everything seemed so quiet and dull. The next few days were very lonely without the company. I wondered whether I should stay out here this winter or go back to town, but then I made up my mind I'd stay.

Soon Ira returned from Santa Barbara and handed me a large *Morning Press* envelope. "Mr. Rogers sent this to you because you helped out his party. He said if you think this is not enough, to let him know and he will send you the balance." It was a check for fifty dollars.

"Enough?" I said. "I didn't expect any pay! If I couldn't pitch in and help when they were in such a fix, I'm sure I could not call myself human." There was also a large package with wonderful story books for Vera. I'm sure that none of them cost less than $1.25, for that price was marked on them. I was so happy. No one could guess how big that fifty-dollar check looked or how far it went. Now we were assured of having enough groceries for almost the whole crawfish season.

Ira said, "That's not all. One of the party, Mr. Lamb, sent us a hundred-pound sack of Spanish beans, and said when that was used up, to let him know and he would send us another."

Well, now I was astonished. Beans were eight dollars a sack, so this was a small fortune. I decided we must send both gentlemen, Mr. Rogers and Mr. Lamb, some crawfish from our first catch of the season. Then Ira pulled out another long envelope, opened it, and handed me the check for his boat hire: $350.00 for thirty-five days' work.

We hadn't seen so much money at once for a long time. Ira would be able to pay the bill for the *Sam Pan*'s lumber, and we would start the crawfish season not owing a dime to anyone. Now we could afford to live a little better than we had at Willows, but I was perfectly happy and satisfied with the way we had lived camping at Dick's.

Margaret Ann Holden, late 1890s.

Potter Hotel, Santa Barbara, 1902–1921.

The *Gussie M.*

Wedding, 1903; left to right—Lillian Eaton, maid of honor; Roscoe Seeley, best man; Juanita Eaton, ring bearer; Margaret Holden; Ira K. Eaton.   Photo 4.

View of Santa Cruz Island near Orizaba, when approaching from Santa Barbara. Photo 5.

6. Beach at Little Pelican.

7. Fisherman's cabin at Willows, taken after the windows were added.

8. A similar view of Willows in 1980.

A fisherman's camp on the south side of the island.

10. Valdez Harbor, where the *Irene* was wrecked.

11. Along the north shore, passing between Fry's and Dick's Harbors.

12. Dick's Harbor, Santa Cruz Island.

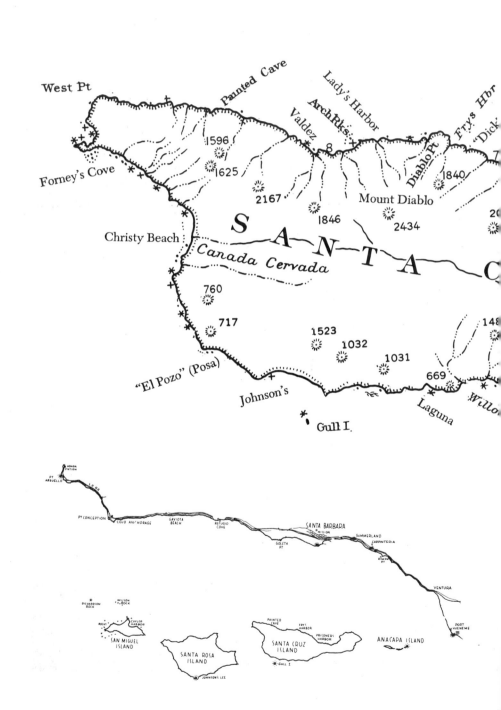

West Pt

Painted Cave

Lady's Harbor

Frys Hbr

Arch Rks.

"Dick

Valdez

Diablo Pt.

1596

1840

7

1625

Forney's Cove

2167

Mount Diablo

2434

S   A   N   T   A   C

1846

20

Christy Beach

Canada Cervada

760

717

1523

148

1032

1031

669

"El Pozo" (Posa)

Johnson's

Laguna

Willo

Gull I.

HONDA STATION

PT ARGUELLO

LO RES

PT CONCEPTION   COJO ANCHORAGE   GAVIOTA BEACH   REFUGIO COVE   SANTA BARBARA

SUMMERLAND

GOLETA PT

CARPINTERIA

VENTURA

RICHARDSON ROCK   WILSON ROCK

PORT HUENEME

ROCKS   CUYLER HARBOR

PAINTED CAVE   FRYS HARBOR

SAN MIGUEL ISLAND

PRISONERS HARBOR

ANACAPA ISLAND

SANTA ROSA ISLAND

SANTA CRUZ ISLAND

GULL I.

JOHNSONS LEE

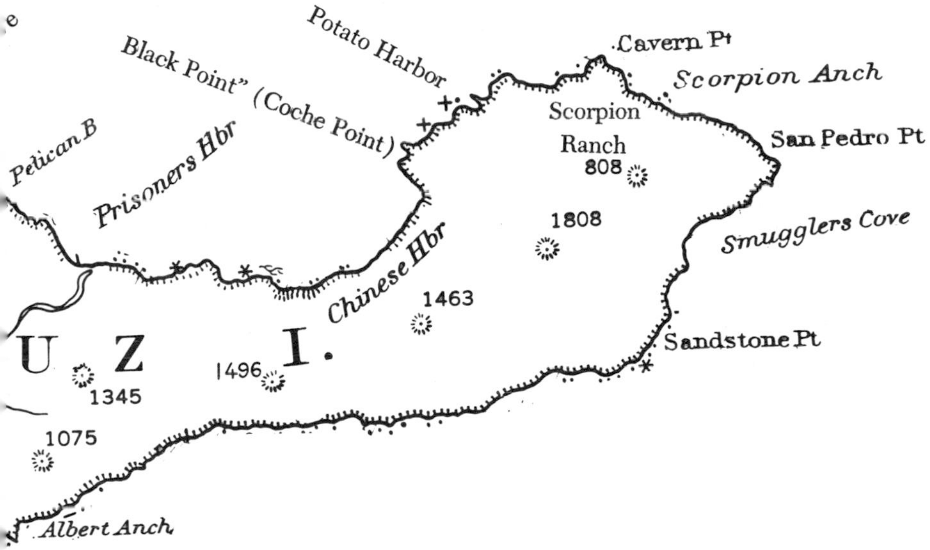

Potato Harbor
Black Point" (Coche Point)
.Cavern Pt
Scorpion Anch
Scorpion
Ranch
808
San Pedro Pt
Pelican B
Prisoners Hbr
1808
Smugglers Cove
Chinese Hbr
1463
Sandstone Pt
U Z I.
1496
1345
1075
Albert Anch

PHOTO CREDITS

Photo no. 2 is courtesy of William Yule Jr.

Photos no. 5, 7, 9, 10, 11, 12, 14, 16, 17, 21, 22 and 31 are from the archives of the Santa Barbara Museum of Natural History.

Photo no. 25 is from *California's Sea Frontier* by Mabel Rockwell (McNally & Loftin, 1964).

Photo no. 38 is from *The Legendary King of San Miguel* by Elizabeth S. Lester (McNally and Loftin, 1978).

All other photos are from the author's collection.

13. Vera Eaton on the beach at Dick's Harbor, 1909.

14. A camp site at Dick's.

15. The Prisoner's Harbor wharf.

The slough at Prisoner's Harbor, showing the watchman's hut on the hill.
Photo 16.

17. The north shore east of Dick's.

18. The schooner *Santa Cruz*.

19. The one-room fisherman's shack at Pelican Bay, about 1910.

20. Inside the shack. Vera at center, Margaret and Ira Eaton at right.

The east end of the island. Scorpion Anchorage is at the top. San Pedro Point lower right, and Hungryman's Gulch lower left.   Photo 21.

22. Lady's Harbor, Santa Cruz Island.

23. Stearns Wharf, Santa Barbara, August 1914.

24. Red Craine back in town with Santa Cruz Island hogs.

The steamer *Santa Rosa* on the rocks, just north of Pt. Arguello, 1911.

26. Ira Eaton's sheep of Anacapa Island, 1917.

Four cabins on the Pelican Bay Point, 1919.

28. The Pelican Bay Camp in 1920.

29. View of camp site in 1980.

Pelican Canyon, note row of fig trees.

31. Fry's Harbor, a favorite movie location.

32. Pelican Bay Camp, when used by film production crews.

William Boyd in pre-Hopalong Cassidy days
at the camp.   Photo 33.

Scene from the 1924 movie "Peter Pan,"
filmed on Santa Cruz Island.   Photo 34.

Augustine, skipper of the *Miramar*. John Barrymore's fishing guide in 1925.   Photo 35.

36. Ira Eaton and Red Craine.

37. A view of the *Sea Wolf* from the Pelican Bay dining room.

38. The *Cuba* aground on San Miguel Island, September 1923.

39. The *Sea Wolf* along side the *Cuba* for salvage.

Ira and Margaret Eaton, 1920.

CHAPTER VI

Fishing at Scorpion Anchorage

Winter, 1909–1910

ONCE AGAIN we started packing to move to a new camping
place. This time it was to be Scorpion Anchorage at the east
end of the island. Ira made another trip to town to buy our
groceries and lumber for the traps. He and his new partner
Jenny Larco returned to find me all ready to move. Our fifty
chickens were the last thing left on the beach. Together we
put them in boxes, loaded them into the skiff, and got them on
board the *Sam Pan*. Then we headed eastward for Scorpion.

At Pelican Bay the blue heron was still perched on the rock
in the kelp bed and did not make a move as we passed. He must
have known he was safe. We came to the marine gardens,
which are superior to those at Catalina Island, then on to
Prisoners' Harbor. We honked the horn and waved at the
ranch hands who were at work with the donkey engine repair-
ing the wharf. Trolling along the way, we caught two nice
large bass and three mackerel, assuring us of breakfast, lunch
and supper for a few days.

Down the coast at Chinese Harbor, five or six Japanese
fishermen standing on the beach waved to us and we waved
back. On a place like an island, everyone is friendly. We could

not afford to high-hat anyone; only the owners could, and I had not met or seen any of them so far. Chinese Harbor—"China" or "China Bay" for short—was an open harbor where all the driftwood from Santa Rosa and San Miguel Islands landed. Just east of it were very high black bluffs with a seal rookery at the base. I think the seals were frightened at our little boat—they started barking and dove off the rocks into the ocean. Then they poked their heads out of the water and barked some more, as if to say, "This is our territory— why come here and disturb us?" Our little fox terrier, standing in the stern of the boat, started barking at the seals, and they barked back in answer.

We continued on to Potato Harbor, which is a small bay with steep cliffs on both sides and a little shack built on the side of the hill. It seemed to be holding on for dear life, as though a strong puff of wind might blow it into the water. The hills around Potato were a light grey and very barren, but there were a great many sheep on top of the hill. They were grazing so near the edge you would think they would tumble down into the ocean.

Rounding another point, we saw Scorpion Anchorage—our new home. To me, it looked about half as large as Prisoners' Harbor, but there were no trees here. As we entered the harbor, on the left were high bluffs; the land to the right was more level. There were herds of sheep and cattle grazing all over the country. There was a fine wide road on the side of the hill to the left of the canyon. The part I could see was nothing but solid rock-work. Some stonemason who knew his business built that road. It was used mostly by the cowboys at the Island Company's Scorpion Ranch farther up the canyon. Up to the right was a space of about a hundred feet long and twenty-five feet wide. This was to be our camping place.

We had lived for two years in canyons; now we were to live on a bluff overlooking the beach. This was the fourth time I had moved since coming to the island, and I was used to it by now. In camping here we would have a wooden floor in our tent for the first time. Ira explained it was necessary to have a floor here because the northeasters were so bad that they would blow the tent to pieces if it was not fastened down. And since there were no trees for shade, he would rig up a tarpaulin over the tent so we would be out of the blazing sun. I would have to wear my straw hat and Vera her sunbonnet all the time, or our fair skin would get badly burned. We dropped anchor, put our camping gear into the skiff, and went ashore.

While Jenny and Ira were unloading, Vera, easily amused, sat on the cobblestone beach and enjoyed herself throwing cobblestones or sticks into the water. The little fox terrier would run out and bring them back. I knew I need have no fear of Vera going very far away, for she was a real mama's baby. She was always in sight, or as soon as I called she would answer, "Here I is, Mamma!"

The first piece of furniture to get ashore was our little wood stove. Standing on the beach and looking around, I noticed there was quite a little driftwood, and I knew I had my old job back, supplying the camp with wood. It was no time before I had dinner ready—fish fried in olive oil, stewed tomatoes, French bread, and pure cold water from the spring at Dick's Harbor.

Piled on the bluff, the amount of junk we had put into this fishing and camping business made it look like we were going to camp for a lifetime; but we dared not throw anything away, for it might be needed later. The first job was to lay the tent floor and set up three redwood boards on each side as walls. Ira was young, strong, and very active, and with Jenny helping him our tent was soon up. A red cotton ingrain rug from a second-hand store gave the white tent a cheerful look. Under the rug I spread quite a few newspapers to help keep out the cold. With the tarpaulin over it and a coal oil stove inside, the tent would be warm enough in the winter. What better home could anyone want? We had no kitchen, but just cooked and ate in the open. Jenny's tent was set up about ten feet away from ours, for the camping space was small. The chickens were turned loose by the hill across the creek. And so our life began at Scorpion.

Soon the boys started building their traps, getting ready for the crawfish season to open. When finished, the traps were dropped in the bay to allow the new lumber to soak. This new partner that Ira had was not as much help as Frank had been; I sized him up as plain lazy. While the men fished, I did my share of work ashore. It was no easy matter, cooking for two men and trying to have a variety for Vera and myself. We were up against it here for fresh meat. There were no wild hogs on this part of the island so we lived on crawfish: one day fresh fish, fresh fish the next, and canned meat on Sundays.

At first I only went off the bluff to feed my chickens across the creek. I felt cramped. This was nothing compared to Willow Canyon, which I considered my home and longed to go back to. I could not take the same interest here that I had at Willows, although I did not neglect anything connected with the camp work. Here the men did the water carrying. They brought brackish water for washing down from the horse-trough tap. The drinking water came from the pump in the fig orchard half a mile further up. Another thing was that in Willow Canyon I had never noticed many mice, but here at Scorpion the place seemed full of them. You had to be mighty careful or they would chew up everything you had. I often thought of Sir Reggie the writer when Ira took him camping, and he said Anacapa Island was "overrun with vermin"— little field mice. I wondered what he would think if he were here!

One day a short and squatty, smiling old man came up onto the bluff carrying a quart lard pail. In broken English he introduced himself as Bourago, a Frenchman, one of the cooks for the Santa Cruz Island Company. He had brought fresh milk for Vera. I was thrilled! I could have just hugged him, even if he was all greasy and dirty and looked as if he never took a bath. I asked him to sit down on an apple box—it seemed we still could not afford chairs. Then he reached under his coat and brought out a brown paper sack, set it on the table, and said he had brought us a nice leg of lamb. He told me it was very good meat, and to be sure to roast it in the oven. I offered to pay him for it, but he said no, he knew Ira and Jenny very well, and they had recently given him half a sack of crawfish. I thanked him very much, and then he left.

When Ira and Jenny came back from pulling their traps, I opened the oven door and showed them what the French cook had brought me—a nice leg of lamb for our dinner. Both men laughed and thought it a good joke on me. "Why Margaret," said Ira, "don't you know better than to let the old fellow put one over on you? This is a shoulder of mutton, and a very old one at that. You'll have to boil it; if you roast it, it will be just as tough as leather. Anyhow, it would not have hurt the old fellow to give us a leg of lamb, because we have kept the ranch hands in crawfish since the season opened."

Outside of the flies bothering us, our New England Dinner of boiled shoulder of ram, cabbage, onions, carrots and potatoes tasted fine. Jenny remarked that it would improve the meat to put about six cloves of garlic through the shoulder, so I agreed to try it next time. I asked if that was garlic I had smelled on the cook's breath; there had been a distinct aroma about him that was not pleasant. Ira said it was probably garlic mixed with dago red. The company allowed all the ranch hands a quart of wine with their meals; on Sundays they were allowed a quart of the best wine. Some men took half wine and half coffee for breakfast. The cook often diluted the men's wine with water so he could have more for himself.

I made bread regularly as I had learned to do at Willows. By now, baking had become routine and I hardly had to think about it, but everyone who tasted my bread said it was good homemade bread. We ate it three times a day. One particular morning I got up early to mix the bread sponge, as the night had been a little cool. I had it all ready to raise the second time and the coffee made when the men came in. Jenny said to me, "I hope this batch of bread will be just as good as the last one." Taking it as a compliment, I said I hoped so too, then went ahead and baked the batch and put it away.

At supper toward the end of the week, Jenny asked if this was the new batch of bread that we were eating. I told him it was. "I think it is even better than usual," he said. "Do you want to know why it is better?"

"Why, yes, but I baked it the same as always."

"Well, in the night I heard a noise outside and got up to see what it was. There was a civet cat in your dishpan of bread sponge. I just took him out and threw him down the beach, then covered up your bread again."

I was horrified. "Why didn't you tell me? I would have thrown the whole batch over the bluff."

"Well," said Jenny, "I didn't think you would let a little thing like a skunk bother you. You said that out camping you didn't mind anything. The other morning when I came in early to make coffee, I looked at your sponge and there were two little field mice in your dishpan. That does not hurt your bread." From then on, the bread came into my tent to raise for the night.

After we had been at Scorpion for awhile, Ira and Jenny went up to Chinese Harbor for a boatload of driftwood and built us a kitchen. It was like the cabin in Willow Canyon— eight by ten feet, with no window. The door was a wood frame covered with gunny sacks and held up by leather hinges. It didn't have a wood floor, but by sprinkling the dirt floor with my dishwater I was able to keep the dust down. For shelves to put pots, pans, and groceries on, there were apple boxes set one on top of the other. Our dishes were kept on the table covered with a clean dishtowel.

I began to feel better about this camping place. So far the weather had been fine, with no wind or swell, and the view! You could not ask for anything more beautiful. To the right from our camp was the peak of Anacapa Island, looking like an ice cream cone turned upside down. Out in the harbor was a rock about fifty feet high, which was always covered with pelicans and seagulls. If they were not perched on the rock, they were hovering overhead. It was a pretty sight. I loved to watch the sun rise in the east, its rays flashing on the ocean. And always there was the steady voice of the sea as it rushed up against the bank. Vera and I would sit on boxes in front of the tent and never tired of watching the freight and passenger vessels as they went up and down the channel. On clear days they seemed to be very close, and we could sometimes read their names—the *Yale,* the *Harvard,* and the letter *A* on the *Alexandria.* In the evenings, no gold in this wide world could be so fine a color or so beautiful as those sunsets were to me. At night when the moon was full, she looked like a large golden plate. The reflection of her light on the water was simply grand, especially as the large steamers passed through it.

I would sit there and dream, and compare this to the nights when I as a youngster sat on our back kitchen steps and watched the St. Lawrence River flowing on and on. Living on an island like this one, a paradise of beauty, I should be thankful. Our table had always been loaded with the best of food, a variety of fish and other seafoods as well. The island was a wonderful spot to live, for no one need be without food—all they had to do was go out and get it; or as Mr. Cameron Rogers said, "farm the sea."

From time to time the ranch foreman or the cook Bourago would ask Ira to help them repair water pumps and things around the ranch. Always there would be a shoulder of mutton in exchange for the work. Once it arrived neatly cut into chops. Still they had to be stewed; if they were fried we would not be able to chew them. But I thanked the cook for the wonderful chops and did not complain about the age of the animal they came from.

We had two weeks of unusually warm weather, and one night Ira said he smelled a northeaster. At suppertime he asked me to fix up a box of food for him to take aboard the *Sam Pan.* He wanted to be ready to leave in a hurry if necessary, as the boat would not be safe in our bay in such weather. He turned in early, saying that the clouds from the east didn't look good.

About nine o'clock Ira woke up. "Whenever you hear that swell on the beach, that is warning of a storm. Jenny and I will have to take the *Sam Pan* and beat it for Potato Harbor."

They left quickly. I heard the skiff being shoved off the beach, the splash of the oars, then the sound of the engine for a long time as they passed the point.

The wind began to come up, and did it blow and blow and blow! The tent swayed from side to side and seemed about to blow away, but I knew the flooring held it. I could hear Jenny's tent fill with wind, quiet down for a few moments, then blow up again. I got up and stuck my head outside the tent flap, but made haste to pull it inside again. Outside there was one cloud of dust swirling all around. I heard the kitchen door banging —the boys must have left it open. I would have to get it closed, or by morning there would be no door left. I heard bottles and pans rattling all around. Dressing, I went out. The kitchen door was hanging on one hinge. I straightened it up and put some boxes against it, then filled them with all the empty fruit jars and bottles that lay between the house and the bank. I looked out toward the ocean; it was a mass of whitecaps, and my golden moon could not be seen for the dust. This storm is what you call a Santa Ana. I went back to the tent, but there was not much sleep for the balance of the night. I heard Jenny's tent blow once more and knew it was down.

Early in the morning I got up and cleaned out my kitchen. I couldn't afford to use fresh water so I went to the beach and dipped my bucket in the ocean to sprinkle the kitchen floor.

About eight o'clock, Ira walked into the kitchen. I looked at him so queerly and thought, has he lost the *Sam Pan*? "How did you get here?" I knew there was no boat in the harbor.

"I walked over the hill from Potato Harbor to see how everything is. Jenny is on the boat and she is riding all right. There are about six other boats from the south side of Santa Cruz and Anacapa Island anchored there. The men are visiting and swapping the news from the different fishing camps. About three o'clock I'll walk back over the hill to the boat and have supper with Skinny, an immense fat man."

The next morning I heard all the boats going back to their different fishing camps to be on the grounds for the early morning catch.

One evening we had gone to bed and were just about asleep, when we heard a great commotion on the beach. It sounded as if our skiff was being shoved off. Ira and Jenny went down to the beach to see what could be the trouble. I heard the French cook's voice raised above the others. Then there was the sound of rowing and more shouting. At last the skiff was hauled up on the beach. I heard the men say "Adiós," and the Frenchman say "T'ank you, Ike." This was very strange indeed.

Ira came in and explained what all the fuss was about: Bourago had gone into the cave to get some wine and found a skunk eating a large cake of fresh cheese he had made that day. He caught the skunk and put it in a sack, tied the opening, and brought it down here, took our skiff, and threw the sack into the ocean. But there was no weight to the sack with just that little civet cat in it. When Bourago saw that it did not sink, he became frightened and started to bless himself. That explained all the shouting.

The excitement over, we settled in for the night. There came a bark, then another bark. The little fox terrier Gypsy, who always slept on the foot of Vera's bed, woke up, hopped out of the tent, and ran to the end of the bluff barking. I thought, what next?

"Those are the seals that we passed on our way down here," said Ira. "They are going over to the smelt hole a little further down the beach where they roost for part of the night. Then early in the morning they'll come by again on their way to the rookery at the black bluffs." The seals had barked just as soon as they came around the point. When Gypsy heard it, she headed straight for the beach and ran back and forth, yapping constantly. The seals barked too, and it was hard to tell who was answering whom.

This became a regular occurrence. Passing back to the black points early in the morning, the seals swam and dove right in front of the camp. If the little dog did not come out right away, the seals would stay in the same spot until she did. Ira or I would say, "Sic'em, Gypsy!" and she would make a beeline for the beach and swim out a little way. When she got

just so far, the seals barked as if to say, "You cannot hurt us!"
Then they would dive out of sight. They would continue this
game until they thought they had the little dog tired out. I
think they remembered her barking at them when we had
passed their rookery, and again when the boys had gone up to
China for wood.

About once a month the company's schooner, the *Santa
Cruz,* came down from Prisoners' Harbor to bring a new supply of wine and groceries to the Scorpion Ranch. There would
be five or six barrels of wine, many boxes of macaroni, sacks
of flour, and grain for the horses. The freight was unloaded
onto a pontoon, and a heavy rope run from the schooner to a
deadman on the beach. Then the captain and two of the crew
—the same ones who serenaded me on my first night on Santa
Cruz Island—would get into the pontoon and bring it ashore,
guiding themselves by the rope, while the straw boss, with a
team of husky, light grey horses, dragged the pontoon up to
the water's edge. The ranch hands would unload the supplies
into a low sled with iron runners underneath. It had no side
boards or seat; the driver just stood on the sled and held the
reins. With much hollering of "Whoa, Bill" and "Get up, Bill"
the horses were started on their way up to the ranch where
the sled was unloaded.

The schooner usually arrived about noon, and Ira always
invited the captain and crew up to our kitchen to have a bite to
eat. Generally it was crawfish cioppino. They would tell us all
the news of any importance from town, as well as how many
sheep, ponchons of wine, and large sacks of wool they hauled
to town. Then they would head back for Prisoners' Harbor.

Once a week regularly, Ira had to take the *Sam Pan* and
leave the harbor at night, between ten and eleven o'clock, on
account of the dry northeasters. Then I'd hear the chug-chug
of all the little boat engines passing the bay on their way to
Potato or China, there to lay until the storms were over.
There was no sleep for me on account of the terribly hot wind
and dust. The next morning I would go through the same
performance of cleaning up the mess caused by the storm.

Then, stopping to say hello to Bourago, I would go up past the ranch to the fig orchard to spend the day, as that was the only cool place around.

This same time last year at Willows we had rain, but here at Scorpion it was hot and there was no shade whatever. The old-timers said that every fifth year was a dry year, and this surely seemed to be one. At night the sheep came to graze on the short stubble on the hill back of our tent and we could hear them calling, bah! bah! all night long. I told Ira that if one of those sheep should happen to fall and break its leg or neck, we could have a whole sheep to eat. Ira said we could not do that, for the sheep did not belong to us but to the company that owned the island.

One morning I took Vera up to the orchard for a walk, and we counted thirty-five dead sheep sprawled out all over the ground. When we got back to camp I told Ira and he said that it could not be helped, that this was a dry year and there was no feed for them. That night we heard two baby lambs calling their mother for hours. We could not sleep, and finally Ira got out of bed, dressed, and went out. He caught the two baby lambs, tied a small rope around their necks, then tied them to the tent post. The little fox terrier licked their noses, and they seemed satisfied and lay down on the ground, the little dog beside them.

The next day Vera and I had a new job on our hands. We fed the two baby lambs out of a small medicine bottle, with nipples made out of pieces of clean dishrags. They were fed that way for quite awhile, and then when they were older we fed them on crushed barley. We named them Rue and Rube. The first time Ira went to town he bought two little bells, which we tied around their necks with some of Vera's hair ribbon. It was no trick to teach them to feed out of Vera's hand, and they followed her around all over the place. Everywhere they went there was the tinkle of the bells, and by listening I could tell where Vera was. At mealtimes, we tied them to a stake to keep them out of the kitchen. At night Vera would throw some grain outside the tent for them, and with Gypsy beside them, they never whimpered and were content for the night.

We missed having pork to eat, so Ira bought two wild hogs from the ranch. We had such good luck raising hogs in Willow Canyon that I was willing to try again. Ira and Jenny made another trip to China Harbor for wood to build a pigpen, and on Ira's next trip to town he bought two sacks of whole corn and barley to fatten our hogs.

The ranch had their own pigpen, with four wild pigs that had been caught when they were very small. They were now quite tame. There was always a flock of large black ravens perched on the fence up there, and they would hop down into the pigpen and eat the ears of corn that Bourago threw to the pigs. The pigs would get mad and try to shoo the ravens away with their snouts, but the birds just hopped a few feet away and then came right back. This amused Vera very much.

One day Bourago told Ira that he would supply all the ammunition that was necessary, if Ira would shoot all those damn ravens. So Ira would sneak up on the ravens. They were very smart. Sometimes he was able to shoot a few, but usually when they saw him coming they would fly away until he left the pen. Then they were back in no time.

Bourago was so pleased to be rid of some at least, that he gave Ira a loaf of hot home-made bread. The loaf was a foot long, and not round like American loaves but flat. It had a wonderful thick crust all around it. We had it for supper, and I never tasted any bread so good. Ira said, "I'll bet there is not another ranch in the state of California where you can get such good bread." The cook had to bake quite a lot of bread every week to feed the seven men at the ranch.

I asked to watch Bourago when he made his next batch of bread. So the following Monday morning at seven o'clock he called me and I went up to the ranch house, a long, two-story adobe building. A small room at the end was the bakery; it was used only to store the flour and to bake the bread and keep it after baking. In this room two deep bread troughs made of sugar pine, as white as milk. The sponge had been mixed into dough the night before. The cook cut a chunk off this mass of dough, put it on his bread board and started kneading it, explaining as he worked that this was the way they made bread over in Brittany, France, where he was born. Next he molded the loaf and placed it on a clean, coarse sack, and then drew up part of the sack to form a sort of support, instead of putting the bread into bake pans to raise. He molded twenty-five loaves in this way. He said he always saved a piece of dough and threw it back in the flour trough to start his yeast for the next baking. At five o'clock that morning, he had started the fire in the large oven; its four sides were made of white brick and it had a large iron door. I had never seen an oven like that before. He filled the top oven with wood, and what large pieces he put in! Closing the door, he said he would ring the dinner bell to let me know when he was ready to bake.

I went back to camp, and an hour later heard the bell. In a few minutes I was again at the bakery door waiting. Bourago opened the oven door and shoveled all the coals out into a tub on the floor. Then he set one loaf on the end of a four-foot-long wooden spatula and raised it into the piping hot oven. When his twenty-five loaves were all in the oven he said he would leave them there one hour or longer, until they were done. In another hour he rang the bell again, and I went to watch the last performance. By the time all the loaves were taken out, put on the bread board, and covered with more clean sacks, it was eleven o'clock.

Bourago was a very interesting man. He was a harness-maker and shoemaker by trade, and had worked at the Main Ranch up the creek at Prisoners' Harbor for many years. When the families came down from San Francisco to spend the summer at the ranch, he mended their shoes too. Then the baker at the Main Ranch took sick, and the superintendent asked Bourago to take the baker's place and bake their bread

the same way they did in good old France. When the cook at
Scorpion Ranch died, he came here and had been here for
seven years.

It was the custom for the straw bosses from the different
ranches on the island to ride over to the Main Ranch every two
weeks to report on the work done and to receive orders for the
following two weeks. One Sunday morning the foreman from
the Scorpion Ranch came down to our camp on horseback and
asked Bourago if the surplus butter and cheese were ready to
take over to the Main Ranch. Bourago told him it was not
ready but it would take only a few minutes, and went up the
canyon. The foreman stayed on the beach and waited. After a
short time Bourago came down, smiling, and he had the most
wonderful roll of yellow butter wrapped in fine salt sacks. I
gave him some newspapers to wrap around the outside of the
package, and he put it in the straw boss's saddlebag.

Later, Vera and I were sitting on the beach. Vera as usual
was amusing herself throwing small stones or sticks into the
water, and Gypsy was running out into the water bringing
them back. Bourago came down to the beach again, and this
time he had a civet cat by the tail. It was all white, looking as
if it had come out of a pan of milk. Remembering the performance on the beach a few nights earlier, I asked him, "Where
did you get that one?"

"Oh, I find the son of a gun in my cream crock this morning. The straw boss come and say make butter, so I take him
out of cream and make the butter. Now I tie a rock around his
neck." He did so and threw the thing out in the ocean. After
that trick, we went back to canned milk. Every little while,
Bourago brought me fresh milk, and I would thank him, but
after he left I would feed it to the chickens.

One morning as I was feeding and watering the pigs and
chickens, Bourago came over on horseback and leading another horse. He asked if Vera and I would like to ride over to
Smugglers' Cove, as he was going there to start the pump to
have water for the cattle. Assuring me it was a gentle animal,
he helped me and Vera up on the horse and then mounted his.

We rode up the long steep wagon road that ran alongside the high bluff, up the hill, and over the hay fields to Smugglers' Cove. After a great deal of tinkering and hammering, the cook got the pump started. We did not rush the horses on the way back; Bourago said we had plenty of time, as his work was all done.

When Ira came back from fishing I told him about my outing. He said that was not quite the proper thing to do, to ride over so far with the cook and leave the camp alone. That ended our rides. I would watch Bourago go to tend the pumps every other morning, riding bareback, coatless, hat in his hand for a whip. He would stop at the top of the hill and wave to us, then was out of sight.

Ira sometimes stopped at Hungryman Gulch for water when he was out fishing. On one of these visits, the Japanese fisherman there asked him if he had paid his rent. Ira told him that the Americans should not have to pay the Japanese to fish in their own country. The Jap was very nice about it; he said the big boss would be coming up from San Pedro soon to pick up their fish, and to find out what the American fishermen were going to do about paying their rent. Ira said he was legally allowed fifty feet above mean high water mark and would not be put off the island.[4] Later, when Ira told the other fishermen about this, they agreed with everything he said.

Soon Ira was ready to take his first load of fish to town. I didn't feel as safe here with him gone as I had at Willow Canyon—there were so many different people back and forth. But he just told me not to leave the bluff except to feed the pigs and chickens. He had packed in plenty of water to see us through until he got back. Watching the little boat out of sight, I calculated how long he should be gone: five hours to Santa Barbara, unload early tomorrow morning, a day to run around and buy what is needed for camp, leave Santa Barbara at midnight to be back to pull traps the second morning at daylight. But the *Sam Pan* did not show up until the fourth day at noon.

When Ira came ashore, he asked me to get lunch for four

extra men. Jenny did not come back, but a man named Foster would now fish with Ira on shares. Charley, Arturo, and Cooney had also come along and were going to fish Chinese Harbor. I said, "Ira, you told me every camp on the island was taken. You can't put anyone in China Harbor—the Japs are there."

Arturo said, "We only want Ike to land us and our fishing gear on the beach, then we'll show them who the fishing rights belong to." I asked no more questions—I fixed them a nice lunch, and they all went up the line for China Harbor.

A few days later, one of the Japanese fishermen stopped to talk to Ira and ask him if he knew anything about the receivers of crawfish disappearing up at China Harbor. Ira answered no, he did not, and went over to their camp to look around with them. They found no trace of the receivers of fish. Ira came back to camp and said the Japs were very much discouraged. When the big boat came from San Pedro they all left the island. Finally it dawned on me that the three new fellows had been pirating the fish and selling it in town.

When it was the light of the moon and the fish were not biting so good, Ira decided to go to Anacapa Island and bring back a load of abalones to dry for the market. Before leaving he said, "I'll bring you back some seagull eggs. They are fine in hotcakes or cake." Captain Vasquez had told me what seagull eggs were like, and I figured if Ira wanted to eat cake made from them, that was up to him.

Four days later the boat was back, loaded down. The first thing Ira did was to give Bourago half a sack of abalones, which would be a change from mutton for him. He was very glad to get them. I made cake and hotcakes with the seagull eggs according to plan, but Ira agreed they tasted pretty bad, so they went to the chickens. Next the boys went to China Harbor and brought back two skiffs and the boat full of wood. The pit was dug, the big boiler set up, and the same process gone through as at Willow Canyon. Again it was Vera's and my job to turn the abalones every day.

When our load of abalone was taken care of, our three

friends rowed down from China Harbor with two skiffs full
of abalone that they had picked. They boiled them in our tank.
I told Ira that I did not like the idea of those fellows hanging
around our place. Now that the Japanese were gone, why
didn't they stay at their own camp? Ira said that he would talk
to them, but that I should not refuse them anything they
might ask for out of the camp if he was not around. He would
settle up with them later. Then he left for town.

While he was gone, a fishing boat with two Portuguese
aboard dropped anchor in the bay and began setting out crawfish traps. Ira returned that same evening and asked them
where they were going to fish, as he was fishing here in
Scorpion. They told him that didn't matter to them, they would
fish here too.

There was nothing more said, but the following morning
Ira was up long before daybreak. As he pulled his traps he
noticed that the Portuguese had dropped one trap right alongside each of his. Well, all there was to do was cut them, and
cut he did. When the Portuguese went to pull their traps,
there were none to pull. They weighed anchor and went to
town and were back that same night with another seventy-five
traps, which they dropped where the others had been. This
time they had a trap on either side of ours. Ira went out to talk
to them again, and they said they had decided to stay here and
fish.

"Well," Ira said to me, "this sort of fishing will never do.
If they keep it up there won't be a fish left in the ocean. Those
fellows are up every day before daybreak, work just like
slaves, and do not quit until long after dark. They keep two
traps on the stern of their boat all the time to replace any they
might lose. We got rid of the Japs and now we must show the
Portuguese how to fish like white men."

So on the dark of the moon the boys started out, and when
they finished there was not a trap left for the Portuguese to
pull. The camp got a wonderful supply of new rope, and the
abalone boiler had plenty of good buoys for firewood. The
Portuguese pulled anchor and went up the island.

Next an Italian boat came over from town, went to the south side, and put about a hundred pots in the water. When they awoke the following morning, they were cleaned out as clean as a whistle, so they went back to the coast.

The time came when we butchered our two pigs, which were as fat as butter. We hung the hind legs in Bourago's cheese cave, and I made two large agate bake pans full of head cheese with spice and gelatin. I sent half a pan up to the ranch for their Sunday supper, keeping the rest for ourselves. Ira mentioned giving some to our pirate friends, but I didn't want to have anything to do with them.

Then there was another load of abalones to be boiled and Ira had to go to town. He said the three pirates would take care of them for us. I did not like the idea of those boys around when Vera and I were alone, for they seemed to be drunk all the time. The following afternoon they rowed down from Potato Harbor, and how they made it I could not tell, for it was blowing a gale outside. They came to the kitchen and said they were hungry from the trip, so I got some hot coffee and food ready—Spanish beans, fried sheephead, and plenty of good homemade bread. They sat down to eat and I went back to my tent to stay with Vera.

In a short time I heard them shove their skiff off the beach and thought, I am rid of them for awhile. I went back to the kitchen. The fish dinner had not been touched. I thought, that's funny. Looking around, I discovered my head cheese was all gone. They had eaten half and taken the other pan full with them, and were out of the bay before I discovered what was done.

It was getting towards Christmastime, but I didn't have the same ambition to do things as I had last year over at Willows. I just wanted the day to pass. I fixed a couple of chickens for dinner, and had a few toys and candy for Vera.

At the beginning of the year the boys learned that the Portuguese at Potato Harbor had a good load of crawfish tied behind their boat ready to take to town. The three pirates came down to our camp and stayed around until nine o'clock at night. Next morning the Portuguese rowed in and asked me where the little boat was. Just then the *Sam Pan* rounded the point, dropped anchor and Ira came ashore.

The Portuguese were about crazy. They said someone had stolen their fish and their propeller was gone too, so they were stuck out here without a way to get to town. Ira told them that perhaps their receivers had broken loose and drifted out to sea. They all went back to Potato Harbor and the three boys took turns diving to look for the propeller, but found nothing. They said the current must have covered it with sand.

So the Portuguese boat was towed to town for the sum of thirty-five dollars, and we did not see those fellows again for a long time. The fish had been sunk in Chinese Harbor until it was safe to take them to market.

Every morning when the weather was fine, I would take Vera by the hand, walk up the hill back of our tent and sit there awhile. Everything up there was so peaceful and quiet. Then we would walk over towards Potato Harbor and look down into the bay. We could see the little shack where Old Man Joe lived, clinging to the bare shale hillside, not a green sprig around. The smoke was always curling up out of the stovepipe, carried away in the wind. On clear days we could see all of Santa Barbara and the coast. Out toward the west was beautiful Pelican Bay, the hills covered with towering pines and gnarled oaks. Sitting on the bluff and gazing across there, I would think, well, soon I'll be out of here and back in God's country again.

As the crawfish were biting well and the men all worked on shares, Ira brought in a little heavy-set fellow named Nick to help. There was another ton of abalones in camp, and Ira left for town saying that the three pirates would take care of them. Little Nick was to pull the crawfish traps while he was away. Three days passed and no one showed up. At noon on the third day I saw a skiff with three men rowing down toward the end of the island, but they did not stop. I wondered what mischief the pirates were planning now.

When Little Nick came in, I told him it was up to us to take care of that ton of abalones, as by now they were not smelling too good. Abalone meat was worth 12½ cents a pound and the shells ten cents each, so if they were not tended that would mean quite a loss. Little Nick borrowed two eucalyptus tree stumps from the ranch and nailed abalone bars to them as Ira and Danny had done last year at Willows. Then we both put on our yellow oilskin aprons, sat on boxes, and started taking the ton of abalone meat out of the shell.

We worked on the beach out in the broiling hot sun from daylight until dark for three full days. The ranch hands came down to the beach, saw me working, and could not understand why a woman would have to work like that. Little Nick explained to them in Spanish that the market price was good, so the work just had to be done. Towards four o'clock on the third day we finished. I was slime all the way up to my eyes.

Little Nick filled the boiler with seawater while I packed firewood and started the fire. Then we carried the cleaned abalones the fifty feet over to the boiler, dumped them in, put the wooden cover on, and sat down in all our dirt to draw a long breath of relief. When the abalones began to boil we raised the lid and stirred them from the bottom so they wouldn't burn or stick. When they were done we bailed them out and dumped them on gunny sacks to cool. Then Vera and I spread them out on the wire frames to dry.

After that, I took off my yellow oilskin apron and went to take a bath. I was soon cleaned up, but every bone in my body was aching from the unusual exercise and I was dead tired. I had just stretched out on my bed in the tent when I heard the *Sam Pan* coming around the point. I thought, she *would* come back just when all the dirty work was done. You can imagine what humor I was in when Ira came ashore. I was burned almost like a black berry sitting out in that hot sun for three days. He explained that he had been held up in town with engine trouble. I said nothing but thought that was a good alibi.

Ira said he was very sorry I had to work so hard, and offered to take Vera and me for a ride down to the Blue Banks about twelve miles around the south side of the island. Some

Chinamen on the wharf had given him five dollars to deliver a package to the two Chinamen camped there picking grass for the market. We started out at six o'clock, leaving a light in the tent so we could see to land on the beach when we got back. On our way, Ira pointed out Hungryman Gulch, which looked just like a narrow cut in the hill. Darkness fell after we passed Smugglers' Cove. The ocean was very smooth and I could hear the swishing sound of the little boat cutting her way through the water.

We arrived at Blue Banks and Ira went ashore. While waiting for him I thought about Willow Canyon, which was not far away. I would be so happy back there; that place seemed so much like home. I did not have that same feeling about Scorpion at all. Now I wondered if I had really appreciated Willows enough while I was there.

As I was musing in this way, Ira found the two Chinamen asleep in their bunks, pipes in their mouths; he awakened them and delivered the package. Then he returned to the boat, started the engine, and we were on our way again. Passing outside the kelp, we saw lights in all the fishermen's shacks along the beaches. Everything seemed so peaceful that night. There was no moon, but millions of stars twinkled as if to say, "We see you down there below, and are lighting your way for you." Returning to camp, we landed by the lantern's light and were soon in bed asleep.

One day when Ira was gone, Big Jerry rowed a party of six men ashore. They were from Hollywood and were on their way to San Miguel Island to take pictures of the latest wreck, which had gone ashore on Wilson's Reef two days before. Big Jerry had been telling these picture people about the woman who lived on Santa Cruz Island with her baby, and that he would like me to go along to see the wreck.

The party were delighted to take us along. I fixed them some breakfast, got some blankets for Vera, and closed up the camp; then we were rowed out to the boat. I laid Vera down below on one of the bunks, covered her with the extra blankets, and then tied her in. She was soon asleep. I went back on deck.

Big Jerry turned the wheel over to his crew, helped me into one of his big sou'westers, and we all sat around on deck. Jerry got his fiddle from the pilot house, sat on the stern, and played and sang, keeping time with his feet. The crowd sang with him—"Sailing, Sailing, Over the Bounding Main," "Barnacle Bill the Sailor," "Come Back to Erin," "The Old Apple Tree," and "I Love You Truly."

Coming to Willows, I told how happy we had been there all last winter, and how I had helped with the different fishing activities. Though it was usually smoother on the south side of the island than in the channel, the heavy southwest swell was rolling high, and a stiff northwest wind blowing made the boat plunge and lurch. The clouds of spray covered us all, and the party were enjoying it very much. But going up the channel between Santa Rosa and San Miguel Island, the storm began to get worse. Jerry said when we got to San Miguel we'd be in shelter, and the party believed him. His wink at me told me I was trusted to say nothing.

Arriving at the north side of San Miguel, we saw the ship lying in shoal water, with a line of breakers two or three hundred yards behind her. The rigging on her three masts was in very bad condition and her sails, torn into rags, were flying with the heavy northwest wind. Her bottom was almost all gone from pounding on the jagged rocks; she was still moving up and down with the high swells.

Vera was awake by now and not any worse for the boat ride. The Hollywood people got their cameras and we were all helped into the skiff. Big Jerry rowed us over and we climbed up the rope ladder onto the ship. Jerry showed us around the deck and then up to the bow. We could see the lumber cargo scattered along the beach for a mile or so, and I remarked how it would come in handy for our camp.

The photographers were late in starting to shoot their scenes, as the boat was rocking so much and some of them got seasick. I figured they were hungry. In our hurry to leave camp we had forgotten to bring our lunch, and expected to be back for supper. The party had brought a box of sandwiches and pies, but it had been left on deck and got all soaked with water, so their lunch was not fit to eat. So I went down into the galley, discovered a tin of hardtack, a few tins of meat, and with some of the ship's water we had a bite to eat.

The ship was still pounding heavily on the reef, giving you the same feeling as the quick downward slide of an elevator. The storm was getting worse. Jerry scratched his head and said we might have to spend the night aboard the ship. The fog rolled in very thick and fast. Finally five of the men decided to take their film and cameras back to Jerry's boat. I stayed aboard the ship with Vera, and one young man decided to stay too. Jerry told me not to worry, he would be right back to fetch us as soon as he got the photographers over to his boat.

As they rowed away from us with the spray flying all over them, one man stood up in the skiff and just then a large breaker rolled in, upsetting the skiff and dumping them all into the foaming ocean. Jerry righted the skiff and picked up four of the men, but the fifth one tried to swim back to the ship. A huge wave picked him up on its crest, carried him toward the ship and threw him against its side. He sank, came up twice, then disappeared.

The thick fog engulfed us, and I doubted that Jerry would take another chance and come out for us. The best we could do was make ready for the night. Going down to the galley, the young man, Vera and I finished the hardtack that was left from noon. In the growing darkness we saw the water washing back and forth through the holes in the bottom of the ship, something I had not noticed earlier. I discovered some old hawser rope, hauled it to the side of the ship, and coiled it to make a bed. Then with the help of a rusty butcher knife, the man managed to cut and tear enough ragged canvas to make a covering. I put Vera on this makeshift bed, covered her with my heavy overcoat, then the sou'westers, and lay down beside her. The young man lay a few feet away to break the wind for us.

There was no sleep for us that night. I drew Vera closer to

me to get the warmth of my body. All night the ship rocked, squeaked, groaned, and pounded on that reef. The ground swell lashed against the ship with such force that the spray hit the deck and fell like rain all over us. I kept telling myself, if she stays on this reef until morning, Jerry will get us off somehow. The wind howled and screeched furiously through the rigging, beating the ragged canvas back and forth and making such a din I could hardly hear the tiny voice asking "Mamma, are we all right here till Jerry comes to get us?"

I answered with an assurance I did not feel, "Yes dear, we're all right. Morning will be here soon."

"Oh, Mamma, won't the wind ever stop blowing?" After awhile she fell asleep, and I lay there praying that all really would be well. Then I got up and stood by the side of the ship, looking up at the silver moon trying to shine through the heavy fog clouds, and the angry ocean covered with white-crested waves.

Settling down by Vera again, I heard something scurrying over the deck. Then I heard the noise again, and feet ran over the sou'wester that was covering us. I nearly screeched, but that would awaken Vera. Something ran over me, and I discovered they were big wharf rats; I could hear them scurrying all over the deck. Frank Nidever had told me that as long as a rat stays aboard a ship after she is wrecked, there is no danger of the ship sinking. Thank heaven! If the rats didn't decide to bite us before morning, we'd live through the night.

After what seemed to be an endless space of time, grey dawn broke. The storm was even worse than the day before, but Big Jerry and crew rowed the skiff through that long line of breakers to our rescue. They made one trip for Vera and me, and another for the young man—the ocean was too rough to take us all at once. I told Jerry about our night on the ship, and he said he had known I would make out somehow. When all were aboard his boat again, Jerry decided not to try to find the drowned man's body, as it would take ten days for it to surface. So we left San Miguel.

We made our way back to Santa Rosa Island and anchored

out of the wind at Johnson's Lee. Jerry started his Portuguese stove and we all had hot coffee, after which we felt very much revived. Then we continued down the south side, rounded the east end, then up the island. In no time we were back at Scorpion, and I put Vera right to bed although she had slept all the way down tied into the bunk. I fixed a good breakfast of bacon, eggs, toast and coffee. After resting awhile, the men from Hollywood bid me goodbye and left for the south. Jerry said to me, "I'll bet those picture people never want to see a boat or an island again." I agreed with him.

The following morning before daybreak, I heard the *Sam Pan* way off in the distance. Stepping out of the tent in my nightdress, I went to the edge of the bluff and could see the boat about five miles from shore. Out in the darkness, the dim riding light looked as if someone had struck a match and the wind was trying awfully hard to blow it out. I dressed quickly and had a hot meal ready when Ira came ashore. I did not say anything to him about going to San Miguel, and I knew I'd get hell if he found out.

Ira was still eating breakfast when the *Gussie M.* came into the bay and Captain Vasquez rowed himself and another man ashore. I wondered if they wanted any news from me about the drowning at the wreck, and hoped they wouldn't mention it in front of Ira. But they had come for a different reason. The man was a Fish and Game Commissioner. I made them some hot coffee, then fried raw potatoes and the tails of under-sized crawfish with plenty of garlic, and served it up with some of my good homemade bread. The two men enjoyed a breakfast they couldn't buy on the mainland.

While they were eating, the Commissioner said he was visiting the different fishing camps to pick up first-hand information concerning the Spiny Lobster, or as the fishermen call them, crawfish. He wanted to know if crawfish migrated through the season. They went out to our receivers and brought in over two hundred crawfish. The Commissioner tagged them and paid Ira the market price which was not more than five cents; then the fish were let loose into the ocean. The government was to be notified if any fish were found with the tags on, and in that way they could gather some interesting information about these fish and their habits. Also the Commissioner tagged and let loose one dozen Eastern lobsters, hoping they would live and increase around the islands. After a very pleasant visit, Captain Vasquez and the Commissioner left to visit at Hungryman Gulch, then on to Smugglers' Cove and around the whole island, then on to Anacapa Island.

A couple of months later, Clarence, camping up at Lady's Harbor, found six of the Eastern lobsters in his traps one morning. They had traveled from Chinese Harbor up that distance. Also, eight that had been planted at Hungryman Gulch were caught at the Yellow Banks, having traveled about six miles. Then news came from town that the fish tagged in Santa Barbara had been caught in the traps down at Rincon, eighteen miles from where they were planted.

Two weeks after the night on the wreck, Big Jerry came to visit and said he had been up to San Miguel Island. The Chinamen gathering and drying abalones told him they had found a body on the extreme end of the island in the kelp. It was the man who had drowned when we were there. Knowing that no one would be around for some time, they made a coffin with driftwood and buried him in the sand, marking the grave with a cross.

Ira decided one day it was time to take his two weeks' catch of crawfish and the last batch of abalones to town. Little Nick went along; he had a share in the abalones, as he had helped to take care of them. That left only the man Foster in camp. At the other end of the beach, he had set up a wood stove, a table, his boxes of groceries, and his cot bed out in the open.

Vera and I went to bed early. Later I woke out of a sound sleep; the dog was making a great fuss. At first I thought it might be a seal coming down from the Black Points, but this was a different bark. There must be someone around who did not belong. Striking a match, I looked at the clock: two in the morning. I poked my head outside the tent and saw the three pirates hauling their skiff up on the beach. They had rowed the six miles from Chinese Harbor in the northwest wind and pounding swell. I wondered what in thunderation could have brought them down here at this time of night and in this weather. They had not been to our camp for some time.

I decided I'd have to go out and face them. Throwing on my clothes in a hurry I went over to the kitchen. There I met Charley, who said, "How do you do, Mrs. Eaton. We are so thirsty—we want to make a cup of coffee." All three of them were so staggering drunk they could hardly stand up. I remembered that Ira had said not to refuse them anything, and said all right, but to be careful with the fire. They went into the kitchen, made their coffee, and after prowling about for awhile they rowed away from camp.

I could not understand how they could be rowing around with that storm outside, but thank goodness I was rid of them! I went back to the kitchen; they had very carefully filled the woodbox and stove with wood and closed the dampers as if they expected to come back again. Into the coffee pot that held six cups they had emptied half a pound of coffee. They had eaten one whole salami and two pounds of cheese. I thought, if only they would come when Ira was in camp he could handle them. The rascals knew he was gone, as our boat was not anchored in the bay. I lay, dressed, on top of the bed for the rest of the night, then got up at five o'clock.

Foster had difficulty getting his skiff off the beach through the swells to go pull the traps. Standing there watching him I thought, if Foster could beach or row a skiff half as good as those pirates did even when they were drunk, he certainly would be a good man. He would not make much headway this morning on account of the rough weather. But finally he passed the point and was out of sight.

I heard the exhaust of some boat and waited to see who it was. As she came into the bay I saw it was the Portuguese back again. After Ira had towed them to town, they had gotten a new propeller and gone to fish at Santa Rosa Island. It was so rough they had come to anchor in our bay and had passed Foster, who decided to quit and come back with them. They

were towing his skiff. He said there was plenty of work to do
ashore to keep him busy.

At four in the afternoon, I was standing on the bluff watching the storm out in the channel when once again the pirates
rowed around the point and landed. They came up to me and
asked for something to eat. This time they were past all reasoning; I gave them food and told them to go over to Foster's
camp at the other end of the beach to cook, which they did.
Then Foster came up the bluff and said he would like to stay
in my kitchen until they left. I told him I thought they were
probably good for the whole night. They took out a couple of
bottles of whiskey and set them on the table, and in a few
minutes there was a free-for-all fight going on. I could see the
three of them falling over the stove and table, knocking things
over. They were yelling and calling each other all sorts of
names. Vera was terrified and began to scream and yell as
loudly as she could.

I told Foster to stay with Vera while I went up to the ranch
house to ask the foreman if he would talk to the fellows;
perhaps they would listen to him. If they kept on much longer
I was sure one would murder the other. When I came to the
pigpen, the foreman was standing there watching the fight. I
said, "Mr. C., will you go down and talk to those fellows?
They are so drunk. My husband is in town and I am here alone
with the baby."

"No," he said. "Those fishermen not on company ground.
The beach not belong to the company from here down." He
pointed up the canyon, saying, "There the company ground."

"But Mr. C., you are a man with seven hands working under you. Can't you do something to help me out?"

He just shook his head. "No, no. Can do nothing." And
with that he left me and walked up to the ranch. I knew then
that the ground we were camping on, and the beach where I
had kept my chickens all winter, was tideland and did not belong to any individual but to the government. I followed the
foreman and let loose on him, and what I told that man would
fill a book. I finished by telling him he was nothing but a dirty

coward, then turned away too disgusted to say any more.

Back at the bluff, I told Foster the only thing left for me to do was to go to town and not stay here another night. I knew it was not safe for Vera and me. The fighting seemed to be getting closer to our side of the camp, and I did not know what those pirates were apt to do. I asked Foster to go out to the Portuguese boat and ask them what they would charge to take Vera and me to town. After some effort he got out through the swells and to the boat. He talked with the Portuguese for a while, and I heard their voices raised as if in an argument. One fellow shook his fist in Foster's face. Finally he came back and told me he had had a very hard time convincing them that I had nothing to do with their lost crawfish or their stolen traps. They had at last agreed to take us for twenty-five dollars.

It did not take me long to grab my heavy coat, some warm clothing for Vera, and a couple of blankets. In no time we were on the beach. Foster shoved the skiff to the water's edge, got in and took the oars out. We would have to wait for three more swells to come in before the next calm spell so we could get into the skiff. I counted two, then heard a war whoop from the men at the other end of the beach. Looking around, I saw them running toward us. Foster yelled, "Quick! Into the skiff before they get here!" Holding Vera I jumped in; how I did it I will never know. A swell hit the skiff and she stood straight up on her stern. I was sure we'd fall out and turn the skiff over on us, but the good Lord above was watching over us. We made it over the next swell, and I surely breathed a sigh of relief.

On the beach, the pirates started picking up stones and throwing them at us. One hit Foster in the eye, stunning him. Meanwhile, seeing something was wrong on the shore, the Portuguese had started their engine and got the boat as close to shore as they could. They helped us aboard and tied our skiff to the stern. Shots began whizzing over the bow as the boat began to turn and head out of the bay. I jumped down into the hold with Vera, laid her down, and stuck my head up

out of the hatch to see what was happening. There was the
flash of the gun on the beach—they were still firing. Just as
we were rounding the point, a bullet hit the pilot house; I
ducked and the Portuguese let out an oath.

Then we were out of range, going toward Potato Harbor.
Our two blankets had fallen out of the skiff, so the crew loaned
me two of theirs. For a mattress there was only the sacks of
live crawfish and abalones in the hold. But in our situation a
person could not be too particular. We lay down on this mess
and covered ourselves with the blankets. I noticed the odor in
the boat and could not tell which smelled the strongest: the
mattress of live fish or the blankets that covered us. As I lay
there I thought, I don't care if those men wreck the whole
camp, because I'm not going back there any more. I would
even rather stay in town than at Scorpion. The boat was rolling and pitching. We were not especially comfortable. Foster
was also down in the hold with us, wedged in on one side. His
eyes were swollen shut from the rock that had hit him.

Shortly we came to Potato Harbor. I tried to poke my head
out of the hatch, but the Portuguese said, "No, no, Madam.
You fall overboard. Ver', ver' rough." I certainly agreed with
him. He pulled the hatch cover over us and closed it. My, but
the smell was terrible. I heard the men pulling something
heavy aboard and the boat almost turned over on one side. It
stayed that way for a short time, then shifted over to the other
side. I knew they were loading on some heavy receivers of
crawfish to take to market for Old Man Joe. I wondered if
we'd ever get out of this hold! The boat rolled first to one side,
then the other. But we couldn't fall overboard, that was certain—we were wedged in so tight we couldn't even stretch our
legs out. I was not worrying about myself but about Vera; if
she was comfortable that was all I cared about.

I heard Old Man Joe say "Adiós," and they started up the
engine. Then it seemed as if we were going up in an elevator
and coming down again, but it was only the boat climbing over
the swells and then going down in the hollows. The propeller

made such a noise, whirling around like mad when out of water!

."Mamma," Vera said, "I am so glad we are going away from those bad men and home to Papa."

"Close your eyes Vera, and try to sleep."

"But Mamma, I can't sleep. There is something sticking in my neck. Will it bite me?" I put my hand under her neck to see what it was—only a crawfish squirming around in the sack. He probably resented being lain on! I folded my blanket, told Vera to raise up a bit, and put it over the sacks she was lying on. She said that was much better, then settled down with my arm around her neck. I held her like that for awhile to keep her from sliding down off the sacks on top of Foster. Finally he handed me two sacks of abalones, and I braced her back with them and she fell asleep.

There must have been a big sea running the way that boat tossed around. As she ploughed into the seas the spray washed over the hatch and water poured through the cracks down onto us. The engine stopped for a moment and I thought, oh no, we couldn't have engine trouble on a night like this after all that has happened. It started up again and went pegging along for a few minutes, then decided to stop altogether and take a rest. I heard the Portuguese hollering to one another, "Oh Joe, engine trouble!" "All right, I fix him in five minute."

We wallowed in the trough of the sea, and Vera was seasick. She squirmed and twisted and heaved up everything she had in her system. I was really helpless and couldn't do anything to help her. If that engine would only start! The two men tinkered and tinkered. They hammered first one part of the engine, then the other. I said to Foster, "If they hammer long enough they will surely hit the right part." Then they came back to the hold and asked Foster if he knew anything about engines. He said he didn't and anyway he could not help because he couldn't see. Both his eyes were closed and the pain was terrible. I wriggled up on deck and found a gunny sack and dipped it into the ocean. I gave it to Foster and told him to hold it over his eyes. Salt water was said to be good for sore eyes. In a little while he said the cold salt water had eased the pain.

All this time the boat was being knocked about by the heavy seas as if they were saying, "Why don't you get out of our way? You don't belong out here." The hatch was open now for air. As each swell hit the boat broadside with a bang, the spray showered over us. There was nothing else to do but sit there and take it. Vera had gone to sleep again, for which I was very thankful. I lay there on my back looking out the hatch up at the stars. Twinkling so fast, they seemed to say, "What are you doing out here this time of night on the wild, rough ocean? This is no place for you." Then big black clouds passed over them, moving fast—heavy northwest wind clouds. They dimmed the stars for awhile, then went on their way south.

While the men cussed and tinkered with the boat, I heard a rumbling sound. Even with the wind howling, the sound seemed to be coming nearer and nearer. I pried myself loose from my hard bed up over the edge of the hatch and saw a big ship heading almost straight for us. I looked up to the mast; we had no riding light. I got up on deck and crawled on my hands and knees—I didn't dare stand—to the engine room, calling to the men to bring a lantern, that there was a big ship coming. There was no hope that the horn could be heard in this gale, and the boat did not have one anyhow. The Portuguese came up from the engine room and went to the stern of the boat waving the lantern, just as a railroad man does when a train is leaving the station.

I stood on deck wondering if that big ship was going to mow us down. I could feel the swell from her bow wave as she ploughed through the sea. She was almost upon us. I held onto the mast for dear life; the little boat was almost on her side in the big swells. But the man on the bridge up there saw our light in time. The lumber schooner passed just to the stern of us, only missing us by about fifteen feet. Well, those fifteen feet saved five lives and a Portuguese boat.

Still holding onto the mast I could not move. The Portuguese was still swinging the lantern, letting out all kinds of oaths. He shouted "Sons of guns" and "Sacramento" and words I had never heard before. I asked him where his riding lights were, and he said he only had enough coal oil for one lantern. (In those days boats were not wired for electric lights.) He was in the wrong and knew it. He said he would buy some more oil on this trip to town.

Our close call over, I crawled back to the hatch and down into the hold beside Vera. Foster said, "A hell of a lot of good buying coal oil in town will do us *this* trip."

"Mamma, did those men fight?" asked Vera. "They swear so loud! I am so glad you came back. You were not with me and I thought the boat was turning over." I drew her close and kissed her. She fell asleep again and I had a good cry, after which I felt better. At least we were alive. If that lumber schooner had cut us in two or ploughed us under, we would never have had a chance. I was wet from head to foot, but that couldn't be helped. Anyway, we were better off on the boat than ashore with those drunken pirates.

At last the engine decided to start again and we were on our way. If it did not stop again I knew we would be in Santa Barbara in about four hours. And sure enough, after what seemed an age, I could hear the old whistling buoy mooing, louder tonight on account of the heavy ground swell. I just hoped the men wouldn't make a mistake and run into it.

Putting my head up out of the hatch I saw we were just passing the buoy, and did the lights of Santa Barbara look good! I gathered up my few belongings and Vera, and the men helped us off the boat onto the passenger steps. Then I paid them with very wet money. There was not a soul on the wharf. Foster could see a tiny bit now, and I guided him up the wharf and left him at the first rooming house. I went to stay with friends, not knowing where to find Ira.

Ira, as it turned out, was staying at the same rooming house where I had left Foster. In the morning he came and said he would get a warrant for the pirates' arrest. He went over to the island in the *Miramar* to bring them to town. He found them at their camp at Chinese Harbor, tied them up, and took them aboard the boat. He locked them in the hold with an iron bar across the top and brought them back to town. The judge gave them ten days each. Ira bailed them out with the money they had coming for their share of the crawfish.

I considered that they got off very lucky and told Ira so. And I added, "I will not go back to Scorpion where I have to put up with a bunch of drunken savages. Nothing doing. I am willing to do my part to help, but this is too much."

"All right," said Ira. "We will stay in town a couple of weeks, then we will go back to Pelican Bay." That sounded just fine to me.

The following week Ira went to move what was left of our camping gear from Scorpion to Pelican. The pirates had left the place in a terrible mess. They got into my tent and went through all my belongings. The gun they had been doing all the shooting with was Ira's. They shot six of my chickens and had a feast up in my kitchen. They didn't get the two little lambs, though.

While in Santa Barbara I took Vera to the beach every day. I looked across the channel to the islands and longed to be back there again. I knew that at Pelican Bay everything would be fine. I was tired of town already.

CHAPTER VII

Early Years at Pelican
1910–1913

Coming Home to Pelican Bay — Big Jerry's Big Heart — The *Sam Pan*'s Stormy Trip — Regatta — Mrs. Walters — First Winter at Pelican — Crawfish Pirates — Captain Vasquez and the Seal Net — Moving Picture Companies — The Commodore and His Wife — Jake Nidever Is Drowned — News From Town — We Acquire the *Gussie M.*

WE STARTED AT MIDNIGHT in our little boat, the *Sam Pan,* to get over to the island before the wind started. While I took my turn at the wheel, Ira made a bed in the tiny cockpit for Vera. Then she and I slept all the way across the channel, until we arrived at Pelican Bay at daybreak. Frank Nidever and Big Jerry were waiting, and sang "Pull, Sailor, Pull for the Shore" while Ira rowed Vera and me ashore. They welcomed us back to our island home and said that breakfast was ready.

We all walked up the narrow, stony trail to the fishermen's shack. The kitchen door faced the ocean and we all walked inside. My wood stove was set up in the corner, a good fire burning and the kettle boiling. To the left stood the long table with benches on both sides. A large coffee can acted as a vase, and in it was a huge bunch of wild lilac. The table looked so pretty and inviting. Looking around the room I noticed that a great many shakes and much of the tar paper had been blown away by the storms, but all the openings around the walls and rafters were covered with large bunches of scrub oak, crinkly holly, and tall pine branches. Frank and Jerry had fixed it up just for me. I was thrilled to be back again.

We all sat down to a wonderful breakfast of fried fish, tender wild pork chops, fluffy baking powder biscuits, and a soft boiled egg and hot milk for Vera. Frank, remembering that I did not drink coffee, had made tea for me, and it tasted darned good. I was so happy to be among these old friends in this wonderful place, where I could drink the cool mountain water, listen to all the birds, and be awakened at daybreak by the song of the doves cooing to their mates. Since the first time I came to this lovely, out-of-the-way place, there had not been a day that something interesting didn't happen. And now that I was back, I was not leaving again in a hurry.

We sat and talked for two hours. Frank and Jerry said they missed me so much at Willow Canyon—the place was all run down, there being no woman to take an interest in it. Finally Ira stood up and said we had better start getting settled.

"Don't you worry, Ike," Big Jerry said. "Our three friends are here, waiting to do anything possible to help you." My heart dropped to my shoes. Would I have to put up with those pirates again? Big Jerry knew how I felt. "Ma'am, don't you worry about them being here. They'll have to answer to me if they don't behave themselves. You know these boys must make a living, just like the rest of us. I'll have them come in and promise you to behave." Then, opening the door that faced the hills, he called, "Oh boys, come here and shake hands with the Missus and tell her how sorry ye are, and that nothing nasty like that will happen again."

In walked the three pirates, Arturo in the lead with a grin from ear to ear. Shaking hands, he said they were sorry for causing me such trouble. Then all three of them went out to help unload our belongings and get things ready to start fishing smelt.

I offered to help Big Jerry with the dishes, but he would not hear of it. "No ma'am, not on your life. No woman works while Big Jerry is around. If you had not come, I'd have had to make breakfast anyhow. You'll have plenty to do getting your family settled. When I'm through here, I'll give Ike a hand."

As Jerry washed and cleaned, he sang one old-fashioned song after another and kept time dancing, his big heavy boots making such a noise. He was used to dancing in his working clothes, so the heavy boots did not bother him. Vera and I sang and danced too, and then Jerry said, "Missus, let's you and I dance the Sailor's Hornpipe for the kid," so we did. He was so tall and I so short, it must have been a funny sight. The dance finished, I sad down very tired from the exercise. That was my second home-coming to Pelican Bay.

The following day I was back in my old routine—cooking, baking bread, washing, tending the chickens and gathering wood. I was very happy to be with those good old fisher folks again. The trips to and from Scorpion and the time I had spent there seemed like a dream, soon to be forgotten. Ira, Jerry, Frank and the three pests started fishing smelt on shares. There was a load of fish taken to Santa Barbara almost every day; two men would go to town, and the others would stay in camp mending the nets on the beach at little Pelican. I was willing to do my part to help. When I baked cake, pies, or a batch of bread, all the men always got their share. When the small smelt season slacked off a bit, Frank and Jerry decided to try their luck fishing for the big jack smelt at Santa Rosa Island. Ira was to fish the different beaches around Santa Cruz Island.

Frank and Jerry did not come back when they were supposed to, so Ira decided to run up the island to look for them. Not wanting to stay alone, Vera and I went along. In a dense fog between Santa Cruz and Santa Rosa, we almost ran into a lifeboat with twelve men aboard. Their steamer, the *Dora Bluhm,* carrying lumber from Coos Bay to San Pedro, had hit the rocks on the west end of Santa Rosa Island. In the heavy swells, she had sunk within a couple of hours. We gave the men a hot meal and took them back to Santa Barbara. Then we resumed our search for Frank and Jerry. We finally found the boys anchored in Cuyler Harbor at San Miguel Island.

The following day the swells went down and the ocean was clear. Looking down into the water we saw an anchor and chain lying there in the harbor. Some big yacht must have had to pull out in a storm and had slipped her mooring. With a grappling hook, Ira and I hauled up the 150-pound anchor and thirteen fathoms of three-quarter-inch chain. They were covered with moss, rust and barnacles, but when cleaned up would make a good mooring for our boat. Knowing the boys were safe, we returned to Pelican Bay.

One day Big Jerry came to have lunch with us, and on leaving he backed his boat, catching the skiff line in the propeller. Not stopping the engine, he leaned over to cut the rope loose, the blades of the propeller wheeled around, catching his hand, and he almost lost a finger. Ira gave him first aid and took him to town. The doctor had a hard time stopping the flow of blood and I was afraid blood poisoning might set in; but in a few weeks Jerry came back to the camp.

"You can't down a good man," he said. "I'm much better off at the islands than in town. I want to keep away from *that* place as much as I can."

"Jerry, why don't you find a nice little woman and get married and settle down?" I asked.

"No ma'am, I don't think she would stick by me the way you stick by Ike. And anyway, I don't want to be bothered with any apron strings. I like to come and go as I please. If I got married, after awhile I couldn't do that, and then I'd be sorry."

I asked him about the young lady he had bought the set of false teeth for at Christmas. "Now ma'am, who told you that story? That lady was no particular friend of mine. I was drunk one day, and she told me if she didn't have a good set of teeth, she would lose her job in the eating house where she worked. Not wanting to see anyone without a job, I told her boss I'd pay for the teeth if he wouldn't fire her. I'd have just spent the money on liquor, and would have nothing to show for it but a big head. But she has her job now, and the money went for something worthwhile."

"Well, Jerry," I said, "you certainly have a good, big heart."

A fishing boat came into the bay from China Harbor with a fifty foot whale caught and drowned in their net. When it was untangled, they towed the whale out in the channel to let it float down the coast. I said, what if some yacht traveling at night ran into it? But the Italian fisherman just shrugged his shoulders and said it didn't make any difference to him; at least the whale was out of his way.

Our first thunder and lightning storm came, and a dark cloud hung over the islands from about three o'clock until six. One afternoon a northwester was blowing forty miles an hour, and the men had two tons of smelt washed down and packed aboard the *Sam Pan* for the trip to town. She looked as if she would sink if there was one more fish put on her. Ira put on clean blue jeans rolled to the knees and his light blue work shirt with sleeves rolled to the elbows, collar open at the neck. I told him I wished he would not go over to town in this storm but wait until early morning, when the weather was smoother.

Laughing, he said not to be a goose, that the two tons of smelt would be ruined if he waited. Then he kissed Vera and me and went aboard the boat to leave for Santa Barbara. Jerry, Frank, Vera and I went up the narrow trail and sat on the stone steps, watching the little *Sam Pan* on her way. The little jib sail was hoisted to help steady her. The white-green combers almost covered her, sending spray high into the air. As each one hit the boat, I thought that would be the last of her. I wondered if I would ever see Ira again. Shading my eyes sailor style, I watched the *Sam Pan* gradually fade away in the distance until she was just a tiny speck.

Jerry was telling Frank what a fine sea boat the little *Sam Pan* was, and I asked if there was any danger of her being swamped and Ira drowning. Jerry said he knew it was a terrible storm out in that channel, but we couldn't afford to lose such a load of fish. And he added, "Let me tell you, the lad knows what he's doing, for he has the nerve of hell. You should know that by now. Don't you worry about him, he'll be back tomorrow evening as he said. And if anything should happen to Ike, I guess I'd pick you and the young'un up myself, and care for you both." As he spoke, he stroked Vera's beautiful hair.

"Jerry, you just talk that way to quiet me. because you know I'm nervous."

He said maybe that was so; then he went into the kitchen, brought out his accordion, and started playing and singing that fine old melody, "When Irish Eyes Are Smiling." Frank and I joined in the singing, Vera keeping time with her feet. Next Jerry sang "Turkey in the Straw." After we had supper, he and Frank went aboard their boat for the night. Later on, about twenty fishing boats came into the harbor. The storm outside was very bad. Hearing the *Sam Pan* had gone across the channel, the men shook their heads. The boats with all their lights looked like a little city, and as the men sat on their piles of nets, music and singing floated up to my camp.

The following evening about sundown we saw the *Sam Pan* coming from town. For a moment I thought the little boat was afire, but as she came nearer I realized it was the reflection of the sun through her cabin windows. I thought, in this game if it isn't storms it's something else. Back at camp, Ira said that after he had hoisted the jib he had tied himself to the mast to steady himself, and arrived at the wharf without losing a fish.

George Gourley with a party aboard his *Vamoose* dropped anchor in the bay and brought his guests ashore. They cooked the fish they had caught trolling on the way over, and had their lunch on the flat outside my one-room palace. They said they were from Omaha, Nebraska, and were visiting at San Ysidro. After lunch, a purse seiner loaded down with fish came into the bay, and we all went out in Captain Gourley's little launch. The seiner had aboard a basking shark thirty-five feet long, that they had caught in China Bay where they had a string of nets set. It was necessary to kill the shark and cut off its tail to clear their net. This shark was not the man-eating kind. The party from Nebraska had never seen a shark before, so they watched the performance with great interest.

Back from town one day, Ira said that a regatta was being held in Santa Barbara, and the bay there was covered with yachts and cruisers of every description Even Tom Mix, the great cowboy actor, was there in his cruiser, the *Thomassa*. A great many of the yachts would stop in our bay on the way south. A day or so earlier, a yacht called the *Rayon* had been here, and men yelled out to ask where the Potter Hotel was. They were up for the regatta and were lost. I gave them directions to follow Larco's Dip, as all the fishermen do when they have no compass. Waving goodbye, they had headed for town.

The following morning there was a good breeze outside, and we could see the yachts coming out of the fog halfway across the channel. Then they started coming into the bay. There was the *Sylph, Clipper, Mischief I* and *II, Sea Bird, Wasp, Minerva, Idler, Winsome, Edna, Enchantress,* and many more; all the owners were aboard. They came ashore to give the place the once-over, saying they had a good time in town and expected to come back every year.

A yacht almost as large as the *Enchantress* arrived, and the owner commented that the fog in Santa Barbara was terrible. I told him that very often the fog bank reached only out to mid-channel and that we had sunshine here. He said that from the standpoint of the navigator, the Santa Barbara Channel was the worst spot on the West Coast. He thought it would take some big passenger ship going on the rocks at San Miguel or Anacapa Island to make Congress wake up and realize that this section of coast was practically without protection from the dangers of the sea. From Point Conception down, there was not a foghorn to aid navigators; in trying to avoid hitting the coast, they risked piling up on the islands.

All the yachts had open house that evening, and Ira and I were invited to come aboard and visit them. Ira wore clean blue overalls with a crease in them (they were taken from under the mattress) and a clean blue shirt. We went from one beautiful yacht to another. The ladies were very sociable, and drinks and sandwiches were handed around, but I took ginger ale. Ira did not refuse anything, as it was not every day you saw so much good liquor.

The following morning the yachts, their anchors up and

sails hoisted, sailed for their homes to the south. Standing on the bank, we three waved to them. Now the summer season was over. I supposed that we would be alone for some time, as the next day Ira was going to town to bring a load of lumber back to start making crawfish traps.

That afternoon a large cruiser dropped anchor in the bay. The owner and his wife were Mr. and Mrs. Walters from San Pedro, and with them were their two sons. They said they would like to go walking in the hills, so I went along with them. They stayed the night anchored in the bay. The following morning a northeaster began to come up, and Ira and his two men left for China Bay to escape the storm. I explained to Mr. Walters that our bay was not safe in a northeaster, but he said his boat would ride here all right.

The storm got worse during the day. As it was growing dark, Mr. Walters began to change his mind and wished he had left earlier. Going aboard his boat with his family, he found that the engine refused to start. The boat began to drift toward the landing. With the skiff, they towed her over toward the left-hand corner of the bay, which was their only hope of saving her. By this time Mrs. Walters was hysterical, wringing her hands in despair. I had them put her ashore to spend the night with me. Then I told the young fellow to put out a stern line and give it plenty of scope, as Ira had a cleat in the rock to fasten it to. There was a terrible backwash in the corner.

All night the wind howled and the rain poured down. The shack was only three feet from the edge of the bank, and it shook as if it wanted to blow off into the ocean. Gusts of wind blew off the tree branches that covered the wide spaces in the walls. I emptied my firewood out onto the floor and stuffed the sacks in to close the openings, then stuffed in a heavy quilt as well. The rain came down in torrents and leaked through the roof in a dozen places. As I set pots and pans and pails to catch the rain that poured in, Mrs. Walters commented, "I should think your husband would take time to fix up this house. You and your baby are apt to take your death of cold." But I told her this house was a palace compared to the one we lived in at Willow Canyon, and anyhow the storm would be over in a day or two. Then we'd live outdoors most of the time.

I kept the fire burning in my stove all night. Mrs. Walters and I sat near the fire and she kept asking if I thought the house would blow off the bank. I told her to calm herself; if the house fell off the bank it would fall on her husband's boat. I poked my head out the window to see his riding light, which seemed to be almost at my eye level, the swells were so high. The boat was bouncing around first on the swells, then on the backwash.

Then we heard a terrible crash. I went out and looked over the bank, but the boat was still riding the storm. Mrs. Walters got on her knees asking the Lord to save us all. I told her there was nothing to fear and went out the other door. Coming back drenched, I told her the noise we heard was only a couple of thousand tons of rock falling off a hill down into the creek. I suggested she lie down, but she said she couldn't, not with her poor Johnny out in that storm. She kept raving on, and I said, "Do you know what I think? I think we are a couple of damn fools to sit here worrying and waiting for your husband's body to be washed ashore, instead of going to bed."

"Oh, do you think the storm is as bad as that?" Then she opened another sack of driftwood and filled the stove. That was my last sack of dry wood, but that meant nothing to her. Finally I told her I didn't see any use in sitting up, and I crawled into bed at two o'clock in the morning. At seven I woke to find her on the inside of the bed, sound asleep.

Mr. Walters came ashore a little later and we asked him what sort of a night he had put in. "A hell of a night," he said. "If it had not been for your little light shining out in the darkness I would have thought every moment I was being dashed against the rocks. I don't think the boat or I would be here now if you had not suggested putting out the stern line; she would have been all over the bay."

All that day I had the pleasure of Mrs. Walters' company, as the storm was still raging. We watched the white-crested swells hit the bluff with a bang and throw the spray almost to the top of the hill. It was really beautiful and awe-inspiring to watch. The ocean outside was all whitecaps. That night the fire in my stove went out early and we all went to bed.

The next morning the boat whistle sounded at six, as they wanted to be on their way, and one of the sons came to row Mrs. Walters to the boat. She had used a pound of coffee and five sacks of wood. When she left with a "thank you for your kindness," I thought, old girl, the next time you come here you'll take care of yourself, because I'm through helping you.

I cleaned up the shack and thought I'd have a good rest. But Ira came from town with his lumber and brought three men and their camping outfit. They were to camp under the large oak tree to the left of the creek for a few days until Ira went back to town again. Two of the men were tall, thin and dark and wore glasses; one of them was Dawson, the bird man. The third man was a professor from Oxford, England. A day or two after they settled in camp, the Oxford professor came up the trail wearing striped overalls. He said he would like to have a hot meal, as the other two men just took a cake of chocolate with them for lunch. He had no money with him, but offered to fix our footpath leading down the hill to the spring, if that were agreeable to me. It was.

He started with a pick and shovel, and before long there was a good four-foot-wide trail going down the hill. At five o'clock he had a good warm supper with us. Then he went down to his camp and had a can of pork and beans with hardtack, which was the other two men's supper after hiking all day. He did not want them to know he had been eating with us, and I did not mention it. A week later they left camp for town. Bidding them goodbye, I told the professor, "Every time I go down the trail I'll think of you."

When the terrible northwest winds blew, about twenty of the fishing boats would anchor in our bay looking for shelter. Towards afternoon the men came ashore to stretch their legs and visit. They were all races, Portuguese, Austrians, Italians and Swedes. One brought macaroni, another a couple of pounds of cheese, some meat and French bread, and others four or five gallons of dago red, for no meal was considered any good without a glass of wine. When the meal was ready, those that could not fit around the kitchen table sat on the floor or at the work table. The dishpan was full of macaroni, the wine jug in the center of the table. The wind was howling outside, but inside my little shack all was contentment. There was never a word out of the way from this mixture of nationalities; they were a jolly crowd. They all treated me like a lady, and I treated them as my company. They were pleased if I listened to them talking about the old folks at home, their little farms and vineyards, and the sweethearts they had left behind but not forgotten, who they would send for when they made enough money fishing. They would show me the new woolen socks the old grandmother or sweetheart had knitted for them. It reminded me of my old home and folks back in Quebec.

Winter was on us again, and I wondered what it would be like here. I was hoping we would have a good but quiet home life. Ira fixed the wide open spaces in the shack with driftwood and coal oil cans and boarded up the fireplace so less wind would blow in. I caulked the open cracks in the walls to help keep out the wind and dust. I hung a blanket at the head of Vera's crib to keep the draft out and refilled her mattress with new oat hay. Two lengths of sail canvas were hung on curtain rings made from wire, to divide the room and hide our bed.

So far the fishing had been good, but as usual the market price was poor. Ira and the Linscows, who were working on shares, decided to hold their crawfish until the Thanksgiving trade when prices would be better. One night in bed about eleven o'clock, I heard our watchman the blue heron cawing from his rocky perch. Ira said, "That's funny. The blue heron never fusses at night. There must be someone out in the bay." He got out of bed, slipped on his overalls, grabbed his gun from the rafters, went out to the end of the bluff, and fired several shots out into the bay.

All was quiet for a moment in the darkness, then we heard

someone say, "Jesus Christ! Duck your heads, men—who-ever's shooting means business." By this time I had dressed and come out, and the Linscows were also on the bluff, very much excited as they had an interest in that crawfish, too. Our eyes now used to the darkness, we saw a skiff over by the kelp, heading out of the bay. It was three men from Fry's Harbor, who had been to our camp in the last storm when their anchor broke. We had treated them the best we could, and they had come back in the dead of night to steal our crawfish. Ira fired a few more shots over their heads for good measure, and then I hung a lighted lantern outside the shack to let them know there was someone watching in case they came back.

The following night, Ira and the men decided to take turns sleeping on the *Sam Pan,* to help the blue heron keep watch over the fish anchored in the bay. Ira had first watch, and all night long he hammered, making new traps. The next night Linscow took his turn and he hammered all night, too. In the morning Ira said, "The men will have to find some other way to keep awake. That hammering bothers me so I can't sleep."

I told him his hammering had kept us awake all night, too. They decided to set the alarm every half hour to take a look around to see if there were any pirates after our fish. That night everyone had a good night's sleep, and the following morning the company's boat came to take our ton of fish to the market. The price of crawfish had gone up two cents, and the lot was worth a hundred and forty dollars.

Then the first of the New Year was again on us. The boys went to town with another load of fish, and on account of the storms could not cross the channel to come back. I got so frightened when the wind roared down the canyon and hit our little shack, that I took my mattress and bedding and went down the canyon to a tent Ira had put up for us. We could have camped under the large oak tree, but my fifty chickens roost-ing there might have dropped a card or two on us. I put Vera to bed, crawled in beside her, and lay awake all night, thinking that if the wind should loosen some big rocks on the hill above us, there would not be much left of Vera or me. Next morning my shack was still there, but everything was covered with a couple of inches of dust and dirt.

Ira took me with him one day when he went to the marine gardens to get a mess of abalone for dinner. We saw two octopus clinging to the rocks in a cave; one was quite large, the other smaller. Extending from the oval body are eight tentacles or arms, which, in the octopus of large size, make it a creature of horror. These are used to hold fast any victim coming within their grasp. Ira caught these octopus and traded them to some Austrian fishermen, who considered them a delicacy.

A yachtsman left me the book called *The Sea Wolf,* by Jack London, and I would read it on stormy nights when I couldn't sleep. I was very much interested in the characters, especially the old style captain, who knows how to handle his men. I liked the name of the book and told Ira that if we ever had enough money to buy a new boat, we should call her the *Sea Wolf.* Ira said that if he kept on fishing and catching seal and had no bad luck, someday we would have enough money.

In those days the skipper owned the seal net and would hire a boat captain to go out to fill the seal order. One day a Mr. Rogers got an order for twelve seals, and Captain Vasquez was supposed to fill the order, but he couldn't be found. So Mr. Rogers told Ira if he would catch the seals, he could have the use of the net for future orders. Ira went to pick up the net and as it was in very bad shape, he made a rack at our camp at Pelican Bay and spread the net over it to be mended. Then he caught the seals, took them to town and turned them over to Mr. Rogers. Leaving Vera and me alone at the camp, he told me to take good care of the seal net. At night I had to bunch it all together in a long row and cover it with canvas, for if exposed to the dew at night it would eventually rot. The following morning after sunup I had to uncover it and spread it out the full length of the rack to dry. Through the day I kept shifting it, so that the wind and sun could hit the whole net. It was 125 feet long and 50 feet wide, with a hundred corks and an equal number of two-inch long lead weights. The whole lot weighed two hundred pounds, but it felt like five hundred.

The next day I uncovered the net and spread it to dry in the sunshine, then turned to the task of cleaning up my one-room palace and getting lunch for myself and Vera. At noontime I stepped out of the house and saw a little double-ended twenty-five foot boat rounding the point. Like a flash it dawned on me—that was Captain Vasquez and his men, who were supposed to have caught that order of seal, and now they were coming for the net that Ira had left in my charge.

I flew up the six stone steps and started pulling the net off the rack to get it into the kitchen. As the meshes caught on the edges of the rack, Vera helped free them; I pulled and tugged that net until I had the rack cleared and that huge mess of twine at my feet. Now I still had to drag it twenty-five feet to the top step, down into the kitchen where I knew the men couldn't enter, and then close the door. I took the massive cork line and started pulling it down the stone steps. The meshes kept catching on the rocks that stuck out of the steps, but I couldn't stop to undo each one now. There would be plenty of time to mend those broken meshes later on. All I could think of now was to get that net past the threshold of my door. Through all this excitement, Vera stood by my side, trying her best to help me. As I was working with the net, I could hear the sound of the engine nearing the mooring, the captain giving orders to drop anchor, and what seemed the endless sound of the anchor chain being played out. They would still have to row in two hundred feet from the boat, haul their skiff up on the rock, and walk up the narrow winding trail.

Finally I had the last of the lead line inside of the door, and such a cloud of dust and gravel with it! The perspiration ran from every pore in my body, and my face was one mass of grime. When I looked up, there stood Captain Vasquez on the top stone step, grinning. His crew, one a Portuguese and the other a good-looking young Spaniard, stood on either side of him. "Good morning, Mrs. Eaton," the Captain said.

"Good morning, Captain Vasquez," I answered.

Then he said, "You look as if you have been doing some fast and furious work."

"What do you and your men want here, Captain Vasquez?"

"I've come to take my seal net home."

"This net belong to my husband," I said. "Mr. Rogers said that if Ira caught the seals, he could have the net."

Then the Captain took a paper from his hip pocket. "I've an order for Mr. Eaton to turn that seal net over to me. It belongs to me."

I said, "I expect you understand that I am Mrs. Eaton, not Mr. Eaton." Then I asked if he had seen Mr. Eaton in town. He said he hadn't, and started down the first stone step. In a flash I sprang onto the kitchen table, reached to the rafters and got the gun which always hung there. Whether it was loaded or not I did not know, but I must make him believe that it was. "If you come down another step I'll fill you full of lead."

The Captain stopped where he was. "I mean what I say," he said. "I'll not take the net now, but I'll come back tonight and get it from this house." He turned, took his two men and left.

By then I was just trembling with fear. Vera had been standing in back of me with her arms around my waist, she was so frightened. I turned to look for her, but she had vanished. I called and called, and finally she answered, "Here I am, Mamma." Following the sound of her voice, I found her under the far corner of the bed. "Mamma, when is Papa coming back to take care of us? Will he come before those men come back again?" I assured her that he would be here soon.

I could not rest or sleep that night, as I expected Captain Vasquez and his men to return at any moment. I left my light burning all night and hung a lantern outside the door to let them know I was prepared. Well, somehow we got through the night, and I was relieved when daylight came. I did not attempt to put the net back where it belonged, but left it and the dirt and gravel to keep it company.

Two days later, Ira arrived from town and I explained what

had happened. It turned out that before Captain Vasquez had left for the islands, he had boasted to Ira that he would come back to town with the seal net. But Ira had laughed and told him, "Colís, as long as my wife has possession of that net, I don't think you'll get it."

When Captain Vasquez had gone back to town, he met Ira on the wharf, shook hands with him, and said, "Ira, if I had a wife like yours, with the guts she has, I'd be the happiest man in town." Then Ira had told him to stop in at the camp in a day or so and he would give him the net.

Back at camp, Ira spread the net, measured it, and cut it in half. When Captain Vasquez arrived the following day, he was invited to have lunch with us; on the island you just can't hold any hard feelings toward anyone. He was given the smaller half of the net, and went away thinking he was the winner after all. But I think the laugh was really on him, for he never mentioned the net again, and continued to stop at the camp the same as before.

White Wings, a beautiful sixty-foot yacht, dropped anchor in the bay one day. The party said they would like to stay for some time, it was such a beautiful spot. They caught a great variety of fish: bonita, albacore, barracuda, and a huge swordfish which they gave us to salt down as bait for the crawfish season. They had enough fish aboard their boat to feed the party and crew twice a day for a week.

Later in the summer, the *Gussie M.* came into the bay with a crowd. There was the usual salute from the boat as they arrived. Ashore, Captain Vasquez introduced me to the manager of the Selig Film Company, who was looking for a location on the island to make a picture that thousands would see in their nickelodeons all over the country. The last time they had been in Santa Barbara, they had taken pictures at the Gillespie place in Montecito. The manager said that after they were finished shooting the scenes on the island, they would go up and take pictures of the wreck of the *Santa Rosa* at Point Arguello on the mainland.

He asked if I would like to join the company for the picture; he told me that I made the perfect mother, and he would pay me good wages. I thought he was fooling, but he wasn't. I was so used to roughing it out here, he said, that I would fit in fine in the scenes at the *Santa Rosa* wreck. They could use Vera too, and they would pay us both well. But I couldn't think of letting my little girl go through the misery of being washed ashore in the surf, so I thanked him for his kind offer and refused it. Now I could always say I had been offered a job in movies, and who knows? I might have had my name in bright letters. The company made ready to go aboard then, and they went up to Fry's Harbor. When Ira came home I mentioned that I had been offered a job with a movie company. He told me to forget it, that I was better off here.

Another fall and winter passed without much excitement, and the new year, 1912, arrived. In early March it was very cold. One day I looked across the channel and saw the mountains behind Santa Barbara covered with snow. There were great swells running outside, and plenty of whitecaps. I imagined I saw a tiny speck away off in the distance, stood there a minute, and then went back in the house to get warm. The stove was going full blast. A while later I went out to take another look, and there was the *Gussie M.,* her flag flying, which meant a load of passengers. I put more wood in the stove, changed Vera's dress, and had the kettle boiling when the boat dropped anchor in the bay. It was a party making scenes for a moving picture. I invited them in, and we pulled up benches and crowded around in front of the stove. They were almost frozen.

The picture was called "Heart of My Heart," and in the party were George Knight Carleton, director of the Alhambra Motion Picture Company, Richard Morris the cameraman, Bessie Holt the leading lady, and Edward Peil, the leading man. They had been in Santa Barbara only a short time and hearing so much about the islands, they had decided to come over here to take some scenes. The trip over had been very rough; a heavy swell had hit the boat and a Mr. Illmer was washed overboard. The captain and crew got him aboard again, but naturally that put a damper on the party. They all thought the island scenery was so beautiful. Mr. Carleton said that Santa Cruz Island cannot be surpassed for natural beauty.

When night came, all the women of the party left to sleep on the boat, except for the leading lady, who said she had had many thrilling experiences in her picture career, but never such a time as that trip over. She had been very seasick. She wanted to stay ashore overnight as she had to work in the scene the next day.

The following morning I watched them work. The sun was shining brightly, but they had on sou'westers, oilskins and rubber hip boots. When they finished, I asked them if that scene was supposed to be taken in rainy weather. They said yes, but unlike me, most people would never notice that it wasn't raining. As long as they got good pictures, the film company didn't care. They left for town that same night.

One evening two beautiful yachts came into the bay: the *Yankee,* owned by Captain Miller of San Francisco, and the *Yankee Boy,* owned by the commodore of the Balboa yacht club. Captain Miller had brought the commodore up to see the wonderful sights of our island. When their anchors dropped overboard, all was quiet for a minute, and then I heard a woman holler: "Where's the hotel on this island? I thought you were bringing me someplace that had Catalina beat!"

The lady's husband, the commodore on the *Yankee Boy,* lost no time in beginning to pace back and forth on the deck. The only reason I could see was to show off his handsome uniform, dark blue trimmed with gold braid and brass buttons, and white gloves. Old Captain Miller was on deck on the *Yankee,* dressed as usual in khaki trousers, tan shirt and sneakers. What a difference there was between those two yacht owners!

The following morning, Captain Miller and his wife went to hike over the hills looking for tiger lily plants, which they had spied on their last trip. The commodore and his wife came ashore in their skiff with the help of three sailors. As they came up the trail, one sailor came first, walking backwards and pulling on the lady's hands; two sailors were behind her, their hands on her hips bracing her up. She was a tall, heavy-set woman, and what an effort that climb was! On top of the bluff at last, she was all out of breath. I invited her into my kitchen. The first thing she said was, "Oh, do you live here?"—and what a lot of meaning there was in that "Oh"!

"Yes," I answered, "and we are thankful to have such a wonderful place to live in." Then I got a good look at her face, streaked with blue veins and covered with perspiration from the strain of climbing that trail.

The commodore had already changed out of his uniform and gone with Captain and Mrs. Miller up in the hills. The lady called to one of the sailors, "Boy! My handbag!" He handed it to her, then asked if anything else would be wanted. She said. "One of you boys must stay ashore with me in case I need you." Then the other two ran down the trail as fast as they could, the third watching and wishing he could go, too.

We went to sit outside and I told the lady about Santa Cruz Island. She said that Captain Miller had told her husband that the island was a beautiful place, that all the yachts came up here to get away from the noise of the city. When they went to Catalina it was so noisy and they were followed to see that they did no damage. But Captain Miller had said that as soon as you dropped anchor here, your troubles were over and you could roam all over the island and no one would bother you. The fishing was good, and you were sure of a mess of fish for the table any time of day.

Then she said, "I thought there was a beautiful hotel here and brought all my evening clothes and my high-heeled shoes." She was wearing the nicest white high-heeled shoes you'd want to own. She went on to say that she didn't like camping but liked being where there were crowds and she could entertain. At the last regatta they had entertained a lot and enjoyed it. She hoped Captain Miller wouldn't spoil her husband by taking him in the hills too often, for that would leave her alone. She couldn't climb hills; she wasn't built for that kind of exercise.

It was lunchtime and no one showed up, so I made her a cup of tea and some toast and she enjoyed it. Then she wanted to take a nap. But when the boy started to lead her down the trail to the boat, she got frightened and said she'd rather stretch out on my bed and wait for her husband. After she got comfortable and was dozing, I went out on the flat, where the sailor was leaning against the rock. "What a pill she is," he said. "I don't see how you put up with her. She never had anything in her life until she married the commodore, and now she makes life miserable for everyone around her. She thinks she should live on the yacht the same way she lives ashore."

I said, "What's the difference? If she gets any fun out of all this, let the old fellow pay. From the looks of things, he can afford it."

Then the sailor said, "I'll bet the old man is sleeping under an oak tree not far from camp, having a good time all by himself. He has a magazine to read and is not coming back until Captain and Mrs. Miller come."

At eight o'clock all three came into camp. There was murder in the air, but all the old fellow said was that he lost his way in the hills and it took a long time to find the trail back to camp.

The following morning early, the bay was alive with smelt; jumping out of the ocean, they sounded just like hail on the roof. When the *Yankee Boy* pulled anchor and left the harbor, the commodore was at the wheel in his gold braid, brass buttons, and white gloves. Standing beside him in all her city finery, the flowers bobbing on her hat, was his lady waving a lace handkerchief. From the bank I waved my sailor cap.

That evening, the bay was aglow with phosphorescence. I sat on the bluff enjoing the beautiful sight and thinking about our life on the island. We had had a long hard road, but now at last we were beginning to see our way clear, and would soon be out of debt. Even with the little *Sam Pan,* Ira had been high man this smelt season, having packed tons of smelt over to town. I had learned to mend the smelt nets, which came in from every trip badly torn from the sharks and rocks. I was just as fast and good as any of the men; to me it was just as easy as crocheting. I could stand two or three days at a time doing my share of the mending. I also did all the cooking and cleaning up, and Ira often told me how much help I was to him. If we kept this up, we were bound to get ahead.

The government boat *McCullough* came in the bay one day and sent two sailors ashore to find out who lived here and what we did for a living. I told them my husband fished and was not here very often, but my little girl and myself lived here most of the time. Later, some fishermen told me that the government had an idea that Chinamen and opium were being smuggled into Santa Barbara by fishermen, and was searching every cove and beach on the different islands to find out who was doing the smuggling.

In January, 1913, Captain George Nidever stopped in our camp and brought us the sad news that his brother Jake had drowned. After a New Year's dinner with their families, Captain Nidever and Jake had gone out on the wharf to inspect the freight that was to be taken to the island. Jake had rowed out to the *Santa Cruz* schooner to put up the riding light, and apparently slipped between the skiff and the schooner. I was very sorry to hear of Jake Nidever's death. I had not forgotten the pleasant evening we had all spent together on my first night on the island, when he was one of the men who had serenaded me.

A heavy northwest wind and swells outside, the *Gussie M.* arrived in the bay. Captain Vasquez came ashore with an artist, who said he had put on a diving suit and helmet, and dove down into the ocean around the marine gardens. He had with him waterproof crayons and sketchbooks, and the scenes at the bottom of the ocean were beautiful. He said he would finish them in his studio.

Captain Vasquez said the bathhouse on the west beach in Santa Barbara had burned. We had seen the fire quite plainly the night before. He also told us there was a rumor in town that the alien fishermen would be taxed one hundred dollars a year for fishing. This greatly upset the Italians, Greeks, Portugese, and others who fished from San Luis Obispo to San Diego, as many of them were not eligible for their first papers. The ones hit the hardest would be the Japanese, as they could not become citizens. They sent a man to appear before the Fish and Game Commission in Sacramento, and he said that the Japanese were more skilled than any other nationality at fishing. There was not a large enough supply of fish in the markets, he said, and if the Japanese fishermen were driven out by this tax, the consumer would not have enough fish to eat, and would have to pay a higher price. We could not agree with this, as we thought that the white fishermen could supply the markets. A further hearing was set.

Ira heard in town that a man named Garbutt had gotten the concession rights to Santa Cruz Island from the Caire family and was going to build a big hotel at Fry's Harbor later on. For the present, tents were to be put up to accommodate the crowds. This moneyed man was building a beautiful forty-foot boat for Colis Vasquez, called the *Otter*. She would haul forty passengers to the islands. I asked what was going to happen to the *Gussie M.*, and Ira said her owner, Captain McGuire, wanted to sell her or get someone else to run her. "Ira," I said, "why don't you ask him to let you handle the *Gussie M.* to catch his seal orders, and apply that money as payment to buy her? He knows you will take good care of his boat."

So the next trip to town, Ira spoke to Captain McGuire and made the arrangements I had suggested. The price was set at $1500, and the boat would remain in Captain McGuire's name until paid for. Ira's first order for seals came on Friday, April 18, 1913. In those days, seal orders were large and came in often. In just six weeks, the *Gussie M.* was ours.

Ira brought her into the bay and anchored her, and moved the little *Sam Pan* over to the eastern anchorage. For a long time afterwards, when I looked out in the bay and saw the *Gussie M.* laying at anchor, rolling in the swells—and the old girl could roll some—I'd think, ever since I made my first trip to this beautiful island in that boat, I've wanted Ira to own her. That had always seemed impossible but now, by a stroke of luck, here she was anchored in our bay for good. As I was standing out on the flat watching her that day, Ira came out, put his arm around my waist and said, "A penny for your thoughts, Margaret."

"You know, Ira," I said, "if you make up your mind to do something, you'll always win out if you work hard enough, won't you?"

Ira agreed. "You and I have always worked together ever since we were married, and we've made a good team. I know you deserve something better than I've been able to give you, but I've a feeling that working together in the future as we've done in the past, there's nothing we can't do in this fishing and passenger business. Although Colís has a brand new boat and the wealthy people of Montecito will charter her in preference to our *Gussie M.,* still we'll get our share of the working people, and they'll be easier to satisfy than the rich. Later on, with our sealing money we'll buy a much larger boat. And we'll call her the *Sea Wolf* after the old captain in Jack London's book." Giving my waist a squeeze and kissing Vera, he added, "I just wish we had a little boy to grow up with Vera. In later years when you and I are too old to carry on this business, we'd have someone we could rely on. The two children with our help could take care of things."

I remembered that the doctor had told me not to risk my life attempting to bring another little one into the world, but I only said: "When we get ahead a little, we will have a playmate for Vera and a helper for you. If this rich man, Garbutt, has the sole rights to Fry's Harbor, why don't you write to the owners of this island and ask them for the sole rights to Pelican Bay? If Colís is charging forty dollars a day for his new boat, you can charge twenty for the *Gussie M.;* that will attract the crowds, I'm sure. When you are in town you can buy some lumber to make long tables and benches so the people will be comfortable. They can bring their lunches and eat out on the flat here, and I'll make their coffee on our little stove. Who

knows? They might come a second time. There's no place in
the State of California where there's such a wonderful view—
the beautiful ocean spreading out in front, the hills covered
with tall pines, giant ironwood trees guarding the canyons,
these gnarled old oaks, the huge summer holly trees in bloom,
lovely wildflowers as far as the eye can see—what lovelier spot
could anyone want?"

That sounded like a fine idea to Ira, and he promptly sat
down to write a letter to the Caires.

CHAPTER VIII

The Pelican Bay Camp
1913–1937

Concession Rights — The Wild Man — The Miller Party and the *What the Hell* — Jack London — School — First Camp Improvements — The *Sea Wolf* — Island Visitors — More Film Companies — "Pearls of Paradise" and "Battle of Hearts" — Wes Thompson — Island Closed to Campers — Ira Leases Anacapa — Cabins, Dining Room and Landscaping — "Adam and Eve" — "Male and Female" — John Barrymore — Bootlegging — The Potter Fire — Frank Nidever and Big Jerry are Lost — The *Cuba* — "Peter Pan" — The Earthquake — Barrymore Returns — Graduation — The *Sea Wolf* is Wrecked — "The Rescue" — Barrymore's Third Visit — The Island is Sold

ABOUT A WEEK went by after Ira wrote to the owners of the island. One day I was sitting on the stone steps with Vera beside me, as I usually did when expecting the boat from town. The *Gussie M.* came ploughing her way across the channel and I thought, how lucky we are to have such a good boat; I wonder if Ira had an answer to his letter. As the *Gussie M.* circled the bay to her moorings, Ira stood in the stern, smiles all over his face. He was shouting, "I got it, Margaret, I got it!" Soon he was ashore, hugging and kissing Vera and me. Then he read the letter in which the owners had given him the sole rights and privileges to Pelican Bay. I was so thrilled to think that we could really cater to people this summer.

The very next Sunday, the *Gussie M.* and Captain Colís Vasquez's new boat the *Otter* brought eighty people to our new Pelican Bay Camp, as we decided to call it. I served a fish barbecue down under the large oak tree in the canyon. Colís came ashore to visit as usual, but I told him he just came to show off his new uniform. He looked like an admiral, dressed in a blue flannel double-breasted coat with a double row of brass buttons, and a real captain's cap with "Otter" in letters an inch high and a captain's insignia on top. We complimented him on his appearance and said he must be doing a good business to be able to afford such an outfit.

"It didn't cost me a penny," said Colis. "It was bought and paid for by a man lousy with money, so why shouldn't I wear it? You know I am a pretty good talker and can usually talk my way into getting what I want."

"You didn't talk your way into getting that seal net from me," I reminded him.

"Well, not everyone is as shrewd as that," he admitted. "But I am in this business to stay, and I intend to give you a run for your money in this passenger game, because I've all the money I want to back me."

"That's all right with us," I answered. "All we expect to make out of this business is a decent living, and we will do that regardless of your backers. Our *Gussie M.* is paid for, no strings attached, and Ira will not have to take orders from anyone but Mr. McGuire when he gives an order for seals. That's more than you can say; even the clothes on your back you didn't pay for. If Ira wears overalls, at least they are his own. Your boat is a beauty, and I know anyone with money will take yours in preference to ours, but we're not worried."

Then he had a cup of coffee and a piece of pie, and I told him not to forget the way to the camp, that he was always welcome. Then both boats left for town, amid honking of horns and waving of handkerchiefs. Going back to camp, I had a mess to clean up. That was the worst part of this business, but when you are bound to get ahead, you must work and not loaf. While Vera and I cleared the tables, I sang to keep my thoughts off the argument I'd just had with Captain Vasquez. I was mad clean through. I'd show him we'd get along.

By this time, Vera had grown into quite a girl. She was always running around the camp or climbing the hills barefoot, with her dogs and a pet lamb or two at her heels. She would make the rounds to see if the birds built their nests in the same places as the year before, and gather wildflowers, especially the yellow violets, to replace the wilted ones on the kitchen table. She was no worry to me; she was careful on the trails and never went too near the edge of the cliff.

The Fourth of July came and Ira was on the town celebration committee, but he had to haul passengers to the visiting warships so I took his place. The committee, headed by Jimmy Kimberley, was busy all day turning Plaza del Mar into a restaurant and serving lunch and supper. The booths were lavishly trimmed with colored bunting, long tables were placed in the park for the big feast, and a band played all day. That night we served over three thousand people to a bowl of rock cod chowder, crawfish salad, fresh bread and hot coffee—for thirty-five cents. We all worked like beavers and our party was a great success. All evening there was dancing and the torpedo boat flotilla was dressed up in flags, lying at anchor in the harbor.

A couple of days of excitement in town were enough for me. I was tickled pink when Ira said we would leave at midnight with a large crowd to spend Sunday in our camp. We were about four miles out when the *Gussie M.* rolled and threw a man who was asleep on the deck overboard into the ocean. Someone saw him fall and at once shouted "Man overboard!" Ira reversed the engine and lowered a boat manned by Charley and Arturo. By now all the passengers were awake and watching in the dim moonlight as the struggling man was carried further and further away by the heavy swell and current. He had sunk twice when the men pulled him into the lifeboat, unconscious, and the passengers gave a hearty cheer. Some of the women fainted and were taken down into the cabin, where I took care of them. For a long time we thought the man was dead, but he was revived by the rolling process. When we arrived in camp I served a hot breakfast and the women lounged around while the men caught large numbers of fish from the reef.

After the party had gone, I thought, this passenger business

is not so hot after all. What if a man fell overboard and
through no fault of ours was drowned? Our business would
be ruined and Colis would have the laugh on us. But I must
not get discouraged. Every night and morning I would pray
and ask guidance from Him above, and through the day I
was often singing hymns and silently praying. Then I had
an uplifted feeling, as though I was being guided.

The albacore season opened again and campers came to the
islands in great numbers expecting big feeds for their parties.
We bought three tents and set them up for renting. Ira made
arrangements with another man to help carry his passengers,
and also bought a glass-bottomed boat so the parties could
have a better view of the marine gardens, which everyone said
were in every way superior to those at Catalina.

One day Ira came in and said he had left a man at Lady's
Harbor who wanted to lead the life of a wild man. I asked if
the man was crazy and Ira said no, he was just as sane as we
are, maybe more so. The man had just gotten tired of city life
and wanted to get away from it all. He had brought only a
box of apples and expected to live on fish for the time he was
there. Then Ira left to catch an order of seal, including several
Steller Sea Lions that were very hard to catch and dangerous
to handle.

Captain George Gourley arrived at the camp with a crowd.
While they were having lunch on the bluff, I told them that
Ira had recently left a wild man on the island who wanted to
become a hermit. The party, looking for some excitement, suggested to Captain Gourley that they run up to Lady's Harbor
and have a look at this wild man. They asked if I would care
to go along. I thought it would be great fun, so Vera and I
went aboard.

When we landed on the beach at Lady's, the wild man was
on top of the mountain. Coming down to meet the crowd, he
told us he was a Dane, thirty-five years old. He was only five
feet tall, heavy-set and broad-shouldered, with light curly hair
and blue eyes with bushy eyebrows. The men thought he was
very interesting and handsome for his type. In his hand he

held a hammer he had made with the crudest implements. All he wore was a loincloth made from a sheepskin. He told us that he had no firearms, matches or dishes but had brought plenty of fruit. His aim was to become a real hermit and to live as nearly as he could the life of an Indian. He had built a rude hut with bark and driftwood, and started his fire with flint he had found. He had killed fox, civet cat and wild boar with a slingshot.

The wild man said most of the time he studied botany, of which he claimed to have some knowledge. He told us that a certain fern grew on top of the mountain here that he had never seen except in Scandinavian countries. He had come from Los Angeles, where he had been ill and tried many cures to no avail, and so decided to try going back to nature. He said that he wanted to stay here forever, because in the short time he had been here he felt a hundred percent better than he had on the mainland. He claimed that Nature was akin to the Creator, and that near the mountains and sea one comes in contact with silent and final forces for good. While talking, he kept his toes squirming in the dirt.

After an enjoyable day, the party bid me goodbye. They were from Tulsa, Oklahoma, and said this trip had been different from any other they had during their stay at the Potter Hotel.

Later in July we got news that the boat *Charm* was to bring out the Miller party, wealthy people from Montecito, to camp under the oak trees in the canyon. We thought it was wonderful that they had chosen Pelican instead of some other harbor. Making the rounds of the camp to see that everything was in order, I wondered how their Chinese cook would manage cooking for the large crowd on my small stove. Perhaps they would do some of their cooking on an open fire. The table was set with a new flowered cloth and paper plates.

Just then the boat rounded the point, blowing the whistle to express their pleasure at being at the end of the ride. The boatmen helped the ladies out of the skiff onto the rock. There was laughing when our friend Arturo at the oars said, "Hold on, young ladies, and don't jump 'til I tell you, or you'll get your pretty shoes wet and that'll never do." The ladies were dressed in white flannel skirts, long coats, white silk shirt waists, sailor hats and high-heeled pumps. That was the way they dressed to go camping in those days.

The Chinaman was landed and shown to the kitchen under the oak trees, and you should have seen his smiling face when he saw how it was set up, even to the kettle on the stove boiling and singing away. As the crowd were half starved, it didn't take them long to eat lunch.

Two young men, Bob Doulton and Earl Miller, the son of the Miller family, went up on the hill, and I asked them whose cute little boat that was moored out in the bay. "Oh," said Bobby, "that is Earl's, and her name is *What the Hell*." My expression must have showed that I thought that a rather funny name, because Bobby continued: "We call her *What the Hell* because her engine is always out of commission. In town when we are out for a spin and think everything is running fine, she'll sputter and stop. She did this so often, we got used to saying 'What the hell is the matter with you?' and that name has stuck to her ever since. We've had heaps of trouble with her lately, so we brought her along on this trip to give her engine a good overhauling."

I asked how fast she would go, and Bobby said, "We make thirty-five miles an hour when she is in shape. That speed is considered very dangerous, but she was built back East for racing. We entered her in several races and in almost every one something happened to her engine."

The following morning camp life really started. The party spent their time fishing, hiking, visiting the caves and grottoes, and enjoying themselves all day. But the boys were aboard the *What the Hell*, tinkering from morning to night. When they thought they had her tuned up in fine shape they would make a run to Chinese Harbor, a distance of six miles. Mrs. Miller had three boats chartered for her stay on the island, and the *What the Hell* was never allowed out of sight unless there was another boat in the bay to follow her in case she broke down and had to be towed back to camp.

On Sunday morning at daybreak the *Gussie M.* was in the bay, bringing the news that Mrs. Chase, the mother of Harold Chase who was a member of the party, had been killed in an automobile accident the night before. When the news was broken to the son, he left at once for town on the *Gussie M.*

The day before the party broke camp they trolled outside the bay for two hours and caught one hundred and eighty-seven beautiful barracuda. So Mrs. Miller's many friends in town were treated to a mess of fresh fish.

For the whole last week, Bobby and Earl planned and planned the trip back across the channel in their little boat. The morning they were to leave, there was not a ripple on the ocean and it was so clear you could almost see every house on the Riviera behind Santa Barbara. Earl tried to coax his mother to let him and Bobby make the trip in the *What the Hell* themselves, but Mrs. Miller was very firm and said that Scotty the camp man would take the boat back to town. They made a couple of circles around the bay to warm her up, and then Scotty took over. He was out of the bay with a bang, tearing through the glassy smooth, crystal clear water, and throwing spray high in the air. We watched through the glasses until she was out of sight.

When the party was ready to leave, Mrs. Miller said good-bye to Vera and me, handed me a check for fifty dollars for my kindness to the crowd, and said she hoped to see me the next summer. Then they headed back for town in the *Gussie M.*

The next day Ira was back, and said that Scotty had arrived at the wharf with the bow of the *What the Hell* fully two feet out of the water and thirty feet of spray on both sides of her. She had broken all records by making the trip from the island in fifty-five minutes. Ira thought it was a shame the kids couldn't have made that trip across the channel themselves, as their hearts had been set on it. But on the way back on the *Gussie M.* Bobby and Earl had bet Arturo five dollars that he wouldn't walk up the middle of State Street as far as Diehl's

Store with a life-preserver on him. Arturo said he would, so they put it on him. For a minute they thought they had won the bet, but then some of the "wharf rats" treated Arturo to a drink and he started up the middle of the street. He was almost in front of the store when two cops came along and waltzed him off to jail, and he was fined ten dollars for being drunk. Bobby and Earl had to bail him out, so it cost them fifteen dollars instead of five. They said the joke was on them after all.

Another moving picture company came to our camp in the *Gussie M.* The leading man was Harold Lockwood, a very handsome blond young man. His leading lady, May Allison, was also a beautiful blonde, and both were as sweet as they were beautiful. As usual, my kitchen was the headquarters for all who had a moment to spare.

The company had a burro on board, and they landed him on the beach at Little Pelican and staked him out. One man kept giving him buttered brown paper, which he ate. There was a scene in this picture where the burro was supposed to eat a faked will. When they got ready to shoot the scene, they buttered the faked will and put it in the leading man's pocket. The burro was led up behind him, saw the paper, and nipped it out of the pocket in full view of the camera. The villain turned around just in time to see the last morsel gone. That was not in the script, and they had to start the whole scene over again.

While lounging around, some of the company said that Jack London was supposed to be near the island, fishing and hunting seal with a party of eastern friends aboard his boat the *Sea Wolf*. Late that same night, there was a great commotion at the boat landing—people were trying to come ashore in the dark. I went down with a lantern, and there stood Jack London himself. By lamplight I could see that he was the stocky, sunburned, seafaring type. His accent and manners reminded me of my father. He said he was sorry he had put me to the trouble of coming down that long flight of stairs in the dark, but he had heard that Harold Lockwood, a young actor he'd met in

New York, was here, and he just wanted to say hello. All the party crowded into the kitchen and visited for half an hour. At midnight, Jack London left for the north.

Vera did not start school until she was seven years old, and until that time she had never been away from us. When she reached school age, we knew we would have to start her in kindergarten. So that she could continue her schooling, she was to stay with her grandparents when we were at the island. They still lived in the house on East Victoria Street. When we were in town we lived in one of Father Eaton's houses on Equestrian Avenue, and Vera would come and stay with us. The nearest kindergarten was the Catholic school on Anapamu Street, and during the day the children always attended church across the street on the corner of Anapamu and State Streets.

Gypsy went to school with Vera, and the Sisters didn't mind, as the dog would lie quietly under the bench during school. But one day not long after Vera had started school, there was trouble: in church, Gypsy started crawling under the pews and distracted the children. So Vera was told to take the dog outside and wait on the front steps. She was very upset and when she came home I knew something was wrong. Finally she told me what had happened, and said she did not want to go back to that school again.

That was the end of school for Vera that year, and we all went back to the island. But the following year, dressed in blue gingham and her hair in two braids, she was handed over to Mr. George, the principal of Washington School. She lived with her grandparents, and every chance he had, Ira would bring her over to the island for weekends as well as for her school vacations. Her pets stayed on the island and were always glad to see her. She spent her time visiting all her familiar and special places, and hated to return to Santa Barbara and school.

All through the winter fishing season, Ira talked of building a platform out from our kitchen so people could eat in the shade. So in the spring we built a platform ten by twenty feet, and covered the roof with palm fronds brought from Santa Barbara. The wind was a problem, though, so Ira enclosed the area and bought windows for it at the Potter Hotel after their laundry fire, for fifty cents apiece. We decorated our new dining room with pine boughs and it looked very cozy. We bought a six-hole range to take the place of my little four-hole stove, and put the smaller stove down in the canyon for the use of campers.

With the summer business ahead of us again, Ira knew something had to be done about the water supply. Water had to be carried up the hill from the spring to the kitchen in five-gallon cans; getting the water and packing it up the trail was very hard work. So Ira enclosed the spring with a high cement wall. It took a day for the new spring area to fill, and then we had all the water we needed. Later, a three-hundred-gallon tank was put up on the flat part of the bluff above the kitchen and a five horsepower engine installed. The water was pumped straight up the cliff to the tank and then piped downhill to the kitchen. To me, the sound of that motor was sweeter than any music I'd ever heard, for it meant that part of the hard work of carrying water was behind us.

There were so many people coming to our camp now, and our bed didn't look too good tucked in the corner of our kitchen. Ira built a small one-room cabin with two windows facing the ocean, and moving into our new bedroom made us feel so happy. We were really getting ahead now.

By 1914 our business had grown. Ira had a new boat built by an Italian in Sausalito, near San Francisco; we had our *Sea Wolf* at last. After four months she was finished, and he went up to get her. A crowd of people waited on the wharf to watch her make her home port. The *Sea Wolf* arrived from San Francisco on Thursday, May 28, 1914, after a trip of just under thirty-three hours. For part of the way, she had bucked a southeaster, but never shipped a gallon of water or missed a stroke. The best in her class, she was rigged with a mainsail, foresail and jib, and had two gas tanks, each holding 350 gallons. Ira came in all smiles and said this was the happiest ocean trip he had ever made. He had brought back a lot of camping equipment as we would be catering to more movie crews.

Mr. George Owen Knapp of Montecito brought over a party including a Mr. and Mrs. Coleman and their three children. To fix up the camp for this distinguished group, we bought lumber and put floors in the tents, and equipped each one with a blue rag rug, colored camp chairs, and a water pail and long-handled dipper. We bought blue and white china for the dining room, and I unpacked my silver. The best part was that we paid cash for everything

The boat in the bay looked trim and beautiful with her tan and yellow awning. The weather was perfect. Looking at myself in the mirror, my auburn hair slicked under my cap and a clean bungalow apron on, I thought, I'm not so bad looking. I was ready for the guests. The party fished, visited the Painted Cave and the seal rookeries, rented horses from the Main Ranch, and with Spanish Joe as a guide explored the interior of the island, which they thought was very beautiful.

The second day of their visit was little Agnes Coleman's birthday. We celebrated with a fried chicken dinner, ice cream and a birthday cake with candles. Vera, in a blue gingham dress, was a guest at the party. At Agnes's and Vera's places there were packages—a gold watch for Agnes and a silver one for Vera, a gift from Mrs. Knapp.

When he was leaving, Mr. Knapp said he was more than satisfied with his visit to the Pelican Bay Camp. He told me he had a lodge in the mountains, and if I ever wanted to go there and work he would be glad to have me. He tipped all the help, including Ira and me. Old Spanish Joe got a twenty-dollar gold piece, but when he was taking the horses back to the ranch he lost it out of his vest pocket and couldn't find it again.

Then came the rush from Montecito. We were booked ahead, and party after party came over. Mr. Knapp came back to bring Mr. C. K. G. Billings, just out from the East. Another good booster for the island was Mr. Charles Dabney, Sr.

About every other week he had a party of guests from the East. When he was in camp, he was up every morning at five and out in the kitchen, dressed in khaki trousers and blue shirt, shoelaces flopping, wanting the cup of coffee that was always made and waiting for him. Then he would go out to the point with a tray loaded with a coffee pot and cups for the ladies.

Others who came were Mr. and Mrs. Peter Cooper Bryce, the Slaters, Mrs. Oliver Dwight Norton, Mr. Wyman, Mr. and Mrs John J. Mitchell and Clarence Mitchell. Major and Mrs. Max Fleischmann were frequent visitors at the camp. Mrs. Fleischmann was the first woman ever to bring back a wild boar from a hunt. There were also Fred Harvey, Reginald Reeves, the Dr. C. C. Parks family, Lockwood de Forest, Sr., and Mr. and Mrs. Frederick Forrest Peabody with a party. Almost all the guests who came to the Miramar were brought to the islands.

When Lockwood de Forest, Jr., Buhl Hammet, and Mr. and Mrs. Thayer visited, the boys hiked over the hills. They found a sow with a litter of baby pigs and brought one home for Vera. We decided to call it Ham, short for Hammet. Vera brought it up on a bottle. When her three cousins, Tommy, Harold and Melva, all about her age, came for vacation, the pig followed the children all around the camp.

At this time we also had as visitors Mr. Batchelder, Mr. Breckenbridge, and Mr. Charlie Edwards. Mr. Breckenbridge took a fancy to the pig and asked me what I would sell it for. I told him it belonged to Vera as she had cared for it since it was a baby. He said he would like to take it to his little girl in Pasadena; he would have a harness made for it and the children could lead it around. It would be a novelty for them. When the children came in, I told Vera that Mr. Breckenbridge wanted to buy her pig and take it home with him. She didn't want to sell Ham, and the other children said it wasn't fair. I knew it wasn't fair, but I was looking at the pig from a financial standpoint: Mr. Breckenbridge and the others had been coming here to fish for a good many years and would come many more. So I coaxed and coaxed Vera, and finally it was agreed that Mr. Breckenbridge could have the pig for a dollar, and Ham would live on millionaire row in Pasadena. The day Ham left, he was given a bath and a pink ribbon around his neck, and put in a box padded with excelsior. The children went down to see him off, and when Ira blew the parting whistle, there were four drooping heads and many tears.

That night for supper I made a chocolate cake and let the children eat their fill, hoping to console them. But Vera said, "Mamma, why do you give my pets away? You gave my airedale puppy to a rich lady who came here." I said I hadn't given it away, Vera had traded it for a set of dishes and a book of fairy tales. Then I suggested we have a party the next day and use the dishes, but the children said they would rather have the puppy to talk to and play with all day long. And Vera said, "Mamma, when I see a boatload of people coming, I'm going to take my pets back into the hills and hide them."

The following morning the children were restless and unhappy and I had a guilty feeling about that pig, so I offered to take them fishing. We packed a lunch, Lonny the camp man got the skiff, and we went up the coast. That day I answered what seemed like a thousand questions about the fish we saw— perch, sheephead, bass, bullhead, sculpin, eels and flying fish. We also saw a school of porpoises leaping six and seven feet out of the water. We started back when the sun was setting like a ball of fire, surrounded by clouds streaked with purple, magenta, cerise and gold. The heron, which had been near us all day, flew to his perch on the rock and cawed to tell us he had enjoyed his share of the fish. The *Sea Wolf* was in the bay, and talking all at once the children told Ira about their day of fishing. I cooked all the fish in hot olive oil, and by the time the four had eaten their supper they were ready to turn in after their wonderful day.

In 1915 our camp was made ready for a motion picture company to come up to film the movie "Undine." Henry Otto was the director, and there were eighty people in the company, fifty of them diving girls. The leading lady was Ida Shanell, who had won a swimming and diving contest in Madison Square Garden and was then given a contract by Universal. She was short, thick-set and more fit to play baseball (which she did very well). She was none too popular with the other girls, who could swim and dive better than she could. The leading man, Gerrard Barry, was tall, good-looking, and Irish.

Ida Shanell had a Russian maid furnished by the company, and when the two stood together, you couldn't tell them apart from the rear. One afternoon, squabbling in the kitchen, Fatima (as we called the maid) threw a flatiron at Ida and missed her head by an inch. That settled Fatima, and the next day she went back to town accompanied by my Chilean cook, who was her friend.

The crowd soon settled down to their work. Some mornings the girls practiced diving from the wharf. Our Spanish camp man, Arturo, had been watching them. One day he put on his bathing suit, climbed out on the oak tree twenty feet above them, and dove into the bay. There were many *ohs* and *ahs*— they didn't know Arturo could dive like that.

The girls spent the days posing, diving off Arch Rock and other slippery rocks along the coast, and swimming around the beaches in swells and wind with kelp drapped around their waists. They were glad when the *Sea Wolf* came to bring them back to camp and a hot dinner. They brought their tights and brassieres to the kitchen where the men hung them to dry for the next day's work. Then their legs and feet were treated for cuts and bruises caused by the sharp rocks. They were a mighty brave lot of girls.

Now the moving picture companies came in rapid succession. There was director Reynolds who was a son-of-a-gun for work. He allowed his people to drink liquor only at meals, and it was rationed out to them. One evening just before supper, someone came running up the hill, saying "Clancy had a fit, he's foaming at the mouth!" The director called for anyone who had a bottle of whiskey to bring it quickly, and sent the bottles down to Clancy in the tent. Then the joke came out that the fit was on a bet that he could get all the drink he wanted, and he had won.

The next director, Paul Hurst, was a regular cowboy. His leading lady was Ruth Roland. In this picture, they were supposed to ride a horse off a 110-foot cliff. They rented one of the Island Company horses, but every time they reached the edge of the cliff the horse just stiffened up and refused to budge, so they had to give it up. Miss Roland never complained about her surroundings and was never temperamental. She was such a good scout. She suggested that we bob Vera's hair so that it would grow out stronger. The high chair, scissors, and towel were taken out, and Vera had her first bob from the most adorable moving picture star.

Then came Flying A Studios and the cast of "The Diamond From the Sky" with Irving Cummings and William Russell. Hoot Gibson was in the party too; he was just doing bits then. The *Vamoose* came into the bay with more moving picture people, who told me that our friend Arturo, one of the pirates, had drowned when fishing for crawfish in Mexico. Cooney had been drowned the week before when he fell off the wharf in Santa Barbara. Well, drunk or sober, they both had known their business.

One night the yacht *Cricket* arrived, and the captain introduced himself as Mr. Banning, one of the owners of Catalina Island. He asked me if I could serve supper for him and his eight friends, all boys, so Ira fileted five dozen smelt and I made cornbread, crawfish salad and a cake. They did justice to the meal. While we were eating breakfast the next morning, our little fox terrier made a great commotion running back and forth, barking. We went outside to see what it was all about, and there were four large whales almost at our kitchen door. The boys ran for guns and rifles and fired in every direction, but nary a shot hit the whales. The last we saw of them they were outside the bay, spouting. Before the group left the next day, one of the boys remarked that he had never seen such large blue jays as we had on the island and that they seemed to be a darker color than the mainland ones.

Another party at our Pelican Bay Camp was disappointed because they weren't catching the fish they expected, so I showed them where the rock cod bank was, two miles from camp. We dropped our lines and made ourselves comfortable when we heard a snorting and splashing. Looking around we saw a school of whales, which looked as big as battleships. A young one made a dive for the skiff and came up on the other side, spouting like a geyser. We decided it was time to move on, or there would be no men, women or boat left.

One morning in March, 1916, the sixty-foot, two-masted schooner *Alice* from San Diego dropped anchor in the harbor. She was to be used in a moving picture called "Pearls of Paradise" which Harry Pollard was to make, with Margarita Fischer as the leading lady. The company of forty people was in Santa Barbara and would be over on the *Sea Wolf* that evening. The crew from the schooner helping, mattresses and bedding were hauled from the storeroom and beds set up. I wondered why the company chose the worst time of the year to make a marine picture—I knew there would be days at a time when the company could not move from camp, and I was worried the tents wouldn't stand up in such weather. When the storms kept up, the winds hitting the tents raised them from the ground and then let them flop, and anyone inside would put in a hell of a night. But the crew assured me that Harry Pollard and Margarita Fischer had knocked around quite a bit and were used to those conditions. The company arrived, and after giving them dinner we were up all night storing away supplies.

The weather calmed a bit and the company worked at Valdez Harbor, where Miss Fischer, in a skiff, was chased in and out of the caves by pirates in canoes. A week later, twenty more extras were brought over from Santa Barbara. It would not pay us to buy more equipment for just one week, so the extras slept on wild oat hay in the canyon.

Then there was bad weather again, so the company worked at Orizaba Flats. The captain of the *Alice,* not used to our weather, refused to take his boat out of the harbor, so the company walked the three miles to location and back over sheep trails, up and down canyons and through the pine forest. Coming home some got lost, and when they failed to show up the camp men would take lanterns to light their way and guns to signal, and guide them back to camp. One night the technical director took a notion he would walk back by a new trail. When he hadn't appeared by ten o'clock, the men started out and found him three miles beyond location sitting beside a huge bonfire. The wind was blowing and they asked him if he wasn't afraid of burning up the island; he said he hadn't thought of that, but he didn't intend to freeze to death. It took them half the night to put out the fire and they brought him back to camp at three in the morning.

One day at luncheon there was a terrible bang against the cliff that shook the building. Everyone jumped and yelled, "What was that?" thinking that the dining room was sliding down into the ocean. It was the ground swell at the turn of the tide, hitting the bank with such force that it shook the building and the spray came up on the windows like hail. The company said that if anyone had told them they'd see a sight like that, they wouldn't have believed it. It would have made a fine shot for their film.

Ira had gone to town that day in the *Sea Wolf* to take in exposed film for the studio and bring back fresh film. All day we watched the storm in the channel. The ocean was nothing but huge green combers and the wind howled at forty miles an hour. We watched for the *Sea Wolf*'s riding lights all evening but they didn't appear, so we all turned in. My heart was weary, and I lay awake listening to the wind and pounding swells. Then I heard a boat whistle. As I jumped out of bed and stuck my head out the window, there were three more blasts and five lighter ones, Ira's signal for letting me know how many people he had on board. That meant that tonight he had thirty-five, and every bed was taken; we already had fifty in the Pollard Company.

I dressed in a hurry. The cook and I hustled to the kitchen, lit four dozen lanterns, started the wood range and put over three great pots of coffee. Then I went to meet the crowd. It was the Fox film company, and the assistant director said he had previously arranged with Ira to use the island, but they had only decided the day before to come now. They had been on Catalina Island and a fishing village they had built there had blown down three times. I thought, you jumped out of the frying pan into the fire. Their picture was called "Battle of Hearts" and had William Farnum as leading man. Also in the party were Mrs. Oscar Apfel, the director's wife, and Mrs. De Wolf Hopper; they were the only two women.

My mind was racing, and I kept thinking, My God! Where will I put all these people? William Farnum was one of the leading actors of the day, and all the people would be soaked and freezing. They must be taken care of. I moved the Pollard company's prop man out of his tent so that the ladies would have a place at least. Fortunately, Ira had brought along another boat loaded with tents, cots and groceries.

Two skiff loads of men were landed, and you never saw such a sight. There was not a dry stitch on them; the water oozed out of their clothes and made pools on the floor. They weren't in the best of humor, and you couldn't blame them. Then the ladies came ashore, as wet as the men but much more cheerful. There was not a grumble out of them. In my cabin they changed from their wet silk underclothes into my cotton underwear, put on my bungalow aprons, and thanked me, saying they knew they had come over unexpectedly.

I begged, borrowed, and finally stole all the dry clothes of the Pollard company, and the men went into the dining room to change from wet to dry. Then with the help of the ladies I cooked ham, eggs, toast and coffee, served with pears and cake. The company sat down to supper and talked about the terrible trip they had coming over. Meanwhile the bedding and groceries were unloaded and a tent put up for William Farnum. After supper, mattresses were spread on the tables in the dining room, on the benches pulled together, and even on the floor. The thirty-five were finally bedded down and at three in the morning the camp was quiet again.

While I was helping to cook breakfast for the crowd of nearly ninety the next morning, Ira went off to Santa Barbara for lumber and more men to build a wreck for a shipwreck scene to be filmed at Mussel Rock. The weather was still very rough, and while the wreck was being towed through the passage between Orizaba Rock and the beach, it caught on the rock and couldn't be budged. The scenes were taken there, and almost everyone taking part was washed overboard several times and nearly drowned.

The weather continued to be bad, and the two companies did not mix well. There seemed to be two icebergs in camp. One day at lunch, Miss Fischer held her water glass up high and, speaking so loud everyone could hear her, said, "What is the matter with the water? It looks cloudy and tastes funny."

The waiter came into the kitchen with it and said, "Mrs. Eaton, what *is* the matter with the water?" I agreed that it did look funny. He said, "Miss Fischer says the Fox company put something in the water for spite, but I know they didn't, for we all drink the same water from the spring." I told him to go on with the dinner, then sent a man down to the spring to look.

Back from the spring, the camp man said, "Mrs. Eaton, I hate to tell you, but the twenty extras from the Pollard company took their Sunday bath in the spring, with plenty of yellow soap."

I said, "And with a whole ocean at our front door!" Well, after dinner the spring and water tank were emptied and scrubbed. We didn't have a drop of water until it filled again, late in the afternoon.

The following week the Pollard company finished "Pearls of Paradise" after forty days of work, and left camp. We cleaned the tents and made them up fresh again for the Fox company, who could now move out of the dining room. With all the inconveniences, they were a jolly lot.

Since they worked like Trojans all through their stay, the night before they left camp Ira bought ten gallons of the island's riesling wine at the Ranch and treated the company. They drank to their hearts' content, but there was no disorder.

They were as fine a bunch of troupers as I ever had the pleasure of catering to.

We always had one or more men working for us to help out around the camp. Like fishing partners, each camp man would come and go, working for us off and on over the years. One of these camp men was Wes Thompson, who had driven me to the wharf for my first visit to the island. He was a grand-nephew of the Captain Thompson in the book *Two Years Before the Mast*.

Toward the end of August, 1916, we had to go to town one morning to pick up a party who were to camp on the island. Leaving the table set and covered and the potatoes in the oven ready for baking, I told Wes to start dinner as soon as he saw the boat coming back from town, for the crowd would be hungry. Ira asked me to leave the storeroom keys with Wes, so that he would know we trusted him with the camp supplies. In the storeroom were five gallons of dago red, a gallon of whiskey, and a couple of cases of beer. We both knew Wes had a drinking problem, and by giving him an allowance every day I could keep him almost sober. But I gave the keys to Wes and hoped everything would be all right. As we left I told him to keep the doors to the storeroom locked or the mice would get into the bedding and ruin it.

The following day around noon we turned to Pelican with a party of fifteen people. As we entered the harbor I had a feeling of panic; something was terribly wrong. The storeroom door was wide open, and Wes was not at the landing to meet us with the skiff. I looked at Ira and he looked at me. He said, "Stay aboard while I take the crew and go ashore." They rowed ashore, and we could hear them calling out to Wes. Then they went down the path to the canyon and heard the fox terrier barking. Soon they found Wes. He had fallen over the cliff onto the canyon floor and was dead. Ira covered the body and then returned to the *Sea Wolf* to bring us ashore.

The next day, Wes had his last ride across the channel when his body was taken back to Santa Barbara on the *Gussie M.* for an inquest. Ira stayed in town for a week to look for someone to take Wes's place as camp man, and I was left alone in camp. Every time I went down into the canyon, and especially at night, I had the feeling Wes was hovering around saying, "If you hadn't left the keys, this would not have happened."

Vera had become very fond of Wes and missed him greatly. He had always had a bedtime story to tell her of his early days as a stagecoach driver in the Yosemite and Yellowstone Parks when cars were not allowed. He had been a guide to Stewart Edward White, who used him as a character in the book *The Mountains*. He had also driven the first mule team down State Street in Santa Barbara, long before it was paved. He had been with us for three years and was 65 years old when he was killed.

The Santa Cruz Island Company had been having trouble with hunters and boatmen killing their livestock. In September 1917, they officially closed the island to all visitors other than those who made reservations with us. With this responsibility on us, Ira made sure that either he or one of his men would always act as guide for any wild boar hunting parties. We never had any problems with the hunters; people coming to our camp seemed to realize they were enjoying private property and respected the privilege. This did not always apply to boaters who landed on the island. The Company found it necessary to employ riders to patrol the island, and because of its size and ruggedness this was a very difficult business. The superintendent at that time was Duncan Swain, and he was later replaced by Clifford McElrath.

In this same year, the government asked for bids to lease Middle and West Anacapa Island for a five-year period. Ira bid on it and won. He leased the island for ten dollars per month for the next five years, and would buy the old buildings and the sheep on the island from the present lessee for two thousand dollars, payable at shearing time. It sounded awfully exciting that we were going to be raising sheep, but with all the activities at Pelican Bay Ira would have to depend on Dan Bethune, a Canadian sheepherder who was going to take care of them for us.

Colis Vasquez had long ago explained to me that Anacapa means "ever changing, never the same"; it had always been noted for its mirages. Sometimes it looked as if it was resting on the water, and other times it seemed to be floating in the air. Sometimes it seemed like such a small group of rocks, and then it would change to look like a giant rock. The island was covered with ice plant which contained enough moisture, along with the morning dew, to supply the sheep with water. At low tide there was a spring that supplied the caretaker with his drinking water, but water had to be carried in during stormy weather.

That winter some Austrian fishermen, good friends of Ira's, stopped at Anacapa to visit with the caretaker, filled him with dago red, and stole ninety of our sheep. Those that were left we had sheared so we were able to pay the two thousand dollars. The wool sold for the highest price on the market, sixty cents a pound, for it was the cleanest wool from any of the islands. That venture ended our sheep raising, but Ira leased Anacapa again in 1922. He rented space to fishermen and also took parties to visit the island.

Our business continued to grow so much that Ira, working as he could over a period of time, replaced all the tents with small cabins, twelve by fourteen feet, built from split shakes. There were five cabins side by side out on the point and then four more way out on the tip of the point. The windows could be left open in summer for the view of the bay, and shuttered in winter to keep out the wind and rain. Each cabin had blue and white rag rugs, a dressing table made of two fruit boxes nailed together, with a skirt of white muslin bordered in gingham, and matching curtains. They looked so neat and clean. The hills surrounding the camp were covered with wild oats, and in the winter and spring there were so many different shades of green in the grass and trees. The whitewashed cabins really stood out, making a beautiful sight as one approached Pelican Bay.

Later on, water was piped out to the cabins and flush toilets were built. A second stove was added in the kitchen, which made my cooking so much easier. Finally, the dining room was extended ninety feet along the bluff, open to the bay on one side and to the hills on the other. This building also had removable shutters. At the far end of the dining room a sturdy rock fireplace was built. We put in comfortable camp and easy chairs, and a table with magazines as well as card tables.

Ira also built a pigeon coop and we began to raise carrier pigeons. Whenever Ira went to town he would take one of the birds with him. Then, when a party chartered his boat for a trip to the island, he would send a message back by carrier pigeon to let me know who and how many were coming.

We had plenty of water, especially when there were not too many people in camp, so Ira spaded a large patch of ground near the water tank and we planted a vegetable garden, which did nicely. Mr. Hazard gave us one white and eleven black fig trees, and we put them in near the vegetable garden. To set off our white cabins, I planted white marguerite daisies all along the trail from the kitchen out to the point. As I was setting out the slips, a fisherman came into the bay with news that the World War was over; the Armistice had been signed November 11, 1918.

To keep the dirt and rocks from slipping, I brought ice plant from the garden of Dr. Doremus on East Anapamu Street and planted it above the trails. When the rains were late that winter, the sheep came down from the hills and ate all my plants. In the spring I replanted, and protected the plants with piles of rocks. They did well and the sheep did not uproot them again.

We had only two hours' notice to prepare for the movie company making "Adam and Eve." The lead was a sixteen-year-old girl, accompanied by her mother. As we left Santa Barbara with the company of thirty-five on board, we headed into a heavy northwester, and I asked Ira why the company didn't stay in town overnight. He said they didn't want to pay for rooms and wanted to get on location as soon as possible.

After what seemed like an endless trip, we arrived at Pelican Bay Camp well after dark. As we were rowing toward the rock, we heard something dropping into the bay around the skiff. In the kitchen door stood Scotty, the camp man, throwing plate after plate into the water. Ira said, "I'll bet the kitchen is like a pigpen—Scotty is throwing the dirty plates out before the Missus gets ashore," and shouted to him to cut that out.

Two men, up to their waists in water, helped us out of the skiff. Up in the kitchen there wasn't a stick of kindling to start a fire. The men chopped up the benches, and soon we had a roaring fire going to thaw people out. The following morning at breakfast the men were singing, whistling and making jokes, the night before forgotten. Ira opened the kitchen door, and great draughts of delicious air blew in from the bay. Vera and I stood beside him looking out; the rocks and kelp were covered with pelicans and gulls, our blue heron standing guard. In spite of all the countless trips we had made to this island, it was still hard to believe that the ocean could be so rough one day and so calm the next.

The reason the company wanted to film on the island was that they wouldn't be disturbed here while taking scenes of a young girl with nothing on but a fig leaf. But when the scene was ready to be shot, they decided on no fig leaf, although we had ten fig trees growing in camp. They borrowed Ira's old-fashioned razor and the mother did the job. I thought it was dreadful to pose in the nude, but the mother said that the studio would give the girl better parts later on. To her it sounded just fine.

In May of 1919, Ira had a telephone call to go to the Paramount Studios in Hollywood to make arrangements to cater to a moving picture company which was planning to come to the islands to make a picture called "Male and Female." There would be about sixty people in the company.

Twelve carpenters and laborers came out first to get the location ready. They stayed in the tents. The cabins would be used by the main company when they arrived. We called this "Millionaires' Row." Most of the scenes were to be taken at Fry's Harbor, which was turned into a South Sea Island. Two large barges were towed from San Pedro, loaded with three dozen big palms, coconut trees, banana trees loaded with fruit, rose bushes, and the like. I was pleased to see that the men had come dressed for this kind of heavy work in boots, old working clothes, and bandanna handkerchiefs. Breakfast was at six sharp, and they worked until seven-thirty at night, getting overtime for every hour over eight hours. I did the cooking myself, with a waiter and dish washer to help. We had plenty to eat—homemade bread, pie, cake, good soup, abalone chowder, fritters, steaks and stewed mussels.

The crew were allowed Sundays off; some stayed to work and others went back to Hollywood. On one trip to Hollywood, the head carpenter decided to offer some of the other men at the studio a chance to go camping on the island. But they told him they were not going up there to work all hours, sleep on a pile of wild oat hay, and be fed "rock soup." Well, the head carpenter had been at the island three weeks already and knew about the food and beds, so he asked how they had come to know the island was like that. They said one of the carpenters had come in the Saturday before and told them what a rotten deal the men had up there. It turned out that this carpenter wanted to get all the overtime he could, and figured if he discouraged the other carpenters they would not go to the island. But they were ordered to pack their tools and go or else leave the studio. One in particular was glad he did, for he made enough money to furnish a six-room bungalow.

One Sunday morning, word came that the main company was on its way in the yacht *Skidbladner*. That day the wind started to blow and the swells came up. It was eight o'clock at night when they finally arrived, having bucked the sea all the way from San Pedro; at times the yacht's masts touched the waves when those swells hit her broadside.

When the crowd arrived in the kitchen they were a sorry mess. They looked as if they had just had shower baths, they were so wet and cold, and seasick besides. I had several large pots of coffee ready for them. In the party were Gloria Swanson, Lila Lee, Mildred Reardon, Thomas Meighan, Jennie

McPherson, Jesse Lasky, Cecil B. DeMille, Frank Garbutt, Major Ian Hay, Sam Woods, and that grand old man of the movies, Theodore Roberts.

The female stars of the company huddled together on the kitchen bench, all looking like drowned rats. One of them said with a smile, "Well, we're all sisters under the skin tonight." And when she said "tonight" it was the truth, for the next day when they were all over their seasickness, they certainly did not feel or act like sisters. Some of the men were stretched out on the floor, too sick to move. If we stepped on them in our mad rush around the kitchen trying to get supper, they didn't care.

When everyone had been served supper they felt much better. No matter how seasick they had been, none of them passed up the meal, and the plates all came back empty. They then went to bed but not to sleep, for the wind howled so much they thought the cabins would be blown off the cliff before morning, with them inside. And the waves hit up against the rocks with a deafening noise.

We were working in the kitchen by lamplight when there was a knock at the door. A short, plump man with a pleasant smile came in with a little box. "Mother," he said—this was what all the members of the company called me; Ira was known as "Cap"—"I thought we were coming to a desert island and didn't know how we would fare for food, so I brought some along. But you seem to have the best in the land. Please take these groceries—there's cheese, jelly, and a pound of coffee." I thanked him but said I already had plenty of coffee. He suggested I use it for the stars' table, and added that he was Max Fisher.

There were ten at the stars' table. The following morning I told their waiter that their coffee was a gift from Max Fisher, and they were so pleased. After breakfast two of the men in the cast, Billy Burton and Raymond Hatton, came to the kitchen door asking if there was a cleaning establishment on the island. I had a very humorous Spanish man working for me, and he said, "Right this way, gentlemen," taking the old hand irons from the shelf and putting them on the stove to heat. "When these irons get hot I'll get the ironing board for you, and that is your cleaning establishment. On this island it is every man for himself." And when the irons were hot, those actors did a perfectly good job of pressing their clothes.

Another boat, the *Salt,* came into the harbor that morning from San Pedro. The company doctor was supposed to be on this boat, along with half a dozen goats and some parrots. My helper Lonny and I were making sandwiches to pack for lunch when two young men came to stand in the doorway. Lonny stopped buttering bread to say, "Mister, are you the doctor of this company?" One of them said he was; why? "This is a fine company to bring over sixty people in that yacht in a terrible storm and not a doctor aboard," Lonny told him. "All I have to say is that they seem to think more of their cattle actors than the human ones. Have they got a veterinary surgeon looking after their actors?" That got to be a standing joke while the company was there.

Storms and seasickness all forgotten, the company worked hard. The stars continued to drink coffee from Max Fisher's one-pound can. I sometimes heard them say, "Oh, yes, Mrs. Eaton makes special coffee for our table." Actually we poured their coffee into a special percolator from the large agate pots we made it in.

One day the third assistant came to me and said, "Gloria Swanson should have pure cream with her meals. She is not used to this condensed milk here. I've heard that there is a ranch further down where they have cows, and fresh cream can be had." Trying to be diplomatic, I said I would send the boat down every evening and have fresh cream brought up for Miss Swanson.

Every morning and evening after that, a special pitcher with a string tied around the handle was put in front of Miss Swanson. It contained the finest condensed milk diluted one third with water, and she thought it was cream from the Santa Cruz Island cows. A prominent yachtsman stopped at the island once and asked Miss Swanson to come aboard for lunch and coffee. She asked if he had fresh cream. When he said no, he used condensed milk, she thanked him kindly but refused, saying, "Mrs. Eaton has her boat make a special trip to the ranch every day to get fresh cream for me." (Later, I was invited to go through the studio in Hollywood when they were working on the lot, but Gloria Swanson wouldn't speak to me; the story of the cream and Max Fisher's coffee had gotten back to her.)

Every night, as soon as the tables were cleared after dinner, the stars started a card game. Any time Ira sat down to play, he always won. One evening he won seventy-five dollars from Theodore Roberts, and another time three hundred from the same table. After that they called him "The Sociable Landlord." When bedtime came, the lights flashed three times as a signal and the Ford motor was turned off for the night. Lanterns were hung around the camp so prowlers and spooners wouldn't fall off the cliff into the ocean or down into the canyon.

The actors caused some problems. A pail of water and clean towels were put in each cabin and tent every morning. The first of the stars to reach camp would send her colored maid to get the large galvanized washtub and perhaps four buckets of hot water from the kitchen. Then the maid went from cabin to cabin swiping all the pails of water to cool off the hot water, and taking what towels the star needed for bathing, hair drying and floor mats. When the rest of the company came back and wanted a bath to wash off the ocean grime that had accumulated through the day, there would be a howl. "Mother Eaton! What's the matter? We have no water, no towels!" There would be nothing to do but start all over again. Finally I had a large galvanized tank filled with water and a fire built under it, and that supplied hot water. We made buckets of the gallon cans the fruit and vegetables came in, and anyone could have all the water he needed if he carried his own bucket.

One evening there was a great fuss because Tommy Meighan had no water in his cabin. He made a special trip down to the kitchen to ask why I treated him like a stepchild. I asked what I had done now, and he said there was no water in his cabin to wash off his makeup. It *was* there, but it had been set at the left of the door instead of the right, and he hadn't seen it.

All through the company's stay at the camp, little Lila Lee was the life of the party. She was just a young, sweet girl of about sixteen, and everyone would go out of his way to do her a favor. As I remember, she wore black and white checked riding pants, a white shirt and boots. Gloria Swanson as a rule wore bungalow aprons similar to the ones I wore, which I thought was very sensible.

One evening Ira came over from Santa Barbara and said, "Margaret, who do you think wants to come to our camp for a rest? John Barrymore!"

"John Barrymore, the great actor?" I just couldn't imagine him coming over here. "Where will we put him? There are eighty people here already and every cot in the camp is occupied."

"That is just what I told him," said Ira, "and he said: 'If your cooks sleep on the kitchen floor, I can sleep on the rafters over their heads, and if I fall out during the night I will hit something soft.'"

Well, any man that would make that proposition I could find a bed for. I moved out Tommy Meighan's roommate to make room for our distinguished guest. The following evening when the boat arrived, Mr. Barrymore was aboard. He was so much interested in how Ira handled his crew unloading the baggage and the huge order of groceries that he didn't leave the boat until the job was all finished.

When he came into the dining room I met him at the door. He shook my hands with both of his and said, "Mrs. Captain, I am very happy to meet you." Those wonderful dark eyes of his looked not only at you but through you. My first impression of him never changed from that day so many years ago.

When the company went on location the following day, Mr. Barrymore went along. He was gracious to all the company and paid no more attention to the leads than to the others. He stayed around the camera crew and property men, watching how things were done. He ate his lunch on the sand with the rest of the company. When in camp, he went out of his way to be pleasant to the cook and his staff in the kitchen, always praising them and telling them how wonderful the food was. And what a marvelous appetite he had!

The rock at Orizaba was to be used in the picture—a replica of one half of the yacht *Skidbladner*, built by the carpenters, was to be wrecked there. The time came for the scene to be shot, and the *Sea Wolf* towed the make-believe yacht onto the rock with the stars and cast on it. Everything was in their favor, high tide and swells washing over the rock. There was wonderful water work done that afternoon. After supper that night, the head carpenter said, "If Cap didn't know his business about handling boats and had not had his surf men standing ready with their skiffs, I am here to tell you I would be short seven of my carpenters tonight."

The company finished the picture and left for Hollywood. Mr. Barrymore stayed for a week longer. Our boat the *Sea Wolf* was reserved, so we hired another boat to show Mr. Barrymore the different points of interest. I sent Vera, then thirteen years old, to act as a guide. She took him to the famous Painted Cave and Cueva Valdez, and they had lunch at Fry's Harbor. When the owners of the island heard that Mr. Barrymore was our guest, they sent a rider the seven miles over from their ranch with an invitation for him to have dinner with them. He sent back word that he would come the following day.

The next morning at eleven o'clock he started out for Prisoners' Harbor by boat; he insisted that Vera must go with him. A horse and sulky met them at the dock, and from there they rode up the creekbed to the Caires' home. When Vera got back, she couldn't wait to tell me about the trip:

The sulky driver was dressed up in blue jeans and a jumper, a red bandanna handkerchief around his neck, and a cowboy hat. He looked like a real cowboy. And when we got to the house, all the Caires were out to meet us because they had heard the sulky coming. I sort of won-

dered how they would take my being there, and they didn't look too
thrilled. I thought I could wait outside, but I was scared Mr. Barrymore
would go in and leave me there. He must have known how frightened I
was, because he took my arm and before I knew it we were all inside the
big house. Everyone seemed to talk to him at once, and some of the girls
said they had seen him in the play *Hamlet*. Mamma, I can't imagine Mr.
Barrymore being an actor; he doesn't act like those moving picture people. He is so real and nice to me and my dogs.

We stayed in the front room just a little while, and then went into the
dining room. It was so long, and there were so many people there! When
I saw that table and all those places, I wondered where they would make
me sit. I didn't think I would ever live through that meal if I couldn't sit
by Mr. Barrymore, but, thank goodness, they put me to his left. First we
had a fruit cocktail, then a wonderful salad, then a baby turkey for each
one of us, with all the trimmings; then apple pie and ice cream. And
guess what? I had some wine, and it was so good! All the children had
some, just like the grownups.

There were two maids who waited on the table, one on each side, all
dressed up in black with little white aprons with lace all around them,
and white lace cuffs, and the prettiest little white lace caps on their heads.
And I noticed when the maid passed the food to Mr. Barrymore, he
would look up at her and smile, and at the same time he tugged at her
apron a little. Maybe he thought she was frightened too.

Just wait until I go back to school and tell all the girls in my class that
I had dinner with Mr. Barrymore at the Caire ranch! And that I acted
as his guide around the island!

His vaction over, Mr. Barrymore said, "Mrs. Captain, you
will see me here again, as I expect to come often. I have had a
wonderful time on this beautiful island." Then he left for
Santa Barbara.

The *Sea Wolf* brought back a package for Vera, a present
from John Barrymore. It was a beautiful little sewing box
covered with blue flowered cretonne, and inside were little
compartments filled with tiny spools of thread, pins and
needles, a small pair of scissors and a thimble. Vera was very
anxious to get back to school to show her gift.

Ira needed to stay nearer the waterfront when he was in
town, and we started looking for another house. In 1919 we
bought a two bedroom house on West Gutierrez Street, moving
there from Father Eaton's cottage. Vera was in Intermediate
(Junior) High School now, and could walk home from school
for lunch. An elderly lady stayed with her in the house when

we were gone. It was a wonderful feeling to own our first home. When we were in town during the winter, I was able to have a few chickens, a flower garden, and a small vegetable garden.

One day in 1920 a man named Church came to see Ira and they talked for awhile in undertones. After the man had gone, Ira told me that a party of three men were forming a company to get bonded liquor into Santa Barbara. If Ira would put up the *Sea Wolf* to bring in the goods as his share, the others would put up a thousand dollars each, the profits to be divided evenly. But Ira said he would take one third of the liquor and do what he pleased with it. In those days there weren't many rum runners and I was told there was nothing to worry about; but if Ira were caught it would be terrible publicity for us, and probably the loss of everything we had.

The boat left for the north and I stayed in town to be on hand if anything went wrong. Before Ira left he cautioned me not to mention the nature of his trip and if any inquiries were made, to say he was out at the island. A week later, a friend telephoned, saying that a woman had called him to get word to Ira that the District Attorney's office knew the liquor was to be unloaded and to be careful. Thanking him, I wondered who the woman was. Ira had told me that only the bootleggers themselves and I knew about the load. When Ira came home I asked him about the message, but he just said there must have been a mistake. I didn't think so, and wondered who that woman was.

Now Ira had his share of the liquor to dispose of. Next morning going down State Street, he met a man named Nye who he knew was a bootlegger. Nye had many customers but no liquor, and didn't even have enough money to get his children's shoes soled. So the two formed an unwritten partnership, Ira to furnish the liquor and Nye to sell it. Things went along nicely and Nye disposed of the whole load; then another one was needed. When that one was sold, Nye and the man Church went into partnership and Ira was out for awhile. Was I glad! My mind was much easier without that to worry about.

Early one Sunday morning, we heard an engine in the bay and thought it was a fishing boat. But very soon there was a knock on the door and Ira got up. The Chief of Police served a search warrant on him to look over the camp for liquor or moonshine. So they climbed the hills and went down into the canyon, and Ira didn't even bother to go with them. When they came back we invited them to a good Sunday breakfast. They told Ira that there had been a complaint that Eaton was unloading bonded goods on the beaches at Santa Barbara and had the stuff at the Pelican Bay Camp. But now they were convinced that other boats waiting to unload had started the rumor to throw the officers off their track.

The following day a revenue cutter came into the bay and the men went through our camp, but found nothing. They said there had been rumors that moonshine was being made in large quantities and shipped south. I didn't tell them that if they went to a small canyon on the south side of the island, they would find two men with seven barrels going day and night, one sleeping while the other worked. The stuff they made was shipped to San Pedro where it was sold in the sporting houses of Los Angeles. One fellow made enough at this to buy a purse seiner and went to fish in Panama. The other squandered his share on wine, women, and song.

Prohibition was being enforced, and we kept hearing much about the money to be made in bootlegging. There were two men willing to go on shares with Ira making the stuff at the camp. But I talked him out of that notion—we had a sweet young girl going to school, and if he were caught making the stuff it would bring disgrace on us all. We were law-abiding people and I wanted to stay that way.

"All right," said Ira, "I won't have anything to do with making the stuff. But these two men are making it and will charter the *Sea Wolf* to haul it to town, because if I don't haul it someone else will. There's a ready market for all they can make. I'm loaning them the money and they will pay it back with interest, just like the bank."

That seemed a fair arrangement. The *Sea Wolf* brought

barrels to start the mash. Tons of the island's wine grapes were bought, as well as sacks of sugar, pounds of yeast, ten-gallon copper stills, and grub and blankets for the men. It would take ten or twelve days for the mash to run through the still; then it would be bottled in five-gallon demijohns. All this was done in a cave, and Ira was the only one who knew where it was. You could pass it and never see it, for the entrance was covered. The finished moonshine was loaded in the skiff, for at that time Ira was taking no chances with the *Sea Wolf*. It was unloaded in town between changes of cops and sold in Montecito for twenty-five dollars a demijohn. There would be ten demijohns in a load. This went on for awhile, then the men quit.

A group of Stanford students came to stay at Pelican Bay Camp and explored the island for relics of an ancient race of people. They found all sorts of skeletons of humans and sea elephants, as well as other animals; also they found wampum, shell beads, curious utensils, pipe cups and spear points.

While we were in town for a few days, the camp man left a live fire in a trash pile. During the night it was fanned into flames, and my storeroom with all the camp equipment was burned up in fourteen minutes. Charlie Hansen, a fisherman, was in the bay; he went up and started the pump and kept the hose on the kitchen. If it hadn't been for him, the whole ninety-foot building would have burned. We bought new equipment and started all over again.

One evening as the *Sea Wolf* was coming in with a movie crew from location, a Coast Guard cutter came into the bay from the south. Three men came ashore. One came to the kitchen where I was making apple dumplings and asked where the still was. I said I didn't know anything about a still, and I really didn't; as far as I knew Ira was out of the business. The man introduced himself as Major McReynolds and said they had come to search the camp. Ira went with them and as he went out the door, he said in an aside to me, "Get the still out of the camp man's shack up on the hill."

So I had the camp man get it and anchor it in the kelp. Then Ira and the Major came back from the cave. They had found barrels filled with mash, part of a still and some brandy. Well, they arrested Ira and gave him time to change his clothes and get a few things from the cabin. The Major stood guard. From the way he looked at me, I supposed he thought I would beg for mercy or something. Then Ira was taken to Los Angeles in the fastest car, where he hired Leo Youngworth as an attorney and pleaded not guilty.

Vera was fifteen at the time. She was a great favorite with her nature study teacher at school and was often called on to answer questions because she knew so much about the island. But when Ira was arrested, Vera came home just crushed. "Mamma, this afternoon in nature study class, my teacher just turned as cold as ice and never called on me to recite. I don't want to go back to school—I want to go back to the island with you."

I explained that it was no fault of Vera's that her father had been arrested; from the teacher's point of view I suppose it was a terrible crime, for it was the first arrest for bootlegging in Santa Barbara County.

The trial was not held for eighteen months, and Ira was acquitted since he was not responsible for other people landing on the beach and bootlegging. There had been no search warrant, either. Chief Wall issued a letter to all western officers asking them to destroy the fingerprints and photos of Ira. It was found out later that the camp man and the fishermen had been working together. Thinking that no one would use the cave, they took a chance. That chance cost us plenty.

In April 1921 we came to town to prepare for a party we were to take over to the island and went home to our house on Gutierrez Street. Ira happened to look over toward the Potter Hotel, which was a few blocks away, and exclaimed, "Look at that big cloud of smoke from the rear of the hotel!"

In a few minutes we saw flames leap from the roof. The hotel had had other fires, but nothing like this one—the flames shot two hundred feet into the air. There was a forty-mile-an-hour gale blowing from the northwest, and we knew the hotel was doomed.

The *Sea Wolf* was anchored right in front of the hotel. Ira, afraid that sparks might fall on the deck and canvas, hurried down to the wharf and moved the boat out to anchor in the kelp. All the boats were covered with ashes and cinders, and some damage had been done to the canvas. Men were guarding the wharf with wet gunny sacks to beat out small fires.

We walked down Chapala Street to get a better view of the fire, but couldn't get very close because of the intense heat. It was a sorry sight. The rare palms and other tropical trees were charred and burned. The guests had all been taken to the Arlington Hotel. In the evening the blaze was still enough to light the sky, and the whole town came down to see the last of the Potter Hotel which had been so much a part of Santa Barbara. Soon there was nothing left but ashes and memories.

In those days there was no protection for small boats at Santa Barbara, so whenever a storm came up the fishermen all went to anchor in the lee of the islands. In late January, 1923, a heavy storm was brewing, and all the boats left for the islands. Frank Nidever was in his boat alone, and when he hadn't returned in ten days all the boatmen of Santa Barbara went out to hunt for him. Every nook and cove around the island was searched, but he was never found.

Big Jerry decided to take a last look for Frank's body. He went to the island and picked up our camp man, Ike Newton, and our extra skiff. A week or so later, a body was found floating in the kelp, brought to Santa Barbara and identified as that of Ike Newton. Then a search party was formed to look for Big Jerry's body. It was found in the kelp with a seagull perched on it keeping guard. Ike and Jerry had apparently had engine trouble in a strong northwester and been dashed against the cliffs at Potato Harbor.

It was thought that Jerry had no relatives, but later it was found that he belonged to a prominent Philadelphia family.

Frank Nidever was a descendant of one of the most widely known and oldest seafaring families of the Pacific coast; his grandfather had sailed the coast of California before it became a state. Frank and Jerry were the two finest fishermen friends I had known.

In September 1923, Ira was on the wharf after a trip to Honda where six Navy ships had gone on the rocks, when a Morning Press reporter told him that a South American boat was on the rocks at San Miguel Island. The passengers, a million dollars in bullion, and the ship's papers had been taken to San Pedro. When Ira and the crew got back to camp some time later, he told me what had happened:

As there was nothing we could do up the coast where the Navy boats had been wrecked, I thought I should go see what could be salvaged at San Miguel. I went to Horace Sexton's shop and told him to grab some clothes and spare cash, that we were due for an outing and there might be some excitement. We left Santa Barbara just before sunset and came on the *Cuba* at midnight; she was easy to find for she was ablaze with lights. We couldn't get near her through the reef in the darkness, so I went to South Harbor to wait for daylight.

Looking through the fog, we could see a tent pitched on the beach. Leno the deckhand rowed us ashore, and there we found the captain of the *Cuba*, his third officer, and two stewards. I introduced myself and asked if we could be of any service, but the captain thought there wasn't much chance of saving his ship. "Young fellow," he said, "there is something unknown and sinister in the vicinity of San Miguel. Many times these rocks have taken their toll of ships and men who thought they were on the right course, but found out to their sorrow that they were on the wrong one."

The *Homer*, a freighter, had worked all night transferring bedding, dry coffee, and whatever else they thought worth saving. I noticed there was no guard on the ship and no anchor overboard—the *Cuba* was a derelict and at the mercy of anyone who would board her. When the *Homer* finished loading at nine o'clock, she received a wireless ordering her to go to San Francisco and saying that guards were on the way from San Pedro. So the captain and crew left on the *Homer*.

Well, no sooner was that boat out of sight than we made the *Sea Wolf* fast to the rail of the *Cuba* and started loading whatever took our fancy, expecting to see the guards any minute. After loading the dining room chairs, I found several packages of marijuana hidden in the piano; but I threw them overboard, because if there is anything I hate it is dope.

About that time, a water taxi came bouncing over the choppy sea toward the ship, and I told the boys that was a sign to load fast.

Horace Sexton continued the story for Ira:

There were three men on the water taxi, all with guns on their hips like real bad men. They held the taxi to the wreck with a boat hook and ordered us to put back all we had taken from the *Cuba*. Cap just said: "Keep loading, boys, keep loading." After using some of the choicest profanity I ever heard one of the guards threatened to shoot the first man who moved. He sure meant what he said, and believe me, I was scared. But Cap, perfectly calm, walked to the rail of the ship and said: "Mister, what right do you have to abuse us this way?"

The guard handed Cap a telegram which he read and handed back. Grinning, he told us to keep on loading. Now the guard let out such a string of curses, I thought he would surely shoot us. But Cap, still grinning, walked over to the rail again and said: "That telegram says you are to come here and guard the ship, Mister, and I figure that you haven't arrived yet."

As soon as the guard figured out what Cap meant, he jumped onto the deck of the *Cuba,* and Cap said: "O.K. boys, get aboard the *Sea Wolf.* The guard has arrived, and we are through." He told me to run forward and cast off the big two-inch hawser we had used to make the *Sea Wolf* fast to the ship.

The guard said: "Like hell you will—that line belongs to the Cuba."

Cap went up to him and said: "How can you prove it? One end is fastened to my *Sea Wolf*, and I say it's mine. By the way, are you fellows planning to spend the night on board the *Cuba*? With this heavy swell and the way the rivets are popping, I believe she will break in two before morning."

That gave the guards something to think about; they had not brought a skiff. So Cap made a deal with them, that he would put them and their gear ashore in our skiff if they would help us load the rest of the plunder from the deck of the *Cuba*. The groaning of the ship helped the guards to make up their minds, and after they had helped us load the stuff, they even cast off the hawser themselves and pulled it aboard the *Sea Wolf*.

Then Ira told me that the man with the water taxi was Marcelles, a Greek bootlegger who had often anchored in our bay. When the guards left the *Cuba,* his contract with them would be through, and he had volunteered to help Ira because things were quiet at San Pedro just then. Ira was to get half of whatever Marcelles took away from the wreck and sold.

I asked, "Ira, aren't you breaking the law?"

"Of course I'm not, Margaret. According to maritime law, when the guards leave the ship she is mine if I get there first, and I will."

When Ira went to town, I went with him. He found that Marcelles had brought a load from the *Cuba* and sold it at the wharf, but he refused to divide according to the arrangements. Ira realized he was being double-crossed. In no uncertain terms he told Marcelles where he could go, and dissolved the partnership on the spot.

The following morning Ira took a crew of five men and went out to the *Cuba*. They started to work when along came a purse seiner with Marcelles aboard. He asked why Ira was holding the ship, and Ira answered that he was there first and according to maritime law whoever finds property lost at sea or cast upon the shore is protected against third parties. Then Marcelles went into the pilot house and brought out a gun and threatened to shoot Ira. Leno ran into the pilot house of the *Sea Wolf*, brought out Ira's gun and said, "If there is going to be any shooting, I want to do my share." But the captain of the purse seiner said he didn't want any trouble, so he started his engine and left. When it was all over, Leno tried the gun and it was empty.

Ira packed the *Sea Wolf* full of mattresses, pillows, blue and white spreads, long red drapes from the dining room, tablecloths, napkins, all the copper steam-table pots, silver, and tons of coal. When the stuff was unloaded at our house on Gutierrez Street, the garage and yard looked like a second hand store.

Marcelles went back to San Pedro and said that Eaton had driven him off the ship with guns. Suddenly the papers were full of news about pirates salvaging the *Cuba*. Lloyd's of London asked the Federal Government to intervene as the ship was rightfully theirs. Two men came to the house and asked for Captain Eaton and showed me their badges. I asked them into the kitchen, for the house was filled with salvage. Just then Ira came in, smiling. When I introduced him, the older man said, "Why, Captain Eaton, we expected to meet a big six-footer. You look quite harmless."

Ira showed them over the place and they asked him if he had brought any liquor or drugs from the *Cuba*. He said he certainly had not; Marcelles had taken some drugs and sold them to a drugstore on lower State Street. Then the older man said that Ira had not declared his salvage to customs, and as there was no customs house in Santa Barbara he should have notified the sheriff. There would be a fine of forty dollars, to be paid to the customs house in San Pedro. So Ira put Leno in charge of the *Sea Wolf* and left for San Pedro, thinking that everything was settled.

But the next afternoon two very nice young men came to the house, showed me their badges, and searched the house for liquor or drugs off the ship. When they finished, they said neither Vera or I were to leave the house until they told us we could. Then they wanted to search the *Sea Wolf,* so Leno took them through everything. The boat was loaded with bathtubs, washbasins, and lots of other salvage. The men put the government seal on the hatch and cabin doors and told Leno not to move the boat.

The next morning, they seemed relieved to see their two prisoners still in place. In the afternoon Ira got home from San Pedro and showed them his receipts from the customs house, the *Sea Wolf* was released again and all was well. I breathed a sigh of relief after having been a federal prisoner for a day. Then Ira left for the wreck again.

Two days later, three men came to the door. One of them introduced himself as an agent for Lloyd's of London and said he was going to have Ira arrested for piracy of the seas, because he had looted the ship in spite of the guards. I was just telling them what really happened when Ira stepped into the kitchen. The agent then began to bulldoze Ira, who stood his ground and said, "Gentlemen, now you listen to me. I have just as much right to talk as you have."

Then he told the whole story from start to finish, how the

Homer had taken everything of real value, and how Lloyd's own guards had sold a tug full of painted chains from the ship, as well as helping Ira to load the *Sea Wolf*. Then Ira laughed and said that in a way he couldn't blame the agents for coming to get him—the papers had been full of how Captain Eaton had made ten thousand dollars off the salvage. That had been Marcelles' doing.

So then the agent said that Lloyd's would try to sell the ship as it was and where it was. The bids were advertised and Ira was the highest bidder, at eight hundred dollars. Then he went to San Pedro and registered as owner and master of the *Cuba*. When he went out to the wreck again he took most of the young fellows of Montecito along for the trip, and they all came back loaded with souvenirs.

Then Ira took a crew out to salvage enough brass to pay the cost of the wreck, but the weather was so bad they could not work. He made a deal with some junk dealers to go halves and they worked for a couple of weeks. Ira brought a load of stuff to ship to Los Angeles and went back to the wreck again.

One morning he could tell by the ground swells that there was going to be a heavy wind storm, so he had the men build a raft and on it they loaded all the junk stacked on the deck of the *Cuba*. Then they towed the raft to shore and pulled it high up on the beach. That night they slept on the *Sea Wolf*. When they got up in the morning, the *Cuba*'s pilot house had been swept away by the seas and she had sunk. The *Sea Wolf* was loaded with all the stuff from the raft until her scuppers were awash, and they headed back for town. Ira and the men were glad when they passed the rip tide between San Miguel and Santa Rosa and knew they were safe.

Throughout the 1920's, the island remained a popular location for filming motion pictures. Henry Otto, who had made "Sirens of the Sea" on the island in 1917, returned to make several more pictures—"Temple of Venus" and others. He always had diving girls, sometimes as many as eighty in a picture. The casts included Billie Dove, Mary Philbin, Jack Mulhall, David Butler and William Boyd. Marian Nixon and

Alice Day, just turned sixteen, were the sweetest girls in camp. When they weren't working, they wore blue jeans.

In 1924 we catered to the movie company making "Peter Pan." Herbert Brenon, the director, was a man of many moods, hard to understand, and completely wrapped up in himself. The leading lady was Betty Bronson, who was a very young girl, but for being temperamental she beat anyone who had hit the island. When she arrived at camp, she expected to be met by a brass band. Only a few months back, she had been working as an extra in the company; now all the extras knew they had better keep out of her way. Also in the company were Mary Brian, Theodore Roberts, Anna May Wong, and James Wong Howe.

All told, there were one hundred people, and half of them were diving girls. Valdez Harbor and Painted Cave were used as locations. Mr. Brenon overruled the company doctor when it came to the diving girls—he worked them in rough or mild weather, diving to represent porpoises with their bodies painted silver, or on the beaches posing as mermaids. They had long wigs hanging down to their waists, and they had to be carried out of the water to rest as they couldn't move with the tight mermaid tail fastened from the hips down.

While they were there I had to go into town for groceries one day, and Ira stayed in camp. When I started back there was a gale blowing. With sails all set, the *Sea Wolf* was straining from the wind, and it was a wonderful feeling as she rose to the top of the long swells. Every little while her rail would go under water, and she bucked and pitched like a thing possessed. She didn't seem to make much headway against the mountains of green water. Far above in the sunshine flew an airplane piloted by Earle Ovington, on its way to make the first landing at Scorpion Harbor.

Eventually we felt the joy and relief of coming to anchorage at Pelican Bay. As I came down from the pilot house, the movie men who had gone along with us came out of the cabin and heaved up all they had eaten for weeks. On account of the storm, the company had not been working and they watched us from the shore, the men having bet against the women that I wouldn't come across the channel in that weather. The girls yelled, "Hurrah, hurrah, here comes Mother home again!" Mother looked a sorry sight as she landed, wet from head to toe. They were all glad to see me, especially the girls who had won the bet, but they had been having a good time watching Ira and Anna May Wong and a few others shoot craps until the small hours of the morning.

Anna May was the most popular one of the lot. She was such a good sport you felt you should do anything to make things pleasant for her. One morning Mr. Brenon, feeling irritable, said that anyone not coming to breakfast on time would have to go without. Anna May didn't have to go to work until afternoon, so we let her slip into the kitchen and eat at the help's table.

I was appointed Camp Mother, and every night at ten o'clock it was my job to take a flashlight and go to each tent to see that the girls were in bed. I'd poke the flashlight inside the tent flap and call, "In bed, girls?" There was always someone to answer "Yes, Mother." If a man was also in the tent, that was none of my business.

At Halloween a great party was put on, and everyone wore a costume. Mr. Brenon was dressed to represent Neptune, and the company escorted him from his cabin to the dining room, using every agate basin and soup spoon in camp to give him a serenade. He was declared "King of Santa Cruz Island" for the night and everyone paid him homage. Then the floor was cleared for dancing and everyone enjoyed themselves for hours. There was some excitement when the *Sea Wolf* arrived on a special trip from Santa Barbara to bring Mr. Brenon a telegram from headquarters in Hollywood, complaining about the delay with the work and the extra expense, and asking for an immediate reply. But it was such a beautiful moonlit night, why bother about business? So the fun went merrily on until daylight, and then the boat took back the answer. We had to throw the washbasins over the bank—there wasn't an inch of agate left on them, they had taken such a beating.

One day I made a trip to town for supplies, taking two of the company men who were going to see their dentist in Hollywood. The following afternoon, they got on the boat with a truckload of film packed in deep cartons. Back at the camp, Little Nick the camp man seemed in a big hurry to get me ashore. Later, Leno, who had taken us over in the boat, came to me and said: "Mrs. Eaton, I'm mad clean through. What do you think was in those boxes we brought over? Not film, but Gordon's Gin! Those men didn't make the trip to see their dentist at all. Suppose on the way a cutter had stopped us— we would have been arrested, lost the boat, and wouldn't have known a thing about the deal. They gave Nick ten dollars to unload it, and I didn't get a thing. But the funny part about it is that the police chief, Captain Newman, was on the wharf and watched us load it without realizing it. I think the joke is on him as well as on us."

Mr. Brenon was told about the liquor; he had one of the cases brought up and smashed the bottles, and sent the two men back to Hollywood. They went to the Federal Office and reported that Eaton had brought the liquor to the island and sold it to the movie people to be taken back to Hollywood.

At dinner the next night, very few came to the dining room. Soon one of the girls came to me and said, "Mother, you're wanted up in the girls' cabin." I asked where the doctor and nurse were, and she said the girls wanted me instead. Out to the cabin I went; it held eight cots and a girl was on each one, crying. They had been into the remaining gin. As I tried to soothe them, they told me how hard Mr. Brenon worked them regardless of the nurse's and doctor's orders. Tired out from battling the surf all day, they were becoming irrational. I sent for Mr. Brenon and he sized up the situation; he was very nice to them and asked what he could do. One girl covered her face with her hands and said she had lost her wig. She knew she had swallowed it and she didn't have the money to pay the company the thirty-five dollars for it. He patted her on the shoulder and told her the wig would be charged to the company. Well, they finally slept it off.

A day or two later, another heavy northwester made loading and unloading at Valdez Harbor very risky. After several skiffs had been dumped in the breakers, work was declared off. The speedboat with Mr. Brenon and a few others, including Vera (who went on location every day in charge of the lunches), came back to camp. They could not unload the men from the pirate ship *Jolly Roger* onto the passenger boats because of the high swells. The boats *Ace* and *Salt* were going to tow the *Jolly Roger* down to Pelican Bay, where they would have calmer water to unload and anchor the boat until the storm was over.

We waited and waited, but no boats came. Then at suppertime we saw the three boats about a mile from shore in what we call "Windy Lane" where the wind and swell are strongest. They were going past Pelican Bay and we kept waiting for them to turn in, but they slowly continued on and we knew something was wrong. The *Ace* came into the bay and the captain told us the pirate ship was drifting with most of the company aboard. Neither the *Ace* or the *Salt* had gear strong enough to hold and guide her. The captain of Mr. Brenon's speedboat pulled out of the bay and made his way through the rough seas to the drifting boat, but because of the rolling of the *Jolly Roger* was unable to get close enough to take any of the people off. We watched the boat drifting toward the rocks at Potato Harbor and there was nothing any of us could do to help.

Then the captain of the speedboat saw a steamer out in the channel and went out to see if he could get help. As we watched, the steamer changed course and headed toward the drifting pirate ship. When she was close enough the crew threw a holding rope to the *Ace,* and the men on the *Ace* passed the rope on to the *Jolly Roger*. When the connection was made, the steamer was able to tow the pirate ship away from the rocks. The *Ace* then took over the job of towing the movie ship to Scorpion Anchorage to get out of the storm. By four in the morning, the first group of men arrived in camp, tired but so happy to be alive and safe.

Early in 1925 Ira entered into an arrangement to bring a new fast boat to Santa Barbara. They had her remodeled in San Francisco to carry passengers. Named the *Miss Santa Barbara,* she was registered in Ira's name and he was to have one-half interest in her. She was sixty-four feet long, beautifully trim and fast, and could make it to the island in sixty minutes; it took the *Sea Wolf* three hours. With this boat, charter parties could have much more fishing time at the islands before having to head home. The *Miss Santa Barbara* was also to be used in unloading bonded liquor from the large ships in the channel, and Ira was to receive fifty cents a case delivered to Santa Barbara.

While we were in San Francisco waiting for the work on the *Miss Santa Barbara* to be finished, the news reached us that Santa Barbara had been wrecked by an earthquake, a tidal wave had hit the waterfront and all the boats were beached. As soon as I could get a message through, I wired to Vera that I would would arrive on the first train. She was at the depot to meet me, and what a beautiful sight she was, since I didn't know how bad the damage really was. There had been no tidal wave, all the boats were safe, and my child was unharmed.

Father Eaton had been staying nights at our home on Gutierrez Street so that Vera would not be alone. Each morning he would get up very early, take the streetcar home and have breakfast with Mother Eaton. Vera would get herself ready for school. Father Eaton had already left when the earthquake hit. Feeling the shaking, Vera jumped out of bed and ran out into the front yard. She kept calling her puppy, who had been sleeping at her feet, but he was never found.

What a sight our house was! It had been jolted off its foundation pillars and was resting lopsided. All the furniture had slid to the low side; even the piano had moved across the room. What was left of my jams, jellies and dishes was on the kitchen floor, and the sink was filled with broken glass. A large picture had fallen down onto the bed where Vera had been sleeping, just seconds after she had jumped up. For weeks after the earthquake we slept out in our front yard, as so many other Santa Barbara people did.

When the *Miss Santa Barbara* was finished, Ira brought her down from San Francisco and had twice as much island business as before. Between parties, I had so much work to do at home. We bought the lot next door and had our house turned to face it. The small cottage on that lot and the small apartment in our back yard were both moved down our lot and turned to face next door. Now there were three houses, all facing west, and the lot next door could be used for parking. Our first home was converted into two apartments, and the little cottage in the center became our new home. With additions, it became a three-bedroom house with a fireplace and a step-down dining room and kitchen It was such a nice home, and so much of it was new. Then the little apartment was enlarged into two small bachelor apartments, so we had four rentals and a comfortable home. There was a lot of money, time and work in this project.

We were at home in town when Ira came in one day with a telegram from Holly (Gordon Hollingshead, the assistant to John Barrymore's director) saying to get ready, that Mr. Barrymore was coming to Pelican Bay for ten days; they would be in Santa Barbara the next day. In the morning Ira had a conference with Holly. There would be eight in the party. Ira was to load the *Sea Wolf* and have it alongside the wharf with the engine running, so when Mr. Barrymore arrived he would not have to wait one minute. Holly didn't know we had met Mr. Barrymore before, and Ira didn't tell him. We went uptown and I ordered enough groceries for fifteen people for fifteen days. We had good fun guessing how Holly would take the joke when he found out we had entertained the Great Barrymore before.

Sharp at one o'clock we were on the dock and the *Sea Wolf* was ready to go. Holly introduced Ira and me to Alan Crosland, Bess Meredyth, and the other members of the party; they were going to work on a scenario while on the island. We waited and waited. At three o'clock the engine was still run-

ning and everyone was fidgety Vera and I sat on the dock
enjoying ourselves watching the water. At last a car was seen
coming out on the wharf; Mr. Barrymore was arriving.

There was a general stir and buzz, but Vera and I never
stirred from our position. Then someone slapped me on the
back and a familiar voice said, "Hello there, Mother! And
here is my little island pilot."

"How are you, Mr. Barrymore?" I said, turning around,
and he shook hands with Vera and me.

"I'm fine; where is that son-of-a-gun husband of yours? I
want to say hello to the damned old pirate."

I called, "Ira, Mr. Barrymore is here and wants to talk to
you."

Patting me on the back again and putting his arm around
Vera, Mr. Barrymore said, "Mother, won't you ever learn to
call me 'John'?"

"It would just not seem right, for me to get so familiar," I
answered.

Ira came up the steps, and Mr. Barrymore's eyes just
lighted up, he was so happy to see him. He put his left hand on
Ira's arm when they shook hands. During all this, Holly
watched with astonishment, his mouth hanging open.

The three-hour trip across the channel was very rough. The
waves dashed over the deck of the *Sea Wolf* and through his
Deauville sandals, but the Great Barrymore was not bothered
by wet feet. His valet, an Englishman, was known simply as
"Limey." When talking he would move his forehead up and
down to emphasize his words and rub his hands together
humbly. He was the perfect servant. As he talked to me, he
looked over at his "master" with adoration.

"Another thing I'd be telling you, ma'am, is that my master's very fond of a pot of black tea. If he wants a pot of tea,
I drop everything and make haste to get it, because he does not
like to be kept waiting."

I told him that would be no problem. I would keep water
boiling all the time on my wood stove, and my blue earthen-

ware teapot nearby with tea in it. A pot of hot tea could then be ready at a moment's notice.

"Why, ma'am," said Limey, "you and me will get along nicely trying to please the master."

Looking over to where Mr. Barrymore was sitting, bareheaded, I said, "There isn't a finer man living, do you think, Limey?"

"No, ma'am, Mr. Barrymore is a very fine boss."

In Pelican Bay, Vera and I were the first ashore, so I could check with the camp man and give the cabins the once-over. This trip I found that Jackson had not made up the cabins since the last party had left—now, of all times! I was ready to explode, but did not have time to give him as big a piece of my mind as I wanted to; a cabin had to be made up in a hurry. I flew around like mad, made the bed and gave the room a lick and a promise. Just as I got everything in order, Limey was bringing Mr. Barrymore out to the cabin. I cooked a wonderful dinner in no time, and Vera waited table. Then we arranged for a nine o'clock breakfast of fruit, bacon and eggs, crisp toast, and good coffee.

The party settled into a regular routine of work on the scenario, stopping for dinner at seven; sometimes they worked until two or three in the morning. About the fifth day, Mr. Barrymore said he would like to go fishing. Cap was busy with other matters, so we hired a small boat, the *Miramar,* and loaned them all our fishing gear. When she dropped anchor in the bay, I knew we would have trouble with Augustine, the Italian skipper; he refused to be told what to do.

The first afternoon of fishing, I fixed Mr. Barrymore's lunch in a basket; I made tea in my blue teapot, wrapped it in a clean dishtowel and tucked it in the corner of the basket. I told Limey to be very careful of that teapot as it was given me by some friends who worked in a royal family in England. When I told Augustine that Mr. Barrymore was going fishing, he said, "No, no good fishing. Wind blowing like hell. Him no catch fish."

"Augustine," I said, "Mr. Barrymore is paying for this boat. If he wants to go fishing, that is his privilege."

"All right, we go. I fix him. Him no catch fish." When all were aboard, he took the *Miramar* out of the bay, got outside a bit and deliberately let her wallow in the trough of the sea. I could have murdered him and not felt any pangs about it.

After about an hour and a half the boat came back, and I asked Mr. Barrymore if he had had any luck. Smiling, he said it had been too rough outside. Later I asked Limey how the lunch was.

"Oh, fine, ma'am. Just as soon as we got into those seas I thought of your teapot. The basket of lunch slid out from under the bench and clear across the deck. I got down on my hands and knees and crawled all over that boat on my bloomin' belly to catch the teapot. It went from one side to the other with the swells, but I finally caught it. It hadn't spilled a drop, but the spout was broken off. I poured the master his tea and he drank it and said it was very good."

The second day of fishing was just the same. The third morning Mr. Barrymore wanted to visit the Painted Cave, but Augustine said, "No good. Can't get in. Too much swell. Too much wind."

"You'll go anyhow, Augustine," I said. "Sometimes if it's a little smooth, Cap backs his boat right into the entrance."

But he said, "You want me to lose boat? No, no. I take them up the coast, but no cave." That was that. Mr. Barrymore was very nice about it; he said the Italian probably didn't know where the cave was.

In the mornings Limey usually came down early and had a cup of coffee with the camp man in the kitchen. He was always very talkative, but one morning I noticed he didn't seem anxious to sit and talk. I paid no attention to that, but when Holly came through and said nothing more than "good morning" before he went into the dining room, I said to Jackson, "There seems to be something wrong this morning. Do you know anything about it?"

"Well," he said, "you'll find out sometime, so I might as well tell you now. Mr. Barrymore was almost burned to death last night."

"What!" That was all I could say.

"Yes, ma'am. When you came into the kitchen this morning, Limey was just telling me about it. When Mr. Barrymore went to bed last night, he fell asleep smoking a cigarette. It set fire to the bed and spread to the pillow, bedclothes and curtain before he woke up. About three o'clock this morning Limey heard the faucet running, hopped out of bed, threw his robe around him and went over to Mr. Barrymore's cabin. There in front of the cabin was Mr. Barrymore with all the bedding, trying to put out the fire under the faucet.

"Limey said, 'Sir, why didn't you call me?'

"Mr. Barrymore answered, 'I can manage this myself, Limey. You get back to your cabin and get your sleep. I'm all right here.'

"But Limey couldn't sleep, and about an hour later he went back to see if he was all right. Mr. Barrymore had crawled into the other twin bed, but the fire was still smouldering in the bedclothes. So Limey took them outside again and put out the fire properly. He said Mr. Barrymore was very sorry about it."

"Well," I said, "as long as Mr. Barrymore is not hurt or burned, the bedding won't matter—it can be replaced. Things like that are liable to happen anywhere."

The *Sea Wolf* arrived in the bay, and Cap and Mr. Barry-had a long confidential talk. I got out of the way; I never asked questions. Along about two o'clock in the morning, I heard the low rumbling motor of the speedboat, *Miss Santa Barbara,* on her way into the bay. Now I understood what the talk was about. The boat lay in the bay all day, and I thought, what a chance! If some Coast Guard cutter should come around, what a find they would have, for she was loaded down with liquor. The crew were very excited when they came ashore. Returning from Mexico, just as they were passing Anacapa Island seven shots were fired at them, but they never stopped. There was a very thick fog and they couldn't be seen. They would not have much chance if they were caught.

Cap took some members of the Barrymore party out to the boat and showed them through; their eyes opened when they saw so much good liquor at one time. Every bottle on board was bonded goods—there were two hundred cases of champagne, four hundred of Royal Stag whiskey in earthen crocks with handles, and the balance was Hennessey. Toward evening, the *Miss Santa Barbara* left for the coast. She shot out of the bay like lightning, on a direct course for the Rincon to unload. The next morning, a Santa Barbara yacht dropped into the harbor and picked up twenty-five cases of champagne.

After staying three weeks, the Barrymore party left for Santa Barbara. With much shaking of hands and waving of hats, and "Goodbye, Mother," they promised to see us again soon.

Later, the bootleggers on the *Miss Santa Barbara* reduced Ira's cut from fifty cents a case to thirty-five. He decided that he would not make enough money to risk the excitement of outrunning the Coast Guard. He turned his interest back to them in time—the *Miss Santa Barbara* was fired on by the Coast Guard near San Nicolas Island, and although she could outrun them, her stern was so badly damaged in trying to escape that she was beached.

Vera graduated from Santa Barbara High School in 1926, having done very well in school in spite of being gone to the island so much. I made her white graduation dress, and she got new white shoes; expectations were high over all the activities. But just before graduation, a moving picture company from Hollywood made reservations for Pelican Bay Camp, and both Ira and I had to be at the island and could not attend the ceremony. It was such a disappointment to us, and Vera graduated without any family member present. I know it must have been a very lonely time for her.

Soon after graduation, Vera's cousin Melva asked her to come to Hollywood for a visit. In her first letter to us, Vera said she was working at the studios with her cousin and loved the work; every day was different and exciting. Ira was furious. He didn't want her in Hollywood or working in motion pictures; he wanted her home in Santa Barbara. But Vera was a grown person now and able to make her own decisions, and she stayed in Hollywood.

Business remained as usual for Ira and me, catering to private parties and motion picture people at our Pelican Bay Camp. We also catered to the Dean, Thacher and Cate Schools, whose students came to the islands for years to study the bird and animal life and visit the caves. The boys of the Thacher School seemed to be more disciplined than the others, and when Mr. Thacher made arrangements for his boys to visit, we always closed the camp to any other visitors during their stay.

In December 1927, Vera wrote to say she would come to spend Christmas with us. Ira was late getting home from the islands because of a terrible southeaster, so I bought a Christmas tree myself and had it all decorated by the time he came home. The day before Christmas Vera drove up to the door loaded with presents for her father and me, and we sat up talking until after midnight. All through the night the wind howled and it rained and stormed, reminding me of the early days when I worried about the *Irene*. I couldn't sleep; I kept thinking about the *Sea Wolf* and wondering how she was riding.

Christmas morning came, and after the presents were opened Ira went to the wharf. When he returned, his face was grey and lifeless. He shook his head and said, "Margaret, as long as I've been in this boating game, I've never seen a storm like this one. The *Sea Wolf* has broken her moorings and is drifting slowly ashore."

I asked if there was any way we could save her, and he said no, he couldn't get out on the wharf from State Street. A barge loaded with rocks for the new breakwater had also broken her mooring, drifted toward the wharf, and hit it with such force that she went completely through it. It was impossible for anyone to get across that opening to any of the boats. The breakers were hitting the beach with such force as to make it impossible to launch a skiff. There was just nothing anyone could do.

We all went down and watched in panic, helpless. In our life together we had had many joys and disappointments; but the relationship between a man and his boat is beyond words to describe. I looked at Ira. The tears were rolling down his face. I had never seen him cry before. He stood facing the violent sea, knowing the destruction that was inevitable. We waited. The *Sea Wolf* moved directly but almost reluctantly toward the wharf, and after unmerciful pounding she finally gave up and just disappeared.

After the loss of the *Sea Wolf,* Ira rented the *Santa Cruz* schooner from the owners of the island and continued to take parties to Pelican Bay.

In 1928 Herbert Brenon came out to make "The Rescue" with Ronald Colman and Lili Damita in the leads and a company of a hundred and fifty people. We took care of one hundred at Pelican Bay, and the rest camped in the old adobe at Prisoners' Harbor, through the courtesy of the Caires. They set up a regular South Sea village and shot the picture there.

Of all the companies we had catered to, there was more dissention in this outfit than any other. No matter what you did, they couldn't be pleased. They thought our kitchen staff wasn't good enough for them, so the business manager suggested he bring up from Hollywood a full crew who were used to catering to these crowds on location. I consented to keep peace in the family. The first week or so everything was fine, but after that the staff got careless, and the members of the company complained. That was where I got my satisfaction—I just told them to take their troubles to the business manager.

Then there was no shower or bath room and, although the whole ocean was around the place, they were ready to pull out and go to Catalina Island unless they got one. So at a cost of eight hundred dollars a bath house was installed. But the first Saturday night it was finished, Mr. Brenon's secretary and friend came up from Hollywood and we had to put up a cot in the bath house, so the crowd were deprived of their baths again.

Lili Damita was a darned good sport and everyone in the company thought she was great. Her mother had come along with the company to look after her, and one night about midnight we heard the mother calling, "Lili, my Lili!" I thought I'd better go out and see if I could do anything, but Ira told me not to. He said that Lili was just out strolling with some young fellow, and they could settle their own affairs. Then we heard someone trying to quiet the mother, but it was a couple of hours before peace was restored.

The following morning, Mr. Brenon said the mother must go back to Hollywood, and that this was the last time anyone in his company need bring a chaperone, because as a rule they only made trouble. When the mother heard she was to be shipped back to Hollywood, she absolutely refused to go; she was staying here even if she had to stay in bed with no clothes on, which she did. But that had no effect on Mr. Brenon. He borrowed enough blankets to wrap around her, the prop men carried her to the skiff and put her aboard the *Freda,* and she was sent to Hollywood.

About this time, we heard that Mr. Barrymore had married the actress, Dolores Costello, and I thought, he's married now and will forget all about the camp and old friends. Then in 1930 there was a new arrival in the famous Barrymore family, and I said that would surely end his coming around the islands. Ira didn't think so; he said that Mr. Barrymore had a new steel boat, called the *Infanta,* which cost him about $59,000.

One afternoon at the Pelican Bay Camp, I was looking out from the point and saw a two-masted boat coming up from Potato Harbor. Soon she arrived in the bay and dropped anchor, and I could see the name *Infanta.* Well, I thought, the good old scout really has come back to see us again. I wondered if his beautiful wife was with him. He was standing on the stern waving both hands and pointing up the hill, I suppose to explain which house he lived in when he was here before. I went down the seventy-five steps to meet them. From the skiff, which was about halfway in from the boat, I heard, "Hello there, Mother. I am here at last!"

I called out a greeting to Mr. Barrymore, and if you ever saw happiness and joy on anyone's face, it was on his. All smiles, he just beamed like a big, overgrown boy, happy to get back to a place he had been longing for.

Then he hopped ashore and introduced his wife, and told her that everyone called me "Mother." Mr. and Mrs. Lionel Barrymore and a doctor and wife were also in the party. Coming up the steps, we reached the dining room and Mr. Barrymore said, "Dolores, here is where I had many a good drunk. Didn't I, Mother?"

Next he said, "Dolores, I want to show you where I almost burned up the bridal suite for Mrs. Eaton." We all went to the cabin. "I burned up the mattress, the curtains, the pillow, all the bedding and almost all the wall." Part of the wall was still black from the fire. He explained that everything in the cabin was off the ship *Cuba*; Cap had salvaged the heavy writing desk, leather chairs, the pink rugs, and the curtain rods with the German silver curtain rings from the captain's cabin.

Back at the dining room, Mr. Barrymore asked Jackson if he had a wild pig to cook for dinner for his crowd. He wanted them to have a meal ashore at our camp. Jackson took him out to the woodpile and showed him a black pig we were fattening. Dolores spoke up: "John, I would rather not eat that pig—it is a pet around here." We assured her it was not a pet but being raised for our dining room. Then she turned to the doctor's wife and said, "You wouldn't want to eat that pig, would you?"

The doctor's wife, being agreeable, said, "Certainly not."

Turning to me, Dolores said, "You know, Mrs. Eaton, neither Mr. Barrymore nor myself can eat any pets. We were at a hotel one time and they served us squabs; John looked at me and I looked at him, and I told the waiter to take them away, we could not eat them." I thought, if John had been alone, he would have eaten both of them.

Mr. Barrymore arranged for the group to have a dinner of mussels and abalones the following Thursday. Then he asked if I remembered once having two famous artists over here, "One a heavy-set woman, the other about the handsomest woman you ever laid eyes on, with dark flashing eyes; once you looked at her, she held your attention." I said I remembered them. "Well," he continued, "a couple of years ago I was in a cafe in Vienna and happened to sit at the same table with them. We struck up a conversation, and they said they had been to California, and while there they had visited a little out-of-the-way place on an island, a camp where everything was so peaceful and quiet and the food marvelous. Then I told them that I had been there also, and we talked about Pelican Bay. And on the strength of that conversation we all had such a good time."

After we had talked for awhile, the ladies wanted to go aboard the boat, and I went down to the rock to see them off safely. That was the last we saw of them.

Thursday Mr. Barrymore came in about one o'clock for his dinner of steamed mussel, abalone steak, salad, vegetables and homemade pumpkin pie. As we were eating, we saw the *Santa Cruz* schooner coming back from town. Not quite finished with his dinner, Mr. Barrymore said "I will take this and finish eating on my boat. I am going down to Prisoners' Harbor to see that King of Pirates, Cap Eaton; I want to talk to him about going hog hunting." So, wrapping what was left of his dinner in his napkin, he was off.

Cap took him hunting out back of the camp, and he came in with one two-hundred-pound hog and another of fifty pounds. Mr. Barrymore did not want them for food; he only wanted the sport of hunting. The *Infanta* lay in the harbor for a week, then left for the south.

(Several years later, about 1940, I saw Mr. Barrymore for the last time at a benefit performance in Los Angeles. I went backstage and said he probably didn't remember me; but he said at once, "Yes I do, you are Mother Eaton." And he put his arm around my shoulder in just the same old friendly way, and took time from all his other friends to ask about myself and Vera. This was about two years before his death.)

About 1933, Ira left the *Santa Cruz* schooner and one of the other men, Red Craine, took over. He got another boat after that, but nothing ever seemed to be the same after the loss of the *Sea Wolf*. Ira had started drinking, and I knew he was very unhappy. He seemed so lonely. When he was in town from the island, he would often stay aboard the boat at night. I really had little knowledge of his actions until there was a party to be taken to the island, and then he needed me to take care of the people at the camp.

Just when everything really seemed to be going to pieces in our personal life, in April 1937, we were notified that the island had been sold and we must remove all of our things immediately. Years earlier, the owners had had disagreements among themselves; the island had been divided among them by court order in 1924, giving the largest portion to the Caires. Still, this news came as a shock to us. We had known that the Park System was interested in buying Santa Cruz Island to be included in a Channel Islands Park,[5] but we had never thought the island would be sold to an individual who would want us off. It all happened so fast I just could not believe it, but there was nothing we could do to change the situation.

Finally the last load of beds, bedding, linen and dishes were removed from the Pelican Bay Camp. My beautiful big range had to be left behind, as we did not have enough help to move anything so heavy. Many other items were also left, and of course the buildings could not be removed.

After the last load, I never returned to the island. It was a ghost, and such a sad one, and I would spend the remainder of my life trying to forget it. Ira was lucky, in a way: he returned to his first love, commercial fishing. It was hard work, but he had always enjoyed doing it and he knew it well. This lonely life did not appeal to me, so I left Santa Barbara and went to Hollywood to live with Vera. I would try to make a new life for myself somehow, away from Pelican Bay.

Ira's Death

August, 1938

I HAD BEEN LIVING in Hollywood for about a year when I received a letter from Mrs. Vandevere, a friend in Santa Barbara, saying that Ira was in the hospital for a stomach operation. Later that same day, she telephoned to tell me that he was in serious condition following a hemorrhage. Vera and I hurried to pack a few things and drove to Santa Barbara, going directly to St. Francis Hospital. Vera went in to see her Dad first; I didn't know if Ira would want to see me.

In a short time she came to the door and said that he was asking for me. As I went to Ira's bedside, he smiled his bright smile and said "Hello there!" just like old times. I couldn't keep back the tears as I leaned over to kiss him. He gave my hand a squeeze and whispered, "I'm sorry." I understood. All the years rolled away, and we felt young again. I wondered if I was the one who had been wrong in those earlier years after all. I wanted to tell him I was so sorry if I had failed him, and to ask if there was anything I could do to make things right. But he was too weak to listen to all that now.

Doctors Pierce and Spaulding said that if no complications set in, Ira would pull through, so Vera was filled with hope. She visited him twice every day and ran errands to the wharf for him, to check on his boat *Pelican* and the crew. The operation was on Monday morning. Throughout the week Ira seemed to be gaining, but early Saturday morning Vera called me and said he was worse. When I arrived at the hospital, Ira was already under an oxygen tent, and I knew the end was near. Vera and I just waited and prayed.

About two in the morning, Ira asked Vera if she had been to a dance, and how Fiesta was going (it being Fiesta week). She asked him how he felt, and he told her that he felt good enough to mow the lawn. That was the last he spoke.

As I sat by the bedside watching him I thought, this can't be my brave Ira lying here so helpless; he has never known the meaning of danger or fear. And all that we had once meant to each other came over me. With all our ups and downs, if I had the choice, I would certainly do everything over again. I loved Ira so much.

An old man once said to Ira: "Young feller, when death comes to get you, you won't be in a hurry." And so it seemed, for it was ten hours later that Ira died, August 13, 1938. His wish for cremation was carried out. Our nephew Harold Couch and George Castagnola took the ashes aboard George's boat and scattered them over the channel Ira had loved so well.

And that was the end of a time that would never be again. "No Trespassing" signs are up at Santa Cruz Island, but I am sure that the blue heron or his descendant—undisturbed by wars or other human sorrows—still sits on his perch guarding what we had once called our beautiful Pelican Bay.

TOPICAL INDEX

253

EDITOR'S NOTES

1. There are no records of goats ever having been on San Nicolas Island, but sheep were grazed there beginning in 1857.

2. Torrey pines do not occur on Santa Cruz Island, but on Santa Rosa Island and on the mainland near San Diego. The trees above Twin Harbors are Santa Cruz Island pine.

3. Captain George Nidever's original account states that the lone woman died after seven weeks in Santa Barbara; she was then baptized Juana María. The whereabouts of her feather robe are unknown, according to the late Fr. Maynard Geiger of Mission Santa Barbara.

4. Few people are aware that, by the terms of the original land grant, private ownership of Santa Cruz Island extends to the water line.

5. National Park status for the Channel Islands was proposed several times in the ensuing decades. Finally, in early 1980, the islands of Santa Barbara, Anacapa, Santa Cruz, Santa Rosa and San Miguel were designated as the Channel Islands National Park in a bill passed by Congress and signed by the President. Under the terms of the bill, the area now held by the Santa Cruz Island Company and The Nature Conservancy will continue as privately-owned land within the park. Purchase of the eastern tenth of Santa Cruz Island and of Santa Rosa Island was authorized by the bill, but funds have yet to be allocated as of this writing.